Best Exotic

Baby Names

Best Exotic Baby Names

Allison Jones

Neoteric Publications
Seattle

Best Exotic Baby Names

by Allison Jones

Printed in the USA by DeHart's Media Services

ISBN 978-0-9657338-2-3
2nd printing 2009

www.exoticnames.com

Neoteric Publications
1122 E. Pike St. #931
Seattle, WA 98122

Table of Contents

Appendices

Dedicated to the
multicultural,
highly advanced
children of tomorrow.

"I bow to him who attained Buddhahood,
And who from his realization taught the path,
Fearless and firm, to enlighten the unawake,
And who holds the supreme sword of wisdom,
And wields the thunderbolt of compassion,
Cutting through all the weeds of suffering,
Smashing the great barrier of perplexity,
Buried deep in the jungle of various views."
—Maitreyanatha, India 300 AD.

Maitreyanatha [migh-tray-yah-nah-thah]. (Skt)
Protector of the next Buddha, named Maitreya.
"Maitreya": "Friend" (compassionate).
"Natha": "Refuge" (protection).

Introduction

This book is the end result of an extensive language research project to gather exotic names from around the world, and to learn their true meanings. I have spent the past 15 years hunting names of great beauty, fascination, and inspiration. I study their languages, so I may be sure of what they mean. This treasure of names that you hold in your hands contains gems of great value for their unique intentions, and for their ability to empower both the bearer and whomever repeats these names.

My interest in knowing the truth about names matured throughout my five pregnancies. I first looked in every book under the sun, constantly finding different meanings for the same names—which made me question every name that I ever read or wrote down. That's when I decided it was time to get serious and take the plunge into research myself, searching for names from exotic lands and back through time, among both legendary and mythological figures. I had to learn the languages from which the names are derived to truly understand them. To accomplish this, I read dictionaries—endless dictionaries—then took my notes from 50 languages to teachers and scholars at language schools and universities from New York to Seattle. They were all native speakers, so I could learn proper pronunciation, meanings, and more. (Apart from English, the only language in which I actually have some fluency is Spanish, which I learned in 1977 when I was living with the Maya Indians in Guatemala.)

Names have stories to tell, through their translations, meanings, and metaphors. For instance, a name that translates into Honey will mean Sweet; Flower means Beauty; Lion means Strength; Shield means Protection. The name for honey in Greek appears like this:

Melia [mehl-lee-ah] Honey (sweet). (Grk)

Melia translates into "Honey," meaning something "Sweet." Adding and joining another name or word adds dimension and depth. Here, all the components of names have been linguistically broken down:

Polymela = Much Honey (very sweet), kindness.

"Poly": "Many" (much) + "Melia": "Honey" (sweet).

7

Some names have meanings that blossom into metaphors, poetic analogies that can contain deep meanings. A beautiful example can be seen in the ancient Sanskrit name Arun. "Arun" translates into the color "Red," which is the color of the dawn, so it means the "Sunrise." And the sunrise is a metaphor for a king, because just as the sun ascends in the sky so does a man ascend the throne to become the king.

Arun [ar-roon] Red (sunrise), a king.
Red is the *translation*
(Sunrise) is the *meaning*
A king is the *metaphor*

The root of the name Arun is from the Indo-European word for red, "Ruh." Through linguistic footprints, names can tell us a lot about human history. By tracing the name Arun, we see how far and wide the Indo-Europeans spread, from India, where the name Arun translates as red and means the sunrise, all the way to Norway, where the name Rune translates as red and means secret wisdom, something carved from the rowan tree (red tree) to record mystical lore.

Long ago, people only had first names and did not have permanent last names inherited by their descendants; last names were just temporary descriptions that were not passed on forever. Such was the case in the United Kingdom up until the 11th century, when Normans (French-speaking Danes from Normandy) took over the island of Britain, which had been named by the Romans, and renamed it England. The Romans had called it "Britain," after the Brythony Celts, refugees of genocide from the mainland; the Normans renamed it "Angland" (angle-land), after the Anglo-Saxon tribes; and Angland evolved into "England." Until then, last names were actually temporary personal descriptions—where people were from, or their title, or trade. But the Norman conquerors instituted a census to tax their new domain, making permanent all those temporary last names. Clifford was a location name, Dean was a title, Spencer was a servant, Cameron meant a crooked nose, Tyler was a tile roofer, and Sawyer sawed wood. There were also destination names made by people giving directions to find someone who lives down the windy road, or by the big oak tree. For example, Graham meant the gray home made of stone.

The American Pilgrims (1600s), Colonists (1700s), and Pioneers (1800s) came out of a darker time in history, when individuality was a death sentence. In 1492 Columbus proved the Earth round and the church wrong, shattering its hypnotic hold on the populace with the truth. This eventually brought the bravest of believers, the Pilgrims, to the shores of America on board the Mayflower. They had already exercised some of their newfound freedom by bestowing upon their children creative names, like Love, Humility, Resolved, Wrestling (with God), Remember (God), and Oceanus, for the boy born in the middle of the sea. They gave them names from the Old Testament or classical Greek literature; or made them up from English, with names like Reliance, Learned, Temperance, and Thankful, for girls; and Experience, Prosper, Greengrove, and Principle, for boys.

Early Americans also gave their children three names, by adding one between the first and the last. They combined the first two names for richer concepts, such as Faithful Comfort, Morning West, and Alpha Jane for their girls; and Reason Round, Enoch Numbers, and Noble Noah for their boys. Early Americans also found that through middle names they could preserve family last names. Many of these worked their way up to become first names, like Clayton, Winston, Taylor, and Travis. And because English last names happen to end in consonants or consonant sounds, their boy names trend toward similar endings. In great contrast, numerous places around the world commonly have boy names that end in vowels, like Romeo in Italy, Diego in Spain, Juma in Africa, Makoa in Hawaii, Sasi in Israel, Teemu in Finland, and Akira in Japan.

The world of names is fascinating, and a great adventure awaits you within the pages of this book. Hang on and join me as your guide as I take you through this sampling of names from exotic lands!

Abbreviation Key

Abbreviation	Word
Ap	Appendices
Cmpd	Compound
fr	from
FN	First Name
LN	Last Name
Mtn	Mountain
N	Name
Nn	Nickname
Orig	Original
Pron	Pronunciation
RN	Real Name
➤	*to become*

Language Key

Arabic	(Ara)	Middle English	(ME)
Early American	(Eam)	Norwegian	(Nor)
French	(Frn)	Old English	(OE)
German	(Ger)	Sanskrit	(Skt)
Greek	(Grk)	Scandinavian	(Scand)
Hebrew	(Hbr)	Serb & Croatian	(Sb-Cr)
Hawaiian	(Hwn)	Spanish	(Span)
Italian	(Ital)	Swedish	(Swed)

Amharic, Basque, Cree, Danish, Estonian, Finnish, Gaelic, Germanic, Hausa, Hindi, Igbo, Ixil Maya, Japanese, Kikuyu, Latin, Lenape, Lithuanian, Mam Maya, Mandarin, Navajo, Norwegian, Quechua, Persian, Russian, Shona, Sioux, Swahili, Tibetan, Turkish, Welsh, Wolof, Yoruba, Yucateco Maya, Zulu.

How Names Are Listed

1 - Some appear below their Root Name:

April [ay-prihl] Opening, the month flowers open.   (Latin)

Apriana [ah-pree-ah-nah] *fr* "April."   (Eam)

2 - Some appear above their Root Name:

Ambretta [ahm-breht-tah] Little Immortal.   (Ital *fr* Grk)

fr "Ambrosia" [ahm-broh-jhah] "Immortal."   (Grk)

Girl Names

A

Aardina [ar-deen-nah] Earth, *fr* "Aarde": "Earth."   (Dutch)
Ardina [ar-deen-nah] Earth.

Aarona [air-roh-nah] Shining Singer, the teacher.   (Hbr)
fr "Zoharon" [zoh-har-rahn] "Shining Singer," the teacher.
"Zohar": "Shining" + "Oneg": "Delight" (joy), singing.
The chanter is teaching by singing sacred songs.

Adaoma [ah-day-oh-mah] Kindhearted Daughter.   (Igbo)
"Ada": "First Lady" (daughter) + "Oma": "Good" (kind).
A father's daughter comes first, she is his first lady.

Adara [ah-dar-rah] Hope.   (Yoruba)

Adela [ah-dehl-lah] Noble.   (Germanic)
Adellinda [ah-dehl-lihn-dah] Noble Protector.
fr "Adellinde" [ad-dehl-lihn-dah] "Noble Shield."
"Adel": "Noble" + "Linde": "Shield" (protector).
Shields were made from hard "Linden" (lime tree) wood.
Adelina [ah-dehl-leen-nah] *fr* "Adellinda."   (Frn)
Adellinde > **Adelinde** (Ger) > **Adeline** (Frn) > Adine.
Adine [ah-deen] Noble Protector, Nn *fr* "Adeline."   (ME)
Diradine [deer-rah-deen] Dear Adine.   (Eam)

Adisa [ah-dee-sah] Goddess, an ancient Nordic priestess. (Swed)
fr "Dess": "Priestess" (goddess); *see* Dessa.
Aerinndis, Aerindis [air-rihn-dihss] Noble Goddess.
"Aerinn": "Noble" + "Dess": "Priestess" (goddess).

Adora [ah-dor-rah] Adored, worshipped.   (Frn)
Adorea [ah-dor-ree-ah] Adored, adored girl.
Madora [mah-dor-rah] My Adoration, worthy of worship.
"Mi": "My" + "Adora": "Adoration" (worship).
Adorabelle [ah-dor-rah-behl] Beauty to Worship.
"Adora": "Adored" (worship) + "Belle": "Beauty."
Adorabella [ah-dor-rah-behl-lah] *fr* "Adorabelle."   (ME)

Aerial [air-ree-ehl] Airborne, *fr* "Aer": "Air," aloft, flying. (Latin)

Akane [ah-kah-nay] Red, the color of the dawn.   (Japanese)

12

Akiko [ah-kee-koh] Bright Autumn Child.   (Japanese)
"Aki": "Autumn" + "-ko" (girl), child.
When leaves fall in autumn, more sunlight comes through.
Akirako [ah-keer-rah-koh] Child of the Light.   (Japanese)
"Akira": "Light" + "-ko" (girl), child.
Alazne [ah-lahz-nay] Miracle.   (Basque)
Aleta [al-lee-tah] Little Wing, *fr* "Ala" [ah-lah] "Wing."   (Span)
Alethea [ah-lee-thee-ah] Truth.   (Grk)
   fr "Aletheia" [ah-lee-thee-ah] "Truth," truthful woman.
   Alethia, Alythia [ah-lee-thee-ah] Truth.
Alexica [al-lehks-zee-kah] Defender of Men.   (Grk)
   fr "Alexander" [al-lehks-zann-dur] "Defender of Men."
   "Alex": "Defender" + "Ander": "Man" (manly), brave.
   Alexander the Great conquered most of the known world
   spreading his name throughout Europe and beyond.
   Alexina [al-lehks-zee-nah] *fr* "Alexandra" (Alexander).
   Alessandrina [al-lehss-sahn-dree-nah] *fr* "Alexandra."   (Ital)
   Alexander > **Alessandra** > Alessina > Alesia > Alice.
   Alessandra [ah-lehss-sann-drah] *fr* "Alexandra."   (Frn)
   Alessina [ah-lehss-seen-nah] Nn *fr* "Alessandra."   (Frn)
   Alesia [al-lehss-see-ah] Defender, *fr* "Alessander."   (Frn)
   Alesia is a famous city in France named after it's founder,
   the legendary conqueror, Alexander the Great.
   Alice [al-leess] Defender of Men, Nn *fr* "Alessandra."   (Frn)
   Alicia [al-lee-see-ah] Defender of Men, *fr* "Alesia."   (Span)
   Aylice, Ayla [ay-leess, ay-lah] Nn *fr* "Alice."   (ME)
   Alifair [al-lih-fair] Fair Alice, fair defender.   (ME)
   "Alice" (alex): "Defender" + "Fair," fair-skinned beauty.
   Alize [ah-lee-zay] Defender of Men, *fr* "Alicia."   (Basque)
   Sandrine [sann-dreen] Nn *fr* "Alessandrina."   (Frn)
   Sandra, Sondra [sawn-drah] Nn *fr* "Alessandra."   (Frn)
   Xandra [zann-drah] Defender of Men, *fr* "Alexandra."   (Ger)
   Xandria [zann-dree-ah] Nn *fr* "Alexandria."   (Ger)
   Andria, Andrea [ann-dree-ah] Nn *fr* "Alexandria."   (ME)

13

Anderia [ann-dair-ree-ah] Defending Men, *fr* "Andria." (ME)

Andressa [ann-drehss-sah] *fr* "Alexandra." (Ger)

Alima [ah-lee-mah] Scholar, to be educated. (Ara)

Allegra [al-lay-grah] Happy. (Ital)

Allika [al-lee-kah] Spring of Water, *fr* "Allikas." (Estonian)

Alma [al-mah]

  1. Soul. (Span)

  2. Nourishing, Nurturing. (Latin)

    "Alma Mater" [al-mah mah-tur] "Nurturing Mother."

Almeria [al-meer-ree-ah] The Mirror, reflecting the sun. (Ara)
"Al" (the) + "Mira": "Mirror."
Where the surface of the sea is like a mirror for the sun.

Alondra [ah-lawn-drah] Lark, a beautiful songbird. (Span)

Alva [al-vah] Elf, a fairy. (Swed)

  Aelfcynn [ehlf-kihn] Elfin Race. (OE)
  "Aelf": "Elf" + "Cynn": "Kin" (kind), race of people.

  Aelfwyn [elf-wihn] Friend of the Elves. (OE)
  "Aelf": "Elf" + "Wine" [wihn] "Friend."

  Elfwina [ehlf-wee-nah] Elf Friend, *fr* "Aelfwyn." (OE)
  Elfwina was born in a Saxon village in 950 AD.

  Alvina [al-vee-nah] Elf Friend, *fr* "Elfwina." (ME)

Ama [ah-mah] Mother. (Tibetan)

  Amala [ah-mah-lah] Honorable Mother.
  "Ama": "Mother" + "La" (veneration), to honor.

Amadea [ah-mah-day-yah] Loved by God. (Latin)
fr "Amadeus" [ah-mah-day-uhss] "God's Love."
"Amor": "Love" + "Deus": "God."

  Amadine [ah-mah-deen] Loved by God, *fr* "Amadeus." (Frn)

  Amadina [ah-mah-deen-nah] *fr* "Amadine." (ME)

Amaechina [ah-may-chee-nah] Do you know tomorrow? (Igbo)

Amala [ah-mah-lah]

  1. Spotless, Purity; another N for Goddess Lakshmi. (Skt)

  2. Hope. (Ara)

  Nur Amalina [nur ah-mah-lee-nah] The Light of Hope.

14

Amalasunta [ah-mah-lah-soon-tah] Strong Tribe.   (Germanic)
"Amali" (tribe) + "Swintha": "Sound" (healthy), strong.
Queen Amalasuntha ruled Italy during the 6th century,
when the Amali tribe brought an end to the Roman Empire.
Amalasunda [ah-mah-lah-soon-dah] *fr* "Amalasunta."
Amalia [ah-mahl-lee-yah] Action (work), to be of service.   (Ara)
  Amaliya [ah-mahl-lee-yah] Action for God.   (Hbr)
  "Amal": "Action" (work) + "Yah": "God."
  Working hard for God, to act for him, and be his hands.
Amalur [ah-mah-lur] Mother Earth.   (Basque)
  "Ama": "Mother" + "Lur": "Earth."
  Amalurra [ah-mah-lur-rah] Mother Earth.
Amani [ah-mahn-nee] Peace, to be safe.   (Swahili)
Amara [ah-mar-rah] Immortal.   (Skt)
  Amarani [ah-mar-rahn-nee] Immortal Queen.
  "Amara": "Immortal" + "Rani": "Queen"; *see* Reyna.
  Ama [ah-mah] Immortal Queen, Nn *fr* "Amarani."
  Amaradeva [ah-mar-rah-day-vah] Immortal Goddess.
  "Amara": "Immortal" + "Deva": "Divinity" (goddess).
  Amrita [ahm-ree-tah] Immortal (ambrosia).
  Amritaka [ahm-ree-tah-kah] Little Immortal, a goddess.
  Amita [ah-mee-tah] Without Measure, the infinite.
Amarachi [ah-mar-rah-chee] Graced by God's Mercy.   (Igbo)
  "Amara": "Grace" (mercy) + "Chi": "God."
Amaranthea [am-mar-rann-thee-ah] Unfading Flower.   (Grk)
  "Amar": "Immortal" (unfading) + "Anthea": "Flower."
  Amarantha [am-mar-rann-thah] *fr* "Amaranthea."
  Amaranda [ah-mar-rahn-dah] *fr* "Amarantha."   (Span)
  Amaraney [ah-mar-rah-nee] *fr* "Amarantha."   (ME)
Amba [ahm-bah] Mother.   (Skt)
  Ambalika [ahm-bah-lee-kah] Little Mother, "-ka" (little).
  Amma [ahm-mah] Mother.   (Hindi)
Ambra [am-brah] Immortality Girl; nectar of the gods.   (Grk)
  fr **Ambrosia** [am-broh-jhah] Immortality; N of a nectar.

15

Amberly [am-bur-lee] Ambrosia, immortal. (ME)

Amberose [am-bur-rohz] Amber Rose, eternal rose. (Eam)

Amica [ah-mee-kah] Friend. (Latin)

Peramica [pair-rah-mee-kah] A Great Friend.
"Peri": "Very" (great) + "Amica": "Friend."

Amicia [ah-mee-see-yah] Friend. (Frn)

Amira [ah-meer-rah] Princess. (Ara)

Amita [ah-mee-tah] Infinite. (Skt)

Amora [ah-mor-rah] Love, to be loving and loveable. (Latin)
fr "Amor": "Love"; *see* Elamor.

Amata [ahm-mah-tah] To Love; N of an ancient queen.
Queen Amata ruled Laurentum in 1200 BC.

Amarosina [ah-mar-roh-see-nah] Rose of Love. (Ital)
"Amor": "Love" + "Rosa": "Rose" + "-ina."

Ananda [ah-nahn-dah] Joy. (Skt)

Anandamaya [ah-nahn-dah-migh-yah] Producing Joy.
"Ananda": "Joy" + "Maya": "Magic" (producing).

Jayananda [jigh-yah-nahn-dah] Joyful Victory.
"Jaya": "Victory" + "Ananda": "Joy."

Sananda [sah-nahn-dah] Excellent Joy, delightful joy.
"Sa": "Best" (excellence) + "Ananda": "Joy."

Andala [ahn-dah-lah] Song of the Nightingale. (Ara)

Andarta [ann-dar-tah] Surpassing Bear, a superior man. (Latin)
"Ante": "Precede," "Surpass" (excel) + "Artos": "Bear."
The bear represents the greatest strength and power.

Andeca [ann-deh-kah] Spirited, courageous. (Germanic)
fr "And": "Spirit," to be spirited and courageous.

Andeona [ann-day-oh-nah] Angel. (Sb-Cr)

Angela, Angella [ann-jehl-lah] Angel, *fr* "Angelus." (Latin)

Angelica [ann-jehl-lee-kah] Angelic.

Bellange [behl-lahnj] Beautiful Angel. (Frn)
"Belle" [behl] "Beauty" + "Ange" [ahnj] "Angel."

Leangela [lay-ahnj-jehl-lah] The Little Angel. (Frn)
"Le": "The" + "Ange": "Angel" + "-la" (little).

16

Angelique [annj-jeh-layn] Angelic; *see* Solange.　　(Frn)

Andela [ann-dehl-lah] Angel.　　(Russian)

Andelika [ann-dehl-lee-kah] Little Angel.　　(Russian)

Andelina [ann-dehl-leen-nah] Angel, angel girl.　　(Russian)

Anica [ah-nee-kah] Respected, to be a Buddhist master.　　(Skt)

  Anicadarshan [ah-nee-kah-dar-shawn] Seeing the Master.

  "Anica": "Respected" (master) + "Darshan": "Perceive."

Aniqa [ah-nee-kah] Elegant, beautiful.　　(Moroccan Ara)

Anisa [ah-nee-sah] Friendly, great to spend time with.　　(Ara)

Anka [ahnk-kah] Eagle; *see* Qorianka.　　(Quechua)

Anpowin [ann-poh-wihn] Dawn Woman.　　(Sioux)

  "Anpa": "Daylight" + "O" (place of) = "Anpo": "Dawn."

  Ampoa [am-poh-wah] Dawn Woman, *fr* "Anpowin."　　(Eam)

Antandra [ahn-tahn-drah] Against Men; N of an Amazon.　　(Grk)

  "Anti": "Against" + "Andra": "Man."

  A woman like a man, but not a man, an Amazon woman.

Anyachi [ahn-yah-chee] Eyes of God, watching over us.　　(Igbo)

  "Anya": "Eye" + "Chi": "God."

Apriana [ah-pree-ah-nah] April Ann.　　(Eam)

Arabella [ar-rah-behl-lah] Beautiful Altar.　　(Latin)

  "Ara": "Altar" + "Bella": "Beauty."

  Araceli, **Aracely** [ar-rah-sehl-lee] Altar of Stars.

  "Ara": "Altar" + "Ciel" [see-ehl] "Sky," celestial, many stars.

  Aracelia [ar-rah-sehl-lee-ah] Altar of Stars.　　(Span)

  Aricella [ar-rih-sehl-lah] Altar of Stars.　　(Frn)

Araminta [ar-rah-mihn-tah] Altar Mint, sacred mint.　　(Latin)

  "Ara": "Altar" + "Mint," an aromatic herb left on altars.

  Araminda [ar-rah-mihn-dah] *fr* "Araminta."　　(Span)

Aratama [ar-rah-tah-mah] Rough Jewel.　　(Japanese)

  "Ara": "Rough" + "Tama": "Precious Stone," jewel.

  A precious stone in the rough, like a diamond in the rough.

Arcadia [ar-kay-dee-yah] Bear, powerful bear woman.　　(Grk)

  fr "Arkada" [ar-kay-dah] "Bear," symbol of great power.

Archana [ar-chah-nah] Honored, *fr* "Archa": "Worship."　　(Skt)

17

Arendina [ar-rehn-deen-nah] Eagle, *fr* "Arend." (Dutch)

Argenta [ar-jehnt-tah] Silver, shiny silver. (Span *fr* Latin)
fr "Argentum" [ar-gehnt-tuhm] "Silver." (Latin)

Aria [ar-ree-ah] Air (melody), a song, the singer. (Ital)
Arietta [ar-ree-eht-tah] Little Song.

◦ **Arian** [ar-ree-ahn] Silver, shiny stars in the sky. (Welsh)
Arianhrod [ar-ree-ahn-rahd] Silver Wheel, galactic stars.
"Arian": "Silver" (stars) + "Rhod": "Wheel" (spiral).
N of the Goddess of the Galaxy, who receives her power
from the stars that spin around her, like a silver wheel.
Rhodica [roh-dee-kah] Wheel, spin power; N of a mystic.
fr "Rhod": "Wheel" (spiral), Celtic symbol of power.

Ariella [ar-ree-ehl-lah] Lioness of God. (Hbr)
"Ari": "Image of a Lion" + "El": "God"; *see* Ap1: Ariel.

Aristina [ar-rih-steen-nah] Excellent Woman. (Grk)
fr "Aristos": "Excellence," to have a splendid lifestyle.

Arkadina [ar-kah-deen-nah] Solar Day, sunny day. (Skt)
"Arka": "Ray" (solar) + "Dina": "Day."

Artemis [art-teh-mihss] Muscular (arteries); N of goddess. (Grk)
Immortal twins "Artemis" (moon), goddess of the night,
and "Apollo" (sun), god of the day, were sacred hunters
whose arrows always saved their worshippers just in time.
Artemisia [art-teh-mee-see-ah] Muscular, *fr* "Artemis." (Frn)
Artima [art-tih-mah] Muscular, *fr* "Artemis." (Frn)
Artemissa [art-teh-meess-sah] Muscular, *fr* "Artemis." (OE)
Artissa [art-tihss-sah] Muscular, *fr* "Artemissa." (Eam)

Aruna [ar-roon-nah] Sunrise, *fr* "Arun": "Red," dawn color. (Skt)
Arunika [ah-roon-nee-kah] Little Sunrise.
"Aruna": "Red" (sunrise) + "-ka" (little).
Arunima [ar-roon-nee-mah] Sunrise.

Asha [ah-shah] Wishes, Hope. (Skt)
Asheni, Ashenee [ah-shehn-nee] Angel. (Cree)
◦ **Astara** [ah-star-rah] Star, to strew stars across the sky. (Skt)
The Gods have strewed the stars across the universe.

18

Astarana [ah-star-rah-nah] Star.

Sterla [stur-lah] Little Star. "Star" + "-la" (little).   (Latin)

Stellara [stehl-lar-rah] Star, *fr* "Stella": "Star."   (Ital)

Istara [ee-star-rah] Star, *became* **Ishtar** in India.   (Persian)

"Istara" (Persian) *became* **Ester, Esther** (Hbr), Astro (Grk).

Starleen [star-leen] Star, star girl.   (Eam)

Astinemoon [ah-stehn-nah-muhn] Hope.   (Cree)

Athena [ah-thee-nah] Female Strength.   (Grk)

fr "Athenamy" [ah-theh-nah-mee] "Female Strength."

"A" (opposite) + "Thenamy": "Strength."

Strong women come from the feminization of male strength.

Athenea [ah-thee-nee-ah] Female Strength, *fr* "Athena."

Ateena [ah-teen-nah] Female Strength, *fr* "Athena." (Finnish)

Atieno [ah-tee-ehn-noh] Guardian of the Night.   (Swahili)

Atisha [ah-tee-shah] Luminous Splendor.   (Persian)

fr "Atish" [ah-teesh] "Fire" (light), luminous splendor.

Atossa, Atoosa [ah-toh-sah, ah-too-sah] *fr* "Atisha."

Audrica [awe-dree-kah] Little Noble Might.   (OE *fr* Germanic)

fr "Adeldreda" [ah-dehl-dray-dah] "Noble Might." (Germanic)

"Adel" (aethel): "Noble" + "Dryd" (thryth): "Might."

Audrey [awe-dree] Noble Might, *fr* "Adeldreda."

Audrina [awe-dree-nah] Noble Might, *fr* "Audrey."   (ME)

Auderia [awe-deer-ree-ah] Noble Might, *fr* "Audrey."   (ME)

Audera [awe-deer-rah] Noble Might, *fr* "Auderia."   (Eam)

Avallon [av-vah-lahn] Island of Apples.   (Welsh)

"Afal" [ah-vahl] "Apple" + "Glan" [lahn] "Shore" (island).

Avalon [av-vah-lahn] Island of Apples, *fr* "Avallon."

Avani [ah-vah-nee] Ground, Earth.   (Skt)

Avanipala [ah-vah-nee-pahl-lah] Protector of the Earth.

"Avani": "Ground" (earth) + "Pala": "Protector."

Avatara [ah-vah-tar-rah] Descent, from heaven.   (Skt)

A divine being that appears on earth is an Avatar.

Awele [ah-weh-lay] Lucky.   (Igbo)

Ayame [i-yah-may] Iris Flower.   (Japanese)

B

Bailara [bigh-lar-rah] Valley. (Basque)

Basanti [bah-sahn-tee] Goddess of Spring. (Hindi *fr* Skt)
   fr **Vasanta** [vah-sahn-tah] Brilliant Season, springtime. (Skt)

Bashara [bah-shar-rah] Bringer of a Sign, bringer of news. (Ara)
   "Ba": "Comes" (brings) + "Shara": "Sign" (news).

   Ishara [ee-shar-rah] A Sign, good sign. (Swahili)

Basilissa [bass-sihl-leess-sah] Queen. (Grk)

   Basilia [bay-sihl-lee-ah] Queen. (Latin)

Beilin [bay-leen] Treasure Rain. (Mandarin)

Bellamira [behl-lah-meer-rah] Wondrous Beauty. (Latin)
   "Bella": "Beauty" + "Mira": "Wondrous" (miraculous).

   Bellezza [behl-leez-zah] Very Beautiful. (Ital)

   Belisima [behl-lee-see-mah] Very Beautiful. (Span)

Beza [bay-zah] Sparkle, like dew or jewel in the sun. (Zulu)

Bhavani [bah-vah-nee] Giver of Life, the power of nature. (Skt)
   fr "Bhava": "Coming into Existence," able to feel love.
   N of a Creator Goddess, who is like Mother Nature.

Bia [bee-yah] Force (power); N of a mighty goddess. (Grk)
   Goddess of Force, winged enforcer for her father Zeus;
   her siblings were Nike, Kratos (power), and Zelos (rivalry).

   Eurybia [yur-ree-bee-yah] Great Power.
   "Eury": "Grand" (great) + "Bia": "Force" (power).

   Eurybe [yur-ree-bee] Great Strength, *fr* "Eurybia."

Bilina [bee-lee-nah] Iris of the Eye, pretty eyes. (Amharic)

Bindi [bihn-dee] Drop, auspicious sign on the third eye. (Skt)
   fr "Bindu" [bihn-doo] "Drop" (mark), brings fortune.
   Marking the third eye with a bindi drop brings good luck.
   "Auspicious" means to be favored by the gods & goddesses.

   Bindiya [bihn-dee-yah] Drop, an auspicious sign.

Blesinde, Blesinda [blehss-sihn-dah] Blessing. (Germanic)
   fr "Bleis": "Bless," to be blessed by the gods.
   Princess Blesinde of the Suevi tribe was born in 350 AD.

Brinna [brihn-nah] Superior Sword (warrior).   (Germanic)
fr "Brinnan": "Burn" (fire), forging a magical sword.
Fire is used to make a superior sword for a superior warrior.
Brendike, Brendika [brehn-dee-kah] Little Warrior.
"Brand": "Burn" (warrior) + "-ke" (little).
Brandika [brann-dee-kah] Pron N *fr* "Brendike."
Brandina [brann-deen-nah] Warrior, *fr* "Brandika."   (OE)
Briolana [bree-yoh-lah-nah] Brilliance, radiance.   (ME *fr* Frn)
fr "Brio" is *fr* "Brillant" [bree-yah] "Brilliance."   (Frn)
Brilliana [brihl-lee-ah-nah] Brilliance, radiance.
Brisa [bree-sah] Breeze, a gentle breeze.   (Span)
Brisanda [bree-sahn-dah] Gentle Breeze, *fr* "Brisa."
▪ **Brynne, Brynna** [brihn-nah] Armored Warrior.   (Nor)
Putting on armor turns a person into warrior.
Bryndisa [brihn-dihss-sah] Warrior Goddess.
"Bryn": "Armor" (warrior) + "Dess": "Goddess."
Branimira [brann-nih-meer-rah] Peaceful Warrior.   (Sb-Cr)
"Bran": "Armor" (warrior) + "Mir": "Peace."
Budhaniya [boo-dahn-nee-yah] Awake, enlightened.   (Skt)
fr "Budh": "Awake" (enlightened), wise, a Sage.
Bodhani [boh-dah-nee] Awake, enlightened woman.
Bodhiya [boh-dee-yah] Awake, to be enlightened.

C

Cadence [kay-dehnss] Rythmn, song.   (Frn)
Kadence [kay-dehnss] Rythmn, song.   (ME)
Caelesta [kigh-lehss-stah] Celestial, heavenly.   (Latin)
Caelia [kigh-lee-ah] Celestial, heavenly.
Gemma Caeli [jehm-mah kigh-lee] Gem from Heaven.
Caelesta (Latin) > **Celestina** > **Celestine** > **Celine** (Frn).
Celestria [sehl-lehss-stree-ah] Celestial, heavenly girl.   (ME)
Cailin, Caileen [kigh-leen] Girl.   (Gaelic)
Caileen Alainn [kigh-leen al-lihn] Beautiful Girl.

21

Calandra [kah-lahn-drah] Lark, the songbird. (Grk)

Calauria [kal-lor-ree-ah] Nice Air, gentle breeze. (Grk)
  "Cala" [kah-lah] "Nicely" (right) + "Aeras": "Air" (wind).
  Island of the gentle breeze; N of an Aegean island.

Calice [kah-leess] Flower. (Frn)

Calla, Callia [kah-lah, kah-lee-ah] Beauty. (Grk)
  fr "Kallos" [kah-lohss] "Beauty."
  Callisto [kah-leess-stoh] Most Beautiful.
  Calista [kal-leess-stah] Most Beautiful, fr "Calisto."
  Calissa [kal-leess-sah] Most Beautiful, fr "Calista."
  Callithea [kah-lee-thee-ah] Beautiful Goddess.
  "Kallia": "Beauty" + "Thea": "Goddess."
  Callianira [kah-lee-ah-neer-rah] Beautiful Woman.
  "Kallia": "Beauty" + "Anira": "Woman."
  Calliandra [kal-lee-ann-drah] Beautiful Strong Woman.
  "Kallia": "Beauty" + "Ander": "Man" (strong).

Candela [kann-dehl-lah] Candle, candlelight. (Span, Latin)
  Chandelle [shawn-dehl] Candle. (Frn)
  Shandi, Shondi [shawn-dee] Candle, fr "Chandelle." (Eam)

Candelaria [kann-dehl-lar-ree-ah] Candlelight Melody. (Latin)
  "Candela": "Candle" + "Aria": "Melody."
  To sing beautiful songs by candlelight.

Cantoria [kann-tor-ree-ah] Singer, place of song. (Latin)
  fr "Cantor" [kann-tor] "Singer."
  Cantora [kann-tor-rah] Singer, her song. (Span)
  Cantelina [kann-tehl-lee-nah] Singer, singing girl. (OE)

Carissa [kar-rihss-sah] Graced by God. (Grk)
  fr "Kharis": "Graced," favored by God.
  Kharitina [kar-rih-tee-nah] Graced by God. (Russian)

Carita [kar-ree-tah] To Care, Dearness, to be loved. (Latin)
  Cara [kar-rah] Friend, one who cares. (Gaelic)

Cathara [kah-thar-rah] Purity, pure enough for God. (Grk)
  fr "Katharos" [kah-thar-rohz] "Purity"; see Katharia.
  Katharos (Grk) > Catharine (OE) > **Katherine** (ME).

22

Catheria [kah-theer-ree-ah] Purity, *fr* "Cathara."   (OE)
Cathanna [kah-thahn-nah] Purity, *fr* "Catherina."   (OE)
Catarina [kat-tah-reen-nah] Woman of Purity.   (Span)
Kathleen > **Katalina** > **Katelyn** (ME) > **Katella** (Eam).
Caitlin [kayt-lihn] Purity, *fr* "Kathleen."   (Gaelic)
Cedrina [seh-dree-nah] Cedar, cedar woman.   (Ital *fr* Latin)
fr "Cedrus" [seh-druhs] "Cedar," fragrant evergreen.   (Latin)
Cerissa [sair-ree-sah] Goddess of Grain, the harvest.   (Grk)
fr "Ceres" [sair-reez] "Grain," goddess of agriculture.
Goddess Ceres symbolizes plenty and abundance.
Chaika [chigh-kah] Seagull.   (Russian)
Chaitanya [chigh-tahn-yah] Consciousness, intelligent.   (Skt)
fr "Chetana" [chay-tahn-nah] "Conscious" (intelligent).
Chetani [chay-tahn-nee] Conscious, *fr* "Chetana."
Chetaniya [chay-tahn-nee-yah] Conscious, intelligent.
Chandrika [chann-dree-kah] Little Moon.   (Skt)
"Chandra": "Glowing" (moon) + "-ka" (little).
Chandrima [chann-dree-mah] Moonbeam.
Chandira [chann-deer-rah] Moon.
Chandramaya [chann-drah-migh-yah] Like the Moon.
"Chandra": "Moon" + "Maya": "Magic," magically.
Chandramani [chann-drah-mah-nee] Moon Gem.
"Chandra": "Moon" + "Mani": "Jewel" (gem).
Chandrasena [chann-drah-seen-nah] Moonlight Warrior.
"Chandra": "Moon" + "Sena": "Warrior."
Chandramati [chann-drah-maht-tee] Moon Prayer.
"Chandra": "Moon" + "Mati": "Prayer" (devotion).
Channa Dorje [chah-nah dor-jay] Truth in Hand.   (Tibetan)
"Channa": "In hand" + "Dorje": "Thunderbolt" (truth).
A Bodhisattva powerful enough to kill demons.
Chantal [shahn-tal] Song.   (Frn)
Chanteuse [shahn-tooss] Singer, the chanter.
Chantella [shahn-tehl-lah] Little Song.   (ME)
Shantal [shahn-tal] Singer, *fr* "Chantal."   (ME)

23

Chantekiya Win [chahn-tay-kee-yah wihn]. (Sioux)
Encouraging Woman, others take heart, feel courage.
"Chante": "Heart" + "Kiya": "To Cause" + "Win."
Chante Ohitika Win "Brave Hearted Woman."
Chanua [chah-noo-wah] Blossom, Flower. (Swahili)
Charuta [char-roo-tah] Loveliness, a charming woman. (Skt)
fr "Charu" [char-roo] "Agreeable" (charming), lovely.
Chaska [chahss-skah] Star, a large star. (Quechua)
Chaska Nawi [chahss-skah nah-wee] Star Eyes, twinkling.
Chava [chah-vah] Earth. (Ixil Maya)
Chayna [chay-nah] Songbird, the Lark. (Quechua)
fr "Ch'ayna" [chay-nah] "Lark," a sweet songbird.
Cherika [chair-ree-kah] The Moon. (Amharic)
Cherina [shair-ree-nah] Dear, beloved. (Frn)
fr "Chere" [shair] "Dear" (beloved); *see* Ap1: Cher.
Cheriline [shair-rihl-leen] Dear, little dear one.
Chere > **Cherelle** > Cherell > Cherill > Cheryll > **Cheryl**.
Cherubina [chair-roo-bee-nah] Little Cherub. (Russian *fr* Grk)
fr "Cherub" [chair-ruhb] "Celestial Being." (Grk)
Chiemi [chee-ay-mee] Great Knowledge Beauty. (Japanese)
Chikara [chee-kar-rah] Force & Power. (Mandarin)
Chimala [chee-mal-lah] Beauty, *fr* "Chimal." (Ixil Maya)
Chime [chee-may] Eternal. (Tibetan)
Chime Drolma [chee-may drohl-mah] Eternal Goddess.
Drolma is the dancing goddess. "Dro": "Moving" + "Ma."
Chinami [chee-nah-mee] 1,000 Ocean Waves. (Japanese)
Chioma [chee-oh-mah] God is Good, with a kind heart. (Igbo)
"Chi": "God" + "Oma": "Good" (kind).
Chiaka [chee-ah-kah] Hand of God, he helps us.
"Chi": "God" + "Aka": "Hand," a helping hand.
Chima [chee-mah] God Knows, he knows everything.
"Chi": "God" + "Ma": "Knows."
Sochima [soh-chee-mah] Only God Knows.
"So": "Only" + "Chi": "God" + "Ma": "Knows."

24

Chione [kee-oh-nay] Snow Queen; N of a snow nymph.   (Grk)
fr "Chioni" [kee-oh-nee] "Snow."
Christiana [krihss-stee-ah-nah] Christian; *see* Xristina.   (Grk)
fr "Chrizo": "Anoint" (consecrate), to mark as sacred.
   Chrisana [krihss-sah-nah] Christian; *see* Krisanna.   (OE)
   Christana [krihss-stah-nah] *fr* "Christian."   (Eam)
   Chrisona [krihs-soh-nah] Nn *fr* "Christian."   (Eam)
   Cristeny [krihss-steh-nee] Nn *fr* "Christian."   (Eam)
Chrysogenia [krihss-soh-jeh-nee-ah] Golden Child.   (Grk)
"Chryso": "Golden" + "Genia": "Generation" (child).
Chrysanthea [krihss-sann-thee-ah] Golden Flower.
"Chryso": "Golden" + "Anthea": "Flower."
   Chrysantha [krihss-sann-thah] Golden Flower.   (OE)
   Crisanda [krihss-sahn-dah] Golden Flower.   (Span)
Ciara [kee-ar-rah] Darker, dark hair and complexion.   (Gaelic)
fr "Ciar" [kee-ur] "Darker," the twilight or darker colors.
Cima [see-mah] Summit, Mountaintop, the pinnacle.   (Span)
Cionarra [kee-ahn-nar-rah] Love, beloved.   (Gaelic)
fr "Cion" [kee-ahn] "Love," to be loved.
   Cionda, Cianda [kee-ahn-dah] Love, beloved.   (OE)
Claire, Clara [klair, klair-rah] Clarity, luminous.   (Frn *fr* Latin)
fr "Claritas": "Clear," shining through, luminous.   (Latin)
   Chiara [kee-ar-rah] Clarity, pron N *fr* "Clara."   (Ital)
   Kalare [kah-lar-ray] Clarity, *fr* "Clara."   (Basque)
   Clarity [klair-rih-tee] Aware, to be able to see.   (ME)
Cosima [kah-zee-mah] Cosmos, *fr* "Kosmos."   (Grk)
   Cosie [koh-zee] Cosmos, infinite stars, *fr* "Cosima."   (Eam)
Cythera [sigh-theer-rah] Guitar, symbol of love.   (Grk)
fr "Kithara" [kih-thar-rah] "Guitar."
A guitar is used to play love songs, the music of Aphrodite.
N of the island where Aphrodite rose from the sea.
   Cytherea [sigh-theer-ree-ah] Guitar, symbol of love.
   Sitara [sih-tar-rah] Guitar, Sitar.   (Skt)
   Kithara (Grk) > Cithara (Latin) > Guitare (Frn) > Guitar.

D

Daima [digh-ee-mah] Always, to live forever. (Swahili)

Daina [digh-ee-nah] Song. (Lithuanian)

Dakini [dah-kee-nee] Sky Dancer Goddess; *see* Khandroma. (Skt)

Dakotawin [dah-koh-tah-wihn] Allied Woman. (Sioux)
fr "Dakoda," orig N of the Sioux tribe, allies to each other.
"Dakoda": "Friend" (ally) + "Win": "Woman."

Damisa [dah-mee-sah] Leopard. (Hausa)

Danica, Dannica [dahn-nee-kah] N of a star goddess. (Russian)
fr **Dennica** "Little Sun"; N of the Morning Star Goddess.
The Sun is a Day-Star. "Den": "Day" (sun) + "-ka" (little).

Darshana [dar-shahn-nah] A Vision of Holiness. (Skt)
fr "Darshan" [dar-shahn] "Percieve," a vision, to appear.
To see the holy appearance of a spiritual master.
Darshini [dar-sheen-nee] A Vision of Holiness.
Darshani [dar-shahn-nee] A Vision of Holiness.
Darshanika [dar-shahn-nee-kah] Little Holy Vision.
Sudarshana [soo-dar-shahn-nah] A Great Vision.
"Su": "Good" + "Darshan": "Perceive" (vision).

Dawa Lhamo [dah-wah lah-moh] Moon Goddess. (Tibetan)
"Dawa": "Moon" + "Lhamo": "Goddess."

Deandra [dee-ann-drah] Goddess, in human form. (Grk)
"Deo": "God" + "Andra": "Man" (strong).
Deondra [dee-ohn-drah] Goddess; *see* Theosa.
Deoma [dee-oh-mah] My God, a prayer to the gods.
Every neighborhood worshipped their own god or goddess.

Dechen [day-chehn] Great Bliss. (Tibetan)
"Dewa" [day-wah] "Bliss" + "Chen": "Great."

Deena [deen-nah] Judgement. (Hbr)

Deianira [day-yah-neer-rah] Divine Woman. (Grk)
"Dei" [day] "Divine" + "Anira": "Woman."
N of a famous Amazon warrior, wife of Hercules.
Dejanira [day-jhah-neer-rah] *fr* "Deianira." (Latin)

26

Dayanira [day-yah-neer-rah] *fr* "Dejanira." (Span)

Delicia [dehl-lee-see-ah] Delight, a joy to be around. (Latin)

Delice [dehl-leess] Delight. (Frn)

Delissa [dehl-leess-sah] Delight. (Frn)

Dendra [dehn-drah] Forest. (Grk)

fr "Dendro": "Tree" (branches), forest; *see* Druantia.

Dessa [dehss-sah] Young Maiden, young goddess. (Finnish)

"God" + "Dess" = "Goddess": "Priestess for the Gods."

N for a goddess; *see* Adisa, Bryndisa, Geiradisa, Gudisa.

Desta [dehss-tah] Joy. (Amharic)

Destina [deh-steen-nah] Destiny. (Frn)

Devani [day-vahn-nee] Heavenly, divine woman. (Skt)

fr "Deva" [day-vah] "Heavenly" (divine).

Devanika [day-vahn-nee-kah] Little Divinity.

Devamani [day-vah-mah-nee] Divine Jewel of Wisdom.

"Deva": "Divine" + "Mani": "Jewel" (wisdom).

Devasena [day-vah-seen-nah] Divine Warrior.

"Deva": "Divine" + "Sena": "Warrior."

Devatara [day-vah-tar-rah] Divine Star, divine rescuer.

"Deva": "Divine" + "Tara": "Star" (rescuer); *see* Tara.

Devika [day-vee-kah] Little Divinity, little goddess.

fr "Devi": "Divine" (heavenly), a deity, a goddess.

Divoja [dee-voh-jah] Born in Heaven.

"Deva": "Divine" (heavenly) + "Ja": "Born."

Dharma [dar-mah] The Teachings, the truth. (Skt)

Dharma is the truth, the spiritual instruction of Buddhists.

Dharmi [dar-mee] The Teachings (truth), *fr* "Dharma."

Dharmika [dar-mee-kah] Little Truth.

Dharmasutra [dar-mah-soo-trah] True Speech.

"Dharma": "Teachings" (truth) + "Sutra": "Thread."

Sutras are the spoken teachings of the masters, spoken
jewels of wisdom strung along together on symbolic thread.

Diantha [dee-ann-thah] Flower Goddess. (Grk)

"Deos" (dio): "God" + "Anthea" [ann-thee-ah] "Flower."

27

Diona [dee-ohn-nah] Goddess.

Diondra [dee-ohn-drah] Goddess. (Ital)

Diosa [dee-oh-sah] Goddess. (Span)

Dilaram [dihl-lar-ruhm] Heart Soothing, a sweetheart. (Persian)
"Dil": "Heart" + "Aram": "Resting" (tranquil), soothing.
A Sweetheart is soothing to the heart she loves.

    Dilara [dihl-lar-rah] Heart Soothing, *fr* "Dilaram."

    Delara [dehl-lar-rah] Heart Soothing, *fr* "Delaram."

Distira [dih-steer-rah] Radiance, radiant woman. (Basque)

Divina [dee-vee-nah] Divinity, divine being. (Latin)
    fr "Divinitas" [dee-vee-nee-tahss] "Divinity."

Dolina [dah-lee-nah] Valley. (Russian)

Dorica [dor-ree-kah] Of Gold, golden. (Ital)
    fr "D'Orica" = "Di": "Of" + "Oro": "Gold."

    Doradina [dor-rah-deen-nah] Golden. (Span)
    fr "Dorado" [dor-rah-doh] "Of Gold" (golden).
    "De" [day] "Of" + "Oro" [or-roh] "Gold."
    D'Oro > Dorado > Dorada > Doradina.

Dorissa [dor-rihss-sah] Gift, *fr* "Doro": "Gift." (Grk)

    Dorema [dor-ray-mah] My Gift.

    Dorothea [dor-roh-thee-yah] Gift from the Goddess.
    "Doro": "Gift" + "Thea": "Goddess."
    Dorothea (Grk) > **Dorothy** (OE) > **Dorotea** (Span).

    Dorte [dor-tay] Gift from the Goddess, *fr* "Dorothea." (Nor)

    Dara [dar-rah] Gift, *fr* "Doro." (Russian)

    Daromila [dar-roh-mee-lah] Dear Gift. (Russian)
    "Dara": "Gift" + "Mila": "Dear" (loved).

Dovana [doh-vah-nah] Gift. (Lithuanian)

Drala [drah-lah] Above the Enemy. (Tibetan)
    "La": "Above" + (the) "Dra": "Enemy."
A sentient being who's above the aggression of the enemy.

Dreolan [droh-leen] Wren, little wren bird. (Gaelic)

Drolma [drohl-mah] Dancing Goddess, a rescuer. (Tibetan)
    "Dro": "Moving" (dancing) + "Ma" (female), a goddess.

Druantia [droo-ahn-tee-ah] Queen of the Druids.　　(Grk)
　　fr "Druinos" [droo-ee-nohss] "Oak Trees."
　　The early Greeks were mystified by Celtic shamans, calling
　　them "Druids," because they could vanish inside of trees.
　　Dryade [dree-yah-day] Oak Tree, tree nymph.
　　Dryades are the female spirits that live inside of oak trees.
　　Dryope [dree-oh-pay] Voice of the Tree, a tree nymph.
　　"Dryade": "Oak" (tree) + "Ope": "Voice."
　　　Dryadene [dree-yah-deen] Oak Tree, tree nymph.　(Swed)
　　　Drumasena [droo-mah-seen-nah] Forest Warrior.　　(Skt)
　　　"Druma": "Trees" (forest) + "Sena": "Warrior."
Duva [doo-vah] Dove.　　(Swed)
Duvessa [duh-vehss-sah] Dark Waterfall, deep reflection. (Gaelic)
　　"Dubh" [duhv] "Dark" + "Eas": "Waterfall."
Dyrleif [deer-leef] Dear Love.　　(Scand)
　　"Dyr": "Dear" + "Leif": "Love."

E

Eartha [ur-thah] Earth.　　(OE)
　　Earthuma [ur-thah-mah] Earth Mother.
Eavan [ay-vihn] Pleasant, delightful girl.　　(Gaelic)
　　fr "Aoibhinn" [ay-vihn] "Pleasant."
Ebere [ay-bair-ray] Mercy.　　(Igbo)
Edel [eh-dehl] Noble, symbolized by the eagle.　　(Germanic)
　　Eda, Edith [eh-dah, ee-dihth] Noble, like the eagle.　(OE)
　　Edelfina [eh-dehl-fee-nah] Fine Noble.　　(Span)
　　"Edel": "Noble" (Germanic) + "Fina": "Fine" (Span).
　　Germanic tribes occupied Hispania during the 5th century.
Eden [ee-dehn] Fertile Plain.　　(Sumerian)
　　Edena [ee-dehn-nah] Fertile Plain, *fr* "Eden."　　(Hbr)
　　Edenia [ee-dehn-nee-ah] Fertile Plain, *fr* "Eden."　　(Span)
Ederra [eh-dair-rah] Beauty, *fr* "Eder": "Beauty."　　(Basque)
　　Ederne [eh-dair-nay] Beautiful.

29

Eirana [air-rah-nah] Snow, fair beauty. (Welsh)
 fr "Eira" [air-rah] "Snow," to be white as snow.
 Refined women did not work outdoors, and were pale (fair).
 Gweneira [gwehn-nair-rah] Snow White.
 "Gwen": "White" + (as) "Eira": "Snow."
 Guenora [gwehn-nor-rah] Snow White, *fr* "Gweneira." (OE)
 Jenori [jehn-nor-ree] Snow White, *fr* "Guenora." (ME)
Eitana [ay-tahn-nah] Strong, a muscular woman. (Hbr)
Elama [ay-lah-mah] Life. (Estonian)
Elamor [ehl-lah-mor] The Love. (Span)
 "El": "The" + "Amor": "Love"; *see* Amora.
Eleonora [ehl-lehn-nor-rah] Tough Lion. (Ger)
 fr "Leonhard" = "Leon": "Lion" + "Hard" (tough), strong.
 Elora, Ellora [ehl-lor-rah] Cmpd Nn *fr* "Eleonora." (ME)
 Elenira [ehl-lehn-neer-rah] Tough Lion, *fr* "Eleonora." (Eam)
 Elenoa [ehl-lehn-noh-wah] *fr* "Eleonora." (Eam)
Elewa [ehl-leh-wah] Understanding. (Swahili)
Elina [ehl-lee-nah] Pretty Sound. (Estonian)
Elisheva [ehl-lee-sheh-vah] My Promise to God. (Hbr)
 "El": "God" + "Sheva": "Promise" (oath).
 Elisheva (Hbr) > **Elisabeth** (OE) > Elizabeth (ME).
 Elisaveta [ehl-lee-sah-veh-tah] *fr* "Elisabeth." (Russian)
 Elixane [ehl-lee-shah-nay] Nn *fr* "Elixabete." (Basque)
 Eliska [ehl-lihss-skah] Little Elisabeth. (Czech)
Ellamaija [ehl-lah-migh-yah] Wolf of Mary. (Finnish)
 fr "Ullamaija" [oo-lah-migh-yah] "Wolf of Mary."
 "Ulla": "Wolf" + "Maija" [migh-yah] "Mary."
 "Maija" is Nn *fr* "Marja" [mar-yah] "Mary"; *see* Mariline.
Elodie [ehl-loh-dee] Melody, a singer. (Frn)
 fr "Melodie" [mehl-loh-dee] "Melody" (song).
 Elodine [ehl-loh-deen] Melody, a singer.
 Elodina [ehl-loh-deen-nah] Melody, a singer. (ME)
Elurra [ehl-lur-rah] Snow, beauty white as snow. (Basque)
Emiko [eh-mee-koh] Smile Child, happy girl. (Japanese)

"Emi" is *fr* "Hohoemi": "Smiling Cheek" + "-ko" (girl).

Emine [ay-mee-nay] Trustworthy, Safe. (Turkish)

Emma, Ema [ehm-mah] God is With Us. (ME *fr* Hbr)
fr "Immanuel" = "Im": "With" + "El": "God." (Hbr)
Immanuel > Emmanuel > Emeline > Emely > **Emily**.
Emeline [ehm-mah-leen] God is With Us.
Emalisse [ehm-mah-leess] God is With Us, *fr* "Emaline."

Enya [ehn-yah] Eye of God, god is watching over us. (Hbr)
"Eyin": "Eye" + "Yah": "God."

Eowyn [ay-yoh-wihn] Horse Joy, she loves horses. (OE)
"Eoh" [ay-yoh] "Horse" + "Wyn" [wihn] "Joy."
Aeowin [ay-yoh-wihn] Horse Joy, *fr* "Eowyn."
◦ **Aewyn** [ay-wihn] Horse Joy, *fr* "Aeowin." (ME)

Erelieva [air-reh-lee-vah] Honored Love. (Ger)
"Ehre": "Honor" + "Liebe" [lee-vah] "Love."

Erenay [air-rehn-nigh] Full Moon. (Turkish)
"Erin": "Mature" (full) + "Ay" [i] "Moon."

Erilina [air-reh-leen-nah] Special. (Estonian)

Ernai [air-nigh] Wide Awake, alert guardian. (Basque)

Esmeralda [ehz-mur-rehl-dah] Emerald. (Span *fr* Latin)
fr "Smaragd": "Emerald," exquisite green eyes. (Latin)
Smaragd (Latin) > Esmeraude (Frn) > Esmeralda (Span).
Esme, Esmay [ehz-may] Emerald, *fr* "Esmeralda." (Frn)
Esmerella [ehz-mur-rehl-lah] *fr* "Esmerelda." (Eam)

Esmeray [ehz-mur-righ] Dark Moon, dark beauty. (Turkish)
"Esmer": "Darker" + "Ay" [i] "Moon," symbol of beauty.

Evandra [ehv-vahn-drah] Great Man; N of an Amazon. (Grk)
"Eu": "Good" (great) + "Andra": "Man" (manly), strong.
Evantia [ehv-vahn-tee-ah] *fr* "Evandra." (Romanian)

Evanel [ehv-vah-nehl] Good Angel. (ME *fr* Grk)
fr "Evangelos": "Good Angel," to be evangelical. (Grk)
"Eu": "Good" + "Angelos": "Angel."

Evidalia [eh-vih-dahl-lee-ah] Evidence, proof of God. (Span)
Evidine [eh-vih-deen] Evidence of God. (Eam)

31

F

Fahrunisa [fah-roo-nee-sah] Honorable Woman.   (Turkish)
Fairnisse [fair-neess] Fairness, to be fair and beautiful.   (ME)
   Fairamay [fair-rah-may] Fair Maiden.
   "Faire": "Fair" (beauty) + "Maiden."
Farhana [far-hahn-nah] Joy, *fr* "Farah": "Joy."   (Ara)
Farzana [far-zah-nah] Learned, wise scholar.   (Persian)
Fayola [fay-yoh-lah] Good Fortune walks with Honor.   (Yoruba)
Fazana [fah-zah-nah] Womankind.   (Zulu)
Feyana [fay-yah-nah] Fairy, *fr* "Feya": "Fairy."   (Russian)
Fiamma [fee-ah-mah] Flame.   (Ital)
   Fiametta [fee-ah-meht-tah] Little Flame.
Finabella [fee-nah-behl-lah] Fine Beauty.   (Ital)
   "Fina": "Fine" + "Bella": "Beauty."
Fionna, Fiona [fee-yoh-nah] White (fair), beauty.   (Gaelic)
   Fionnuala [fee-yoh-noo-wah-lah] White Shoulder, a swan.
   "Fionn" + "Gualainn" [goo-wuh-lihn] "Shoulder."
   "Nuala" is pron N *fr* "Gualainn": "Shoulder," of a swan.
   N of a goddess in the legend of The Children of Lir.
   Finuala [fee-noo-wah-lah] White Shoulder, a swan.
   Finola, Fynola [fee-noh-lah] Swan, *fr* "Finuala."   (OE)
Floratina [flor-rah-tee-nah] Flower Girl, *fr* "Flora."   (Ital)
   Florendina [flor-rehn-dee-nah] Flower Girl.
   Florenday [flor-rehn-day] Flower, *fr* "Florendina."   (Eam)
Folasade [foh-lah-shah-day] The Honor of the Crown.   (Yoruba)
   "Fola": "Honor" + "Ade": "Crown"; *see* Sade.
Fontana [fahn-tann-nah] Fountain, *fr* "Fontane."   (Eam)
Forresta [for-rehss-stah] Forest.   (ME)
   Forestina [for-rehss-steen-nah] Forest, girl of the forest.
Fredina [freh-dee-nah] Peaceful Ruler.   (Germanic)
   fr "Frederich" = "Friede": "Peace" + "Ric": "Ruler."
   Fredacia [freh-day-see-ah] Peaceful Ruler.
Frendessa [frehn-dehss-sah] Friend, friendly woman.   (ME)

Friyana [free-yah-nah] Beloved, Loved. (Persian)

Once the Persian and Finnish empires bordered each other
and both cultures worshipped Freya, the Goddess of Love.

⁕ **Freya** [fray-yah] Beloved; N of the Goddess of Love. (Ger)

Freyja [fray-yah] Beloved; N of Goddess Freya. (Scand)

Freydisa [fray-dee-sah] Beloved Goddess; *see* Dess. (Scand)

Priya [pree-yah] Beloved; *see* Priyala. (Skt)

Fronia [froh-nee-ah] Wisdom; Nn *fr* "Sofronia." (Grk)

Sofronia [soh-froh-nee-ah] Wisdom; *see* Sophia.

G

Gabisa [gah-bee-sah] Very Confident. (Zulu)

Gadara [gah-dar-rah] Gatherer, Harvester. (OE)

fr "Gadere" [gah-deer] "Together" (gathers), the harvester.

Gadella [gah-dehl-lah] God's Wonderful Surprise. (Amharic)

Gadina [gah-deen-nah] Flower Garden. (Hausa)

Gaia [gigh-yah] Earth. (Grk)

Gaiana [gigh-yah-nah] Earth, *fr* "Gaia." (Latin)

Gaiania [gigh-yah-nee-yah] Earth. (Russian)

Galani [gah-lah-nee] Milky White, fair-white beauty. (Grk)

fr "Gala": "Milk" (white), *became* "Galaxy": "Milky Way."

Galaxia [gal-laks-see-yah] Milky Way (galaxy), galactic girl.

Galiana [gah-lee-yah-nah] Milky White, fair beauty.

Galina [gah-leen-nah] Milky White, *fr* "Galiana." (Russian)

Galatea [gah-lah-tee-ah] Milky White, a sea nymph. (Grk)

fr "Gala": "Milk" (white), a fair beauty.

Beautiful sea nymph Galatea rode the seas on a giant fish.

Galletha [gah-lee-thah] Milky White, *fr* "Galatea." (OE)

Galene [gah-lee-nee] Calm, like a peaceful sea. (Grk)

Galenia [gah-lee-nee-ah] Calm, peaceful woman.

Galet [gah-leht] Wave of Energy, beaming good energy. (Hbr)

fr "Gal": "Wave" (energy), for energy moves like water.

Galiya [gah-lee-yah] Wave of Energy from God.

"Gal": "Wave" (energy) + "Yah": "God."

Avigal [ahv-vee-gahl] Wave of Energy from God.
"Avi": "Father" (god) + "Gal": "Wave" (energy).

Abigail [ab-bih-gayl] Energy from God, *fr* "Avigal."   (Grk)

Galila [gah-lee-lah] Rolling Hills, an area of lush beauty.   (Hbr)
fr "Galil" [gah-leel] "Roll," rolling hills or surface of the sea.

Ganiyah [gahn-nee-yah] Garden of God.   (Hbr)
"Gan": "Garden" + "Yah": "God."

Ganita [gahn-nee-tah] Garden, garden girl.   (New Hbr)

Geira [geer-rah] Spear (warrior).   (Scand *fr* Germanic)
"Geir" is *fr* "Gerade": "Straight" (spear).   (Germanic)

Geirny [geer-nee] New Warrior.
"Geir": "Spear" (warrior) + "Ny" [nee] "New."

Geiradisa [geer-rah-deess-sah] Warrior Goddess.
"Geir": "Spear" (warrior) + "Dess": "Priestess" (goddess).

Gerdica, Gerdika [geer-dee-kah] Little Warrior.

Geirunn, Geirun [geer-roon] Wise Warrior.
"Geir": "Spear" (warrior) + "Rune": "Secret Wisdom."

Geiruna [geer-roo-nah] Wise Warrior, *fr* "Geirun."

Gergana [gur-gahn-nah] Magic Warrior.
fr "Gargandar" [gar-gann-dar] "Magical Warrior."
"Geir": "Spear" (warrior) + "Gandar": "Magic Staff."

Gelina [gehl-lee-nah] Flower Garden.   (Lithuanian)
fr "Gelynas" [gehl-lee-nuhss] "Flower Garden."

Gemma [jehm-mah] Gem, precious stone.   (Latin)

Gemma Clare [jehm-mah klair] Gem of Clarity, brightness.

Gemma Luna [jehm-mah loo-nah] Moon Stone.

Genea [jeh-nee-ah] Generation, the next generation.   (Grk)

Nea Genea [nee-ah jeh-nee-ah] New Generation.

Gerradina [geer-rah-deen-nah] Tough Warrior.   (Germanic)
fr "Gerardina": "Tough Warrior," strong warrior.
"Geir": "Spear" (warrior) + "Hart": "Hard" (tough).

Gerdina [geer-deen-nah] Tough Warrior.   (Dutch)

Geertina [geer-teen-nah] Tough Warrior.   (Dutch)

34

Gevira [geh-veer-rah] Strong Woman. (Hbr)
    fr "Gevurah" [geh-vur-rah] "Strong."
    Gavriela [gahv-vree-ehl-lah] God is my Strength.
    "Gevurah": "Strong" (strength) + "El": "God."
    Gabriella [gahb-bree-ehl-lah] God is my Strength. (Grk)
    Gabrella [gahb-brehl-lah] *fr* "Gabriella." (Ital)
    Abrielle [ay-bree-ehl] Nn *fr* **Gabrielle** (Gabriella). (Frn)
    Gabray [gah-bray] God is my Strength, *fr* "Gabriela." (Eam)
Ghazala [jah-zahl-lah] Gazelle, graceful girl. (Moroccan Ara)
Giedra [ghee-drah] Calm, calm woman. (Lithuanian)
    fr "Giedre" [ghee-drah] "Calm."
Gita [ghee-tah] Sacred Song. (Skt)
    Gitaka [ghee-tah-kah] Little Sacred Song.
    "Gita": "Song" + "-ka" (little).
    Sangita [sanng-ghee-tah] Sacred Song Singer.
    "San": "Bestow" + "Gita": "Sacred Song."
    Sangeeta [sanng-ghee-tah] Singer, *fr* "Sangita." (Hindi)
Gitana [jee-tahn-nah] Gypsy. (Frn)
Godina [gah-dee-nah] God, God's little girl. (Germanic)
    Goditha [gah-dee-thah] God, God's little girl. (OE)
    Godiva is *fr* "Godgifu": "God's Gift"; *see* Ap1: Godiva.
    Godwin [gahd-wihn] Friend of God.
    "God" + "Wine" [wihn] "Friend."
Golotina [goh-loh-tee-nah] Sweetness. (Quechua)
Gratiana [grah-tee-ah-nah] Graced by God. (Latin)
    fr "Gratias": "Graced," graced by God's mercy.
    We say grace to thank God for his mercy.
    Gratidia [grah-tee-dee-ah] Graced by God.
    Graecina [grayss-see-nah] Graced by God, *fr* "Gratiana."
    Saint Graecina lived in Rome during the 1st century.
    Gracinea [grayss-see-nee-ah] Graced by God.
    Gracina [grah-see-nah] Graced by God, thankful. (Span)
    Gracinda [grah-sihn-dah] Graced, thankful girl. (Span)
Grazina [grah-zee-nah] Beauty, *fr* "Grozis." (Lithuanian)

Gudisa [goo-dee-sah] God's Priestess, a goddess. (Swed, Scand)
"Gud" [goo-d] + "Dess": "Priestess" (goddess); *see* Dessa.
Godessa [gahd-dehss-sah] Goddess. (Modern Eng)
Gudrun [goo-droon] Goddess of Runic Wisdom. (Scand)
"Gud": "God" + "Run" [roon] "Rune," secret wisdom.
Gyde, **Gyda** [gee-dah] Goddess; N for a Nordic priestess.
Gudruna [guh-droo-nah] *fr* "Gudrun"; *see* Runa. (OE)
Gydena [gee-deh-nah] Goddess, *fr* "Gyde." (OE)
Gwen [gwehn] White, fair white skin, a fair maiden. (Welsh)
Gwenith [gwehn-nihth] White, a fair maiden.
Gwenllian [gwehn-lee-ihn] White Linen, in fine clothes.
"Gwen": "White" + "Llian" [lee-ihn] "Linen."
Elegant women wore soft clothes made of fine linen.

H

Hadara [hah-dar-rah] Adorned, a beautiful woman. (Hbr)
Hadira [hah-deer-rah] Glory, glorified woman. (Ara)
Hadiyya [hah-dee-yah] Gift. (Ara)
Haizea [high-zay-yah] Strong Wind, having power. (Basque)
Halima, **Halimah** [hah-lee-mah] Gentle, mild mannered. (Ara)
fr "Alim" [ah-leem] "Gentle."
Hamadrya [hah-mah-dree-yah] Tree Nymph; *see* Druantia. (Grk)
Hamara [hah-mar-rah] Mystical Dawn. (Finnish)
Mystical moment of half-light, pre-dawn & twilight.
Hamsa [hahm-sah] Swan, the mystic swan. (Skt)
Hanami [hah-nah-mee] Flower, beautiful blossom. (Japanese)
Hanata [hah-nah-tah] Peace. (Blackfoot)
Hannah [hann-nah] Grace, graced by God, *became* **Anna**. (Hbr)
Anya [ahn-yah] Nn *fr* "Hannah." (Russian, Scand)
Anka [ahnk-kah] Little Grace. "Anya" + "-ka." (Ger)
Anoushka [ah-noosh-kah] Little Anna. (Russian)
Harumi [har-roo-mee] Spring Beauty. (Japanese)
Hassina [hah-see-nah] Very Beautiful. (Ara)

Helene [hehl-lee-nee] Sun, radiant beauty.　　　　　(Grk)
fr "Helios" [heel-lee-ohss] "Sun" (radiance).
Helen of Troy had beauty as radiant as the sun.
"Helen" *for* girls; "Helenus" *for* boys, powerful as the sun.
Hellenica [hehl-lehn-nee-kah] Culture of the Sun.
N for the Greeks; the sun was central to all ancient religions.
Hilaira [hihl-lair-rah] Sun, radiant beauty; N of a priestess.
Helianthe [hehl-lee-ahn-thay] Sun Flower.
"Helios": "Sun" + "Anthea" [ann-thee-ah] "Flower."
Helica [hehl-lee-kah] Sun-burned, tanned & rugged girl.
Hemithea [heh-mee-thee-ah] Half Goddess.　　　　(Grk)
"Hemi": "Half" + "Thea": "Goddess."
Hermione [hur-migh-oh-nee] Mercury, the messenger.　(Grk)
fr "Hermes": "Mercury," quick messenger for the gods.
Daughter of the legendary beauty, Helen of Troy.
Hermasenda [hur-mah-sehn-dah] Mercury, messenger girl.
Hermosa [air-moh-sah] Beautiful.　　　　　　　(Span)
Hero [heer-roh] Holy; N of a legendary priestess.　　(Grk)
Hiera [heer-rah] Holy, *became* Goddess **Hera** [hair-rah].
Herundina [hair-roon-deen-nah] Little Swallow.　(Span *fr* Latin)
fr "Hirundo" [heer-roon-doh] "Swallow" (songbird).　(Latin)
Himaya [hee-may-yah] Protection.　　　　　　　(Swahili)
Himeko [hee-may-koh] Princess Child.　　　　　(Japanese)
Hiraka [heer-rah-kah] Little Diamond, little mighty one.　(Skt)
"Hira": "Diamond" (mightiest) + "-ka" (little).
Hiradevi [heer-rah-day-vee] Divine Diamond.
"Hira": "Diamond" (mightiest) + "Devi": "Divine."
Hiromi [heer-roh-mee] Big Ocean. Full of Beauty.　(Japanese)
Honora [ahn-nor-rah] Honorable, *fr* "Honor."　　(Latin)
Honorina [ahn-nor-reen-nah] Honorable.
Honorae, Honoray [ahn-nor-ray] *fr* "Honoria."　　(OE)
Onorina [ahn-nor-reen-nah] Honorable.　　　　(Ital)
Hunaja [hoo-nigh-yah] Honey, a sweet girl.　　　(Finnish)
Hurmerinta [hur-mur-rihn-tah] Charming.　　　(Finnish)

I

Ihana [ee-hah-nah] Wonderful. (Finnish)

Iina [ee-nah] Life. (Navajo)

Ijenwa [i-jehn-wah] Journey of the Child, a good life. (Igbo)
"Ije" [i-jay] "Life" (journey) + "Nwa": "Child."

    Ijeoma [i-jay-oh-mah] Good Journey, to have a good life.
"Ije": "Life" (journey) + "Oma": "Good."

Imala [eem-mah-lah] God is With Us. (ME *fr* Hbr)
fr "Immanuel": "God is With Us"; *see* Emma. (Hbr)

Imani [ee-mahn-nee] Faith. (Swahili)

Imarika [ee-mar-ree-kah] Resolute and Strong. (Swahili)
fr "Imara" [ee-mar-rah] "Firm" (resolute).

Imatra [ee-mah-trah] Place of Wonders. (Finnish)
fr "Ihme": "Wonder," something wondrous & miraculous.
A famous destination to see many wondrous waterfalls.

    Imelina [ee-mah-lee-nah] Little Miracle, *fr* "Ime." (Estonian)

Indarra [ihn-dar-rah] Energy, having strength. (Basque)

Indrani [ihn-drah-nee] Conquering, a mighty woman. (Skt)
fr "Indra": "Subduer," "Conqueror"; N of the mightiest god.

    Indira [ihn-deer-rah] Conquering, *fr* "Indra."

    Indramani [ihn-drah-mah-nee] Wise Conqueror.
"Indra": "Conqueror" + "Mani": "Jewel" (wisdom).

    Indrasena [ihn-drah-seen-nah] Conquering Warrior.
"Indra": "Conqueror" (mighty) + "Sena": "Warrior."

Inira [ee-neer-rah] Singer, she loves to sing. (Kikuyu)

    Inithia [ee-nee-thee-ah] Leading the Song and Dance.

Iolani [i-oh-lah-nee] Heavenly Hawk. (Hwn)
"Io": "Hawk" + "Lani": "Heaven."

Ione [i-oh-nay] Purple Woman; N of a sea nymph. (Grk)
fr "Io": "Purple," of purple iridescence.

    Iola [i-oh-lah] Purple, Violet Flower; *see* Veola.

Isadora [ee-sah-dor-rah] Gift from the Goddess Isis. (Grk)
"Isis": "Woman" (first goddess) + "Doro": "Gift."

Isadira [ee-sah-deer-rah] Gift from the Goddess. (ME)

Isadine, Isadene [ee-sah-deen] *fr* "Isadora." (ME)

Isabeau, Ysabeau [ee-sah-bow] Beautiful Goddess. (Frn)
"Isis" (first goddess) + "Beau" [bow] "Beauty."

Isabella [ee-sah-behl-lah] Beautiful Goddess. (Span)
"Isis" (first goddess) + "Bella": "Beauty."

Isella, Issella [ee-sehl-lah] Cmpd Nn *fr* "Isabella." (Span)

Isami [ee-sah-mee] Brave Beauty. (Japanese)

Ishana [ee-shah-nah] Wealthy. (Skt)

Isioma [ee-see-oh-mah] Good Head, smart thinker. (Igbo)
"Isi": "Head" (thinker) + "Oma": "Good" (smart).

Itanya [ee-tahn-yah] Hope. (Kikuyu)

Itewa [ee-tay-wah] Face of Holiness. (Sioux)
fr **Ite Wakan** [ee-tay wah-kahn] Face of Holiness.
"Ite": "Face" + "Wakan": "Sacred" (holy).

Ixmucane [eesh-moo-kah-nay] Goddess of the Dawn. (Maya)
"Ix": "Goddess" + "Mucane" [moo-kah-nay] "Dawn."
Ixchela [eesh-shehl-lah] Goddess of the Rainbow.
"Ix" [eesh] "Goddess" + "Chel" [shehl] "Rainbow."

Ixone [ee-shoh-nay] Quiet One, *fr* "Ixo": "Quiet." (Basque)

Izarra [ee-zar-rah] Star. (Basque)

J

Jachima [jah-chee-mah] Praise the Goodness of God. (Igbo)
fr "Jaachimma" [jah-chee-mah] "Praise God's Goodness."
"Jaa": "Praise" + "Chi": "God" + "Mma": "Goodness."

Jadallah [jah-dahl-lah] Gift from God, from Allah. (Ara)
"Jada": "Gift" + "Allah": "God."

Jahanara [jah-hahn-nar-rah] Beauty in the World. (Persian)
"Jahan": "World" + "Aray": "Adornment" (beauty).

Jahina [jah-hee-nah] Bold & Brave. (Swahili)

Jamani [jah-mah-nee] Friend. (Swahili)

Jamesina [jay-meh-see-nah] James's Girl; *see* Jacobae. (OE)

Jamila [jah-meel-lah] Beauty, *fr* "Jamal": "Beauty." (Ara)

    Jamala [jah-mahl-lah] Elegance, beauty. (Swahili)

Jarunta [jar-roon-tah] Courage. (Hausa)

Jasanse [jah-sahn-say] Comforting Healer. (Eam *fr* Grk)

    fr "Jason" [jay-suhn] "Comforts," a healer. (Grk)

Jasara [jah-sar-rah] Bold. (Ara)

Jata [jah-tah] Star. (Kikuyu)

Jatorra [jah-tor-rah] Loyal, genuinely good person. (Basque)

Jaya [jigh-yah] Conquering, Victorious. (Skt)

    Jayanti [jigh-yahn-tee] Victory, victorious woman.

    Sujaya [soo-jigh-yah] Great Victory.

    "Su": "Good" (great) + "Jaya": "Conquering," "Victory."

    Jayasundara [jigh-yah-soon-dar-rah] Beautiful Victory. (Skt)

    Jaitra [jigh-trah] Victory. "Jai" is *fr* "Jaya."

    Jaimala [jigh-mah-lah] Garland of Victory.

    "Jaya": "Victory" + "Mala": "Garland."

    Jaipriya [jigh-pree-yah] Victorious Love.

    "Jai": "Victory" + "Priya": "Love."

Jedidah [jeh-dee-dah] Friend of God. (Grk *fr* Hbr)

    fr "Yedidah" [yeh-dee-dah] "Friend of God." (Hbr)

    "Yadid" [yah-deed] "Friend" + "Yah": "God."

    Jedeline > **Jadeline** > **Jadalyn** > Jadyn > Jada. (Frn)

    Jedella [jeh-dehl-lah] Friend of God, *fr* "Jedidah." (ME)

    Jedinia [jeh-dee-nee-ah] Friend of God, *fr* "Jedidah." (Eam)

    Jadine, Jady [jay-deen, jay-dee] *fr* "Jedidah." (Eam)

    Jadela [jay-dehl-lah] Friend of God, *fr* "Jedidah." (Eam)

    Jadyn [jay-dihn] Friend of God, *fr* "Jedidah." (Eam)

    Jadah, Jada [jay-dah] Friend of God, *fr* "Jedidah." (Eam)

Jerusha [jair-roo-shah] Inheritance. (Grk *fr* Hbr)

    fr **Yerusha** [yair-roo-shah] Inheritance. (Hbr)

    Jeresia [jair-reh-sigh-ah] Inheritance, *fr* "Jerusha." (Eam)

Jessamine [jehss-sah-meen] Jasmine, flowers. (ME *fr* Persian)

    fr "Yasaman": "Jessamine" (jasmine); *see* Yasmin. (Persian)

    Jessamay [jehss-sah-may] Jasmine, *fr* "Jessamine."

Jessika, Jessica [jehss-see-kah] *fr* "Jessamine."   (Eam)

Jiamei [jee-ah-may] Finest Beauty, the best beauty.   (Mandarin)
"Jia": "Fine" (finest) + "Mei": "Beauty."

Jiva [jee-vah] Life.   (Skt)

    Jivani [jee-vahn-nee] Life, lively woman.

    Jivala [jee-vah-lah] Honored Life. "Jiva" + "-la" (honorable).

    Sanjivani [sann-jee-vah-nee] Bestower of Life.
    "San": "Gain," "Bestow" + "Jivani": "Life Woman."

    Jeeva [jee-vah] Life, *fr* "Jiva."   (Hindi)

Johari [joh-har-ree] Jewel.   (Swahili)

Jolanda [joh-lahn-dah] Violet Flower.   (Latin *fr* Grk)

    fr **Iolantha** [i-oh-lahn-thah] Violet Flower.   (Grk)
    "Io": "Violet" + "Anthea" [ann-thee-ah] "Flower."

    Jolanta [joh-lahn-tah] Violet Flower.   (Frn)

    Jolantha [joh-lahn-thah] Violet Flower.   (ME)

    Yolanda [yoh-lahn-dah] Violet Flower, *fr* "Jolanda."   (Span)

Joli [joh-lee] Pretty.   (Frn)

    Jolicia [joh-lee-see-ah] Pretty Girl.

    Joliange [joh-lee-ahnj] Pretty Angel.
    "Joli": "Pretty" + "Ange" [ahnj] "Angel."

Josina [jahss-seen-nah] Storyteller for God.   (Frn *fr* Hbr)
    fr "Joseph" (Grk) is *fr* "Yosef": "God's Storyteller."   (Hbr)
    "Yah": "God" + "Sipur": "Storyteller."

    Joza [joh-zah] God's Storyteller, *fr* "Joseph."   (Czech)

    Joetta [joh-weh-tah] Little Storyteller for God.   (ME)

Jossara [jahss-sar-rah] Shield of Joseph.   (ME *fr* OE)
    fr "Josserand" = "Joseph" + "Rand": "Shield."   (OE)

Jubilee [joo-bih-lee] Celebration.   (ME *fr* Hbr)
    fr "Yovel" [yoh-vehl] "Jubilee" (celebration).   (Hbr)

    Jubalani [joo-bah-lah-nee] Jubilee, celebration.   (Eam)

Junaina [joo-nay-nah] Little Garden.   (Ara)

Juniper [joo-nih-pur] Evergreen Cyprus Tree.   (Latin)

Jyotika [jee-yoh-tee-kah] Little Light.   (Skt)
    "Jyoti" [jee-yoh-tee] "Light" + "-ka" (little).

K

Kaari [kar-ree] Bow, the archer. (Estonian, Finnish)

Kachina [kah-chee-nah] Spirit Dancer. (Hopi)
Spirit dancers channel all the different elements of nature,
and statues of them (kachina dolls) are carved for altars.

Kahlara [kah-lar-rah] White Water Lily. (Skt)

Kai [kigh] Sea, the ocean. (Hwn)
Kailani [kigh-lah-nee] Heavenly Sea.
"Kai": "Sea" + "Lani": "Heaven."
Kainoa [kigh-noh-wah] The Wide Open Sea.
"Kai": "Sea" + "Noa": "Unrestricted" (wide open).

Kalinda [kah-lihn-dah] Sun; N of a sacred mountain. (Skt)
The source of the sacred Yamuna River is a glacier lake
on top of Mt Kalinda in the Himalayas; *see* Yamuna.
Kalindi [kah-lihn-dee] Sun, *fr* "Kalinda."

Kalliala [kahl-lee-ah-lah] Dear One, Beloved. (Finnish)

Kalyca [kal-lee-kah] Rosebud. (Grk)

Kamala [kah-mah-lah] Lotus. (Skt)
Kamalini [kah-mah-lee-nee] Lotus Girl.
Kamalanetra [kah-mah-lah-neh-trah] Lotus Eyes.
"Kamala": "Lotus" + "Netra": "Guiding" (eyes).
Kamalanayana [kah-mah-lah-nigh-yah-nah] Lotus Eyes.
"Kamala": "Lotus" + "Nayana": "Pupil of Eye."

Kameko [kah-may-koh] Turtle Child, has a long life. (Japanese)
"Kame" [kah-may] "Turtle" + "-ko" (girl), child.

Kanisa [kah-nee-sah] Church. (Swahili)

Kannike [kahn-nee-kay] Violet Flower. (Estonian)

Karrima [kair-ree-mah] Generosity. (Ara)

Kataja [kah-tigh-yah] Juniper. (Finnish)

Katharia [kah-thar-ree-ah] Purity, pure enough for God. (Grk)
fr "Katharos" [kah-thar-rohz] "Pure"; *see* Cathara.
Katharos (Grk) > Catherine (OE) > **Katherine** (ME).
Katrina [kah-tree-nah] Pure, *fr* "Katherine." (Ger)

Katina, Kateena [kah-tee-nah] Pure, *fr* "Katrina." (Ger)

Katriana [kah-tree-ah-nah] Purity. (Ger)

Katrissa [kah-trihss-sah] Purity. (Frn)

Katera [kah-tair-rah] Purity. (Russian)

Katerinka [kat-tur-reenk-kah] Little Katherine. (Russian)

Katinka [kah-teenk-kah] Purity, *fr* "Katerinka." (Russian)

Katixa [kah-tee-shah] Purity, *fr* "Katerina." (Basque)

Katri [kah-tree] Purity, *fr* "Katerina." (Finnish)

Katharan [kah-thar-rehn] Purity, *fr* "Katheria." (ME)

Kathana [kah-thah-nah] Cmpd Nn *fr* "Katharina." (ME)

Kathina [kah-thee-nah] Purity, *fr* "Kathana." (ME)

Katelyn [kah-tehl-lihn] Purity, *fr* "Kathleen." (ME)

Katella [kah-tehl-lah] Purity, *fr* "Kathleen." (Eam)

Kavini [kah-vee-nee] Poet, Insightful, wise woman. (Skt)
    fr "Kavi": "Poet," "Insightful," wise, a Sage.

Kaweche [kah-wee-chay] Kind Helper, *fr* "Kawechehut." (Cree)

Kayla [kay-lah] Beloved. (ME *fr* Gaelic)
    fr "Ceile" [kay-lah] "Beloved." (Gaelic)

Kealoha [kay-ah-loh-hah] The Love. (Hwn)
    "Ke" [kay] "The" + "Aloha": "Love."

Kedara [keh-dar-rah] Meadow; N of a Himalayan mtn. (Skt)
Breathtaking meadows exist in the valleys of the Himalayas.

Keiko [kay-koh] September Flower. (Japanese)

Kelechi [kehl-leh-chee] Grateful for Tomorrow. (Igbo)

Kenia, Kenithia [keh-nee-ah, keh-nee-thee-ah] Happy. (Kikuyu)
    Kenura [keh-nur-rah] Happy.

Keola [kay-oh-lah] The Life. (Hwn)
    "Ke": "The" + "Ola": "Life."
    Keona [kay-oh-nah] Fragrant Fragrance, super fragrant.
    fr "Keonaona" [kay-oh-nah-oh-nah] "Fragrant Fragrance."
    "Ke" + "Ona": "Fragrance" + "Ona": "Fragrance."

Kesa [kay-sah] Summer. (Finnish)
    Kesalla [kay-sah-lah] Summertime.

Kesha [kee-shah] Awake, watching over us. (Swahili)

Keturah [keh-tur-rah] Crown of God; a wife of Abraham.   (Hbr)
"Keter": "Crown" + "Yah": "God."
 Kitra [kee-trah] Crown of God, Nn *fr* "Keturah."
 Ketura, **Kitura** [keh-tur-rah, kih-tur-rah] *fr* "Keturah." (Eam)
 Kittie, **Kitty** [kih-tur-rah, kiht-tee] *fr* "Keturah."   (Eam)
Keya [kay-yah] Turtle; symbol of the land.   (Sioux)
The North American continent sits on the back of a giant
turtle swimming in a great sea that covers the earth,
thus, they call the land they stand upon Turtle Island.
 Keya Tehan Win [kay-yah tay-hahn wihn].
Ancient Turtle Woman. "Tehan": "Long Time" (ancient).
 Keya Woniya Win [kay-yah woh-nee-yah wihn].
Turtle Spirit Woman. "Keya" + "Woniya": "Spirit."
 Keyawin [kay-yah-wihn] Turtle Woman, earth woman.
"Keya": "Turtle" + "Win": "Woman."
 Kayawi [kay-yah-wee] *fr* "Keyawin." "Wi" is "Win."
Khandroma [kahn-droh-mah] Sky Dancer Goddess.   (Tibetan)
"Kha": "Sky" + "Dro": "Moving" (dancing)" + "Ma."
Kia, **Kiania** [kee-ah, kee-ah-nee-ah] Dawn.   (Kikuyu)
 Kianira [kee-ah-neer-rah] Dawn.
Kiama [kee-ah-mah] Magic.   (Kikuyu)
Kiche [kih-shay] Sky, sacred sky.   (Cree)
 Kichemen [kih-shay-mehn] The Great Spirit.
fr "Kiche Mendoo" (Manitou): "Sky Spirit," Great Spirit.
Kichea [kih-chee-ah] Brightness, light returns to earth. (Swahili)
After clouds, the sun comes out and brightens the world.
Kiele [kee-ah-lay] Gardenia Flower, a fragrant flower.   (Hwn)
Kijana [kee-jah-nah] Youth.   (Swahili)
Kiko [kee-koh] Hope.   (Japanese)
Kilinda [kee-lihn-dah] Guardian, Protector.   (Swahili)
fr "Linda": "Guard" (protector).
Kilinya [kee-leen-yah] Mountain of God; Mt Kenya.   (Kamba)
The local Kamba tribe call their mountain Kilinya,
and the first British explorers abbreviated this to "Kenya."

Kenya [keen-yah] Pron N *fr* "Kilinya," Ki(l)inya.　　(ME)

Kimiyo [kee-mee-yoh] Beauty of the Century.　　(Japanese)

Kiriko [keer-ree-koh] Child of the Mist.　　(Japanese)
"Kiri": "Mist" + "-ko" (girl), child.

Kirtana [keer-tahn-nah] Singing, celebrating in song.　　(Skt)
fr "Kirtan" [keer-tahn] "Speech" (recite), glorious songs.
Kirtans are celebrations where everyone sings sacred songs.

　　Keertana [keer-tahn-nah] Singing.　　(Hindi)

Kisa [kee-sah] Sunlight.　　(Ixil Maya)

　　Kisa Oyamal [kee-sah oy-yah-mahl] Gift from the Sun.
　　"Kisa": "Sunlight" + "Oyamal": "Gift."

Kiva [kee-vah]
1. A sacred place in the ground for ceremonies.　　(Hopi)
2. Harmony, Unity.　　(Swahili)

Kiyomi [kee-yoh-mee] Seed of Purity, pure beauty.　　(Japanese)
"Kiyo": "Pure"+ "Mi": "Berry" (seed).

　　Kiyoko [kee-yoh-koh] Child of Purity, she is holy.
　　"Kiyo": "Pure" + "-ko" (girl), child.

Kojika [koh-jee-kah] Fawn.　　(Japanese)

Kosame [koh-sah-may] Fine Rain. "Ame": "Rain."　　(Japanese)

Koya [koy-yah] Queen.　　(Quechua)

Kristanna [krihst-ann-nah] Christian, Anointed.　　(Ger *fr* Grk)
fr "Chrizo": "Anoint" (consecrate), to mark sacred.　　(Grk)

　　Krisanna [krihss-sahn-nah] Christian, *fr* "Kristanna."　(Swed)

　　Kirsten [keer-stehn] Christian, *fr* "Kristanna."　(Swed, Nor)

　　Kira [keer-rah] Christian, Nn *fr* "Kirsten."　(Swed, Nor)

　　Kirta [keer-tah] Christian, Nn *fr* "Kirsten."　(Nor)

　　Kirsiina [keer-seen-nah] Christian, *fr* "Kirsten."　(Finnish)

　　Kierstin [keer-stihn] Christian, *fr* "Kristian."　(Danish)

　　Kiera [keer-rah] Christian, Nn *fr* "Kierstin."　(Danish)

　　Kyranna [keer-rahn-nah] Christian, *fr* "Kierstin."　(ME)

　　Kyra [keer-rah] Christian, Nn *fr* "Kierstin."　(ME)

　　"Kristen" *for* boys; "Kirsten" *for* girls.

　　"Kier" *is* "Christian" (Scand); "Keir" *is* "Darker" (Gaelic).

Kudiwa [koo-dee-wah] Beloved. (Shona)

Kulisa [koo-lee-sah] To Raise, to make someone great. (Zulu)

Kuma [koo-mah] Distant Light, a glimmer. (Estonian)

Kumari [koo-mar-ree] Youth; N for the living goddess. (Skt)
fr "Kumar": "Youth," bachelorette, remaining unmarried.
A Divine Kumari is raised in a temple as a living goddess,
and will never marry, so she can give out advice to all men.
  Kanyakumari [kahn-yah-koo-mar-ree] Young Goddess.
  "Kanya": "Girl" + "Kumari": "Youth."

Kumi [koo-mee] Long Time Beauty, rare beauty. (Japanese)
  Kumiko [koo-mee-koh] Long Time Beauty Child.
  "Kumi": "Long Time" + "-ko" (girl), child.

Kumisa [koo-mee-sah] Courage, courageous woman. (Zulu)

Kusuma [koo-soo-mah] Flower, Blossom. (Skt)
  Kusumita [koo-soo-mee-tah] Flower, she brings flowers.

Kuvala [koo-vah-lah] Honorable Water Lily. (Skt)
fr "Kuva": "Water Lily" (lotus), symbol of truth.
  Kuvani [koo-vah-nee] Water Lily, lotus woman.

Kylissa [kigh-lihss-sah] Archer, she achieves her goals. (Dutch)
"Kyler" is *fr* "Keilen" [kigh-lehn] "Fling," shoot arrows.

L

Ladera [lah-dair-rah] Ladder, climbing up to God. (Span)
Spiritual pilgrims climbed the rocky cliffs of coastal Spain,
rocky ladders that brought them to altars and closer to God.
  Ladeira [lah-deer-rah] Ladder, *fr* "Ladera." (Portuguese)

Ladora [lah-dor-rah] The Gift, the gift from God. (Span)
"La": "The" + "Dora": "Gift."

Laetitia [ligh-tee-shee-yah] Joyful, Cheerful, delightful. (Latin)
  Leticia [leh-tee-see-ah] Joyful, cheerful girl. (Frn)
  Letizia [lay-tee-zee-ah] Joyful, cheerful girl. (Span)

Laka [lah-kah] Goddess of Dance. (Hwn)
Musical God Lono descended on a rainbow to marry Laka.

46

Lani [lah-nee] Heaven. (Hwn)

    Kalani [kah-lah-nee] The Heaven.

    "Ka": "The" + "Lani": "Heaven."

    Kawailani [kah-wigh-lah-nee] Heavenly Water.

    "Ka": "The" + "Wai": "Water" + "Lani": "Heaven."

    Keilani [kay-lah-nee] Heavenly Glory.

    "Kei" [kay] "Glorious" + "Lani": "Heaven."

    Kulani [koo-lah-nee] Standing in Heaven.

    "Ku": "Stands" + (in) "Lani": "Heaven."

    Leolani [lee-oh-lah-nee] Heavenly Voice.

    "Leo": "Voice" + "Lani": "Heaven."

    Noelani [noh-wehl-lah-nee] Mist from Heaven.

    "Noe" [noh-wee] "Mist" + "Lani": "Heaven."

    Noela [noh-wehl-lah] Heavenly Mist, *fr* "Neolani."

Larissa [lar-rihss-sah] Seagull. (Grk)

Larosa [lah-roh-zah] The Rose. "La": "The" + "Rosa." (Span)

Lasai [lah-sigh] Calm, carefree. (Basque)

Lasairfiona [lah-seer-fee-yoh-nah] White Fire. (Gaelic)

    "Lasair": "Fire" + "Fiona": "White," intense fire.

    Lasairiona [lah-sair-ree-oh-nah] *fr* "Lasairfiona." (OE)

    Lassarina [lah-sar-ree-nah] White Fire, *fr* "Lasairiona." (OE)

Lasya, Lasiya [lah-see-yah] Dancer. (Sanskrit)

Laterra [lah-tair-rah] The Earth. (Portuguese)

    "La": "The" + "Terra": "Earth."

Latifah [lah-tee-fah] Fine, Gentle, to be cute. (Ara)

Latika [lah-tee-kah] Little Vine, a graceful beauty. (Skt)

    fr "Lata": "Creeping Plant," with graceful twining tendrils.

Laurea [lor-ray-yah] Laurel, the champion, victorious. (Latin)

    Laurel leaves were used to crown the champions.

    Laurentia (laurel-town) > Laurencia > Laurence > **Laura.**

    Laurelle, Lorelle [lor-rehl] Little Champion. (Frn)

    Lorella [lor-rehl-lah] Little Champion, *fr* "Lorelle." (Frn)

    Laureline [lor-rehl-leen] Little Champion. (Frn)

    Lorinda, Lorana [lor-rihn-dah, lor-rah-nah] *fr* "Laura." (ME)

Laray [lar-ray] Champion, *fr* "Laurea." (Eam)

Laxmi, Lakshmi [lahksh-mee] Goddess of Fortune. (Skt)

   Jayalakshmi [jigh-yah-lahksh-mee] Goddess of Victory.
   "Jaya": "Victory" + "Lakshmi": "Goddess of Fortune."

Leandra [lee-ahn-drah] Lioness Woman. (Grk)
   "Leana": "Lion" + "Andra": "Man" (woman).

   Leonessa [lee-oh-nehss-sah] Lioness. (Ital)

Leora [lee-or-rah] To Light, bringer of light. (Hbr)
   "Le" [lee] "To" + "Ori" [or-ree] "Light."
   Eliora [ehl-lee-or-rah] God is my Light.
   "El": "God" + "Ori" [or-ree] "Light."
   Liora [lee-or-rah] My Light.
   "Li": "My" + "Ori" [or-ree] "Light."

Levana [leh-vah-nah] White; poetic N for the moon. (Hbr)
   fr "Lavan": "White," to be white as the moon.

Lewa [lee-wah] Beautiful. (Yoruba)

Leyenda [lay-yehn-dah] Legend. (Span)

Lilura [lee-lur-rah] Enchantment. (Basque)

Lindeza [leen-day-zah] Very Pretty. (Span)
   fr **Linda** [leen-dah] Pretty, *became* [lihn-dah].
   Lindamara [lihn-dah-mar-rah] Beautiful Sea.
   "Linda": "Pretty" (beauty) + "Mar": "Sea."
   Deolinda [dee-oh-lihn-dah] Beautiful Goddess.
   "Dios": "God" (goddess) + "Linda": "Pretty" (beauty).

Lirica [leer-ree-kah] Lyrical (melody), a musician. (Ital *fr* Grk)
   fr "Lyrikos": "Lyre" (lyra), lyrical music. (Grk)

Liya [lee-yah] My God, *became* **Leah**. (Hbr)
   "Li" (sheli): "My" + "Yah": "God."
   Liyana [lee-yah-nah] My God.

Llewelyn [loo-wehl-lihn] Lion by the Lake. (Welsh)
   "Llewe" [loo] "Lion" + "Llyn" [lihn] "Lake."
   Llewela [loo-wehl-lah] Lion by the Lake, *fr* "Llewelyn."
   Llewelina [loo-wehl-leen-nah] *fr* "Llewelyn." (ME)

Loala [loh-wah-lah] Praise. (Hwn)

48

Locana [loh-kah-nah] Illuminates, makes everything visible. (Skt)

Lorea [lor-ray-yah] Flower. (Basque)

    Lorate [lor-rah-tay] Blooming Season.

    Loradi [lor-rah-dee] Garden of Flowers.

    Loredana [lor-reh-dahn-nah] Garden of Flowers.

Loveta [luhv-veh-tah] Little Love. (Eam)

    Loveina, Lovina, Luvina [luhv-vee-nah] Love.

Lowansa [loh-wahn-sah] Singing. (Lakota Sioux)

    fr "Lowan" [loh-wahn] "Singer."

Loyanne [loy-yann] Loyalty, *fr* "Loyal." (Frn)

Luana [loo-wah-nah] Relaxed, easy living. (Hwn)

Lucana [loo-kah-nah] Light, a radiant woman. (Latin)

    fr "Lucis" [loo-kihss] "Light."

    Luceria [loo-seer-ree-ah] Bringer of Light.

    Lucera [loo-seer-rah] Light, radiant.

    Lucita [loo-see-tah] Little Light. "Luz" + "-ita." (Span)

    Lucinda [loo-sihn-dah] Light. (Span)

    Lucindra [loo-sihn-drah] Light, woman of light. (ME)

    Lucina [loo-see-nah] Goddess of Light. (Swed)

Luka [loo-kah] Harbor. (Sb-Cr)

Luma [loo-mah] Feather. (Basque)

    Lumaia [loo-migh-yah] Feather, beautiful plumage.

Lumina [loo-mee-nah] Luminous. (Latin)

    Luminita [loo-mih-nee-tah] Little Luminosity, little light.

    Lumira [loo-meer-rah] Luminous.

Luvella [luh-vehl-lah] Lovely. (Eam)

Luvica [loo-vee-kah] Cry of Victory. (Germanic)

    fr "Ludvig": "Loud Victor," the victory cry.

    "Luit" [lood] "Loud" + "Vigr": "Victor."

    Luvisa [loo-vee-sah] The Victory Cry, *fr* "Luvica."

    Lovisa [loh-vee-sah] The Victory Cry, *fr* "Luvisa." (Swed)

    Beloved Queen Lovisa of Sweden was born in 1720.

    Ludvig > Luvisa > Lovisa > Luise (Ger) > **Louisa**.

    Luvesa [luh-veh-sah] Victory Cry, *fr* "Luvisa." (Eam)

M

Maakera [mah-kair-rah] Sphere of Soil, the Earth.   (Estonian)
"Maa": "Soil" + "Kera": "Sphere" (globe), planet.

Macaria [mah-kar-ree-ah] Bliss.   (Grk)

Machika [mah-chee-kah] Great Knowledge.   (Japanese)

Madrina [mah-dree-nah] Mother.   (Span)

Magaly [mah-gah-lee] Pearls of Wisdom.   (OE *fr* Grk)
   fr "Margarita" [mar-gah-ree-tah] "Pearls."   (Grk)
   Margarita > Margarete > **Margaret** > **Margery** > Marjory.
   Marjory [mar-jor-ree] Pearls of Wisdom, *fr* "Margery."   (ME)
   Megan [may-guhn] Pearls of Wisdom, *fr* "Margaret."   (Welsh)
   Margetty [mar-geht-tee] Pearls, *fr* "Margaret."   (Eam)

Mahala [mah-hah-lah] Praised by God.   (Hbr)
   Mahalia [mah-hah-lee-ah] *fr* "Mahala."   (Eam)

Maheona [mah-hay-oh-nah] Medicine Woman.   (Cheyenne)
   fr "Maheo" [mah-hay-oh] "Great Spirit" (God).
   The medicine woman channels the power of the Great Spirit.

Maia [migh-yah] Mother; N of a Pleiadian star goddess.   (Grk)
   Daughter of Atlas & Goddess Pleione; *see* Ap1: Pleiades.
   Maiandria [migh-ann-dree-yah] Mother of Men.
   "Maia": "Mother" + "Andra": "Man" (men).

Maika [migh-ee-kah] Dancing Flower.   (Japanese)

Maitea [migh-tay-ah] Beloved.   (Basque)
   fr "Maite" [migh-tay] "Love" (beloved).
   Maitena [migh-tay-nah] Beloved, a darling.
   Mayteana [migh-tee-nah] Beloved, *fr* "Maitena."   (Span)

Maitriba [migh-tree-bah] Love Power, the power of love.   (Skt)
   fr "Maitribala" [migh-tree-bah-lah] "Loving Power."
   "Maitri": "Friendly" (love) + "Bala": "Power."

Majaliwa [mah-jah-lee-wah] Mercy is Granted to Us.   (Swahili)
   "Ma" (us) + "Jaliwa": "Granted," granted mercy from God.

Majaya [mah-jigh-yah] Mother of Victory.   (Skt)
   "Ma" (amba): "Mother" + "Jaya": "Victory."

Maka [mah-kah] Earth, mother earth.   (Lakota Sioux)
   Makamani [mah-kah-mah-nee] Walking Over the Earth.
   "Maka": "Earth" + "Mani": "Walking."
Makalani [mah-kah-lah-nee] Heavenly Eyes.   (Hwn)
   "Maka": "Eyes" + "Lani": "Heaven."
   Makanani [mah-kah-nah-nee] Pretty Eyes.
   "Maka": "Eyes" + "Nani": "Pretty."
Malaika [mah-ligh-kah] Angel.   (Swahili)
Malia [mah-lee-ah] Calmness.   (Hwn)
   fr "Malie" [mah-lee-ee] "Calm."
   Halemalia [hah-lay-mah-lee-ah] Home of Tranquility.
   "Hale": "House" + "Malie": "Calm" (tranquil).
Malina [mah-leen-nah] Raspberry.   (Russian)
   Malinka [mah-leenk-kah] Little Berry.
Malini [mah-lee-nee] Garland.   (Skt)
   fr "Mala" [mah-lah] "Wreath" (garland).
   Sumala [soo-mahl-lah] Fine Garland of Flowers.
   "Su": "Good" (fine) + "Mala": "Garland" (flowers).
Mandir, Mandira [mann-deer, mann-deer-rah] Temple.   (Skt)
   Taramandir [tar-rah-mann-deer] Temple of Stars.
   "Tara": "Star" + "Mandir": "Temple."
   Mandara [mann-dar-rah] Heavenly Temple; N of a flower.
   N of mystical flowers that fall slowly from Buddha's heaven,
   as if dancing in the sky; N for a mystical Sky Dancer.
   Mandarava [mann-dar-rah-vah] Mystical Flower.
   Mandarava was a magical princess back in 700 AD.
Manika [mah-nee-kah] Little Jewel, little wisdom.   (Skt)
   "Mani": "Jewel" (clarity), enlightenment, to see wisdom.
   Buddhists pray for truth and peace in the world, they say,
   "Om Mani Padme Hum" [ohm mah-nee pahd-may huhm].
   "Jewel in the Lotus" means "Wisdom in the Truth."
   "Mani": "Jewel" (wisdom) + "Padme": "Lotus" (truth).
   Mandiramani [mann-deer-rah-mah-nee] Temple of Jewels.
   "Mandira": "Temple" + "Mani": "Jewel" (wisdom).

51

Sumani [soo-mah-nee] Fine Jewels of Wisdom.
"Su": "Good" (fine) + "Mani": "Jewel" (wisdom).
Maniwin [mah-nee-wihn] Walking Woman. (Sioux)
"Mani": "Walks" + "Win": "Woman."
 Zintkamani Win [zeent-kah-mah-nee wihn].
 Walking Bird Woman. "Zintka": "Bird" + "Mani."
Marica [mar-ree-kah] Sea Nymph, *fr* "Mare": "Sea." (Latin)
Lovely nymph of a sacred grove by the Mediterrean Sea.
Mariko [mar-ree-koh] Pure Knowledge Girl. (Japanese)
Mariline, Marilene [mair-rih-leen] Bitter Seed. (Frn *fr* Hbr)
 fr "Maryam" [mar-yahm] "Bitter Seed." (Hbr)
 "Mar": "Bitter" + "Yam": "Seed" = MRYM (myrm).
 A bitter seed germinates from the slavery experience.
 MRYM > Miryam > Mir(y)am > **Miriam** > **Mary**.
 Marilyn [mair-rih-lihn] Bitter Seed, *fr* "Marilene." (ME)
 Aarilyn, Aaralyn [air-rih-lihn] Bitter Seed, *fr* "Marilyn." (ME)
 Marilea [mair-rih-lee-ah] Bitter Seed, *fr* "Marilyn." (Eam)
 Maralua [mair-rah-loo-wah] Bitter Seed, *fr* "Marilea." (Eam)
Marinda [mar-rihn-dah] Evening Star. (Shona)
Marisol [mar-ree-sohl] Sea & Sun, sparkling sea. (Span)
 "Mar": "Sea" + "Y" [ee] "And" + "Sol": "Sun."
 Marisa, Marissa [mar-rihss-sah] Nn *fr* "Marisol."
 Marisela [mar-ree-sehl-lah] Sea & Sun, sparkling sea.
 Maristella [mar-rih-stehl-lah] Sea & Stars. (Ital)
 "Mar": "Sea" + "Stella": "Stars," reflected upon the sea.
 Marisoleil [mair-ree-soh-lay] Sea & Sun. (Frn)
 "Mer" [mair] "Sea" + "Soleil" [soh-lay] "Sun."
Marvella [mar-vehl-lah] Marvelous. (ME *fr* Frn)
 fr "Marvaile" (merveille): "Marvel." (Frn)
Marwa [mar-wah] Spring of Water. (Ara)
Matoaka [mah-toh-wah-kah] RN of Pocahontas. (Powhatan)
 Bright Stream between the Hills.
 Matoaca, Matowaka *fr* "Matoaka." (Eam)
Matowakan Wi [mah-toh-wah-kahn wee]. (Sioux)

52

Sacred Bear Woman. "Wi" is Win": "Woman."
"Mato": "Bear" + "Wakan": "Sacred."
Matricia [mah-tree-see-ah] Mother. (ME *fr* Latin)
fr "Matrix": "Mother," what brings forth life. (Latin)
   Matracy [mah-tray-see] Mother, *fr* "Matricia." (Eam)
Maxanda [maks-zann-dah] Highest Degree, the best. (Latin)
Maya [migh-yah] Magic, the great illusion of reality. (Skt)
   To be a supernatural being with extraordinary powers.
   Both Hindu and Maya believe reality is an illusion; *see* Naiya.
   Mayadhara [migh-yah-dar-rah] Skilled in Magic.
   "Maya": "Magic" + "Dhara": "Holding" (possessing).
   Sumaya [soo-migh-yah] Excellent Magician.
   "Su": "Good" (excellent) + "Maya": "Magic" (magician).
   Mayadeva [migh-yah-day-vah] Magic from the Gods.
   "Maya": "Magic" + "Deva": "Divine" (gods), divine magic.
   Mayadeva (Maya) was mother of Guatama the Buddha.
Mayumi [migh-yoo-mee] True Beautiful Wisdom. (Japanese)
Medea [meh-dee-ah] Cunning, *fr* "Meda": "Cunning." (Grk)
   Princess Medea was a great sorceress, who lived in 400 BC.
   Andromeda [ann-droh-meh-dah] Cunning Woman.
   "Andra": "Man" (woman) + "Meda": "Cunning."
   Andremela [ann-dray-mehl-lah] *fr* "Andromeda." (Ital)
Meganira [may-gah-neer-rah] Great Mighty Woman. (Grk)
   "Mega": "Great" (mighty) + "Aneira": "Woman."
Mehana [may-hah-nah] Warmth. (Hwn)
Meishan [may-shahn] Great Beauty. (Mandarin)
   "Mei": "Beauty" + "Shan": "Good" (great).
   Meiwei [may-way] Always Lovely.
   "Mei": "Beauty" (lovely) + "Wei": "To Maintain" (always).
Melanthea [mehl-lann-thee-ah] Dark Colored Flower. (Grk)
   "Mela": "Dark" (dark-colored) + "Anthea": "Flower."
   Melantha [mehl-lann-thah] *fr* "Melanthea," *became* **Melanie**.
Melia [mehl-lee-ah] Honey (sweet), a sweet girl. (Grk)
   Melita, **Melitta** [mehl-lee-tah] Little Honey, little sweetie.

53

Melitina [mehl-lih-tee-nah] Honey, sweet woman.
Melina [mehl-lee-nah] Honey, sweet woman.
Polymela [pah-lee-mehl-lah] Very Sweet, very kind.
"Poly": "Many" (very) + "Meli": "Honey" (sweet).
Mellea [mehl-lee-ah] Honey, *fr* "Melia."   (Latin)
Melania [mehl-lahn-nee-yah] Honey, sweetness.   (Latin)
Melanija [mehl-lahn-nee-yah] Honey, *fr* "Melania." (Russian)
Melinda [mehl-lihn-dah] Honey, *fr* "Melina."   (Frn)
Melika [mehl-lee-kah] Beauty.   (Turkish)
Melissa [mehl-lihss-sah] Honey Bee, makes things sweet.   (Grk)
fr "Melia" [mehl-lee-ah] "Honey" (sweetness).
Melicia [mehl-lee-see-ah] Honey Bee, *fr* "Melissa."   (Ital)
Melisende [mehl-lih-sehn-day] *fr* "Melissa."   (Frn)
Mendira [mehn-deer-rah] To the Mountain.   (Basque)
fr "Mendi" [mehn-dee] "Mountain."
Merella [mair-rehl-lah] At Sea, *fr* "Meri": "Sea."   (Finnish)
Meribah [mair-ree-bah] Quarrel, tested by God.   (ME *fr* Hbr)
fr "Meriva" [mair-ree-vah] "Quarrel," to feel angry.   (Hbr)
One who quarrels with God, for being tested by him.
Meriby [mair-rih-bee] Quarrel, *fr* "Meribah."   (Eam)
Miadora [mee-ah-dor-rah] My Adoration, of God.   (Latin)
"Mi": "Mine" + "Adora": "Adore" (worship).
Maydora [may-dor-rah] My Adoration, *fr* "Miadora."   (Eam)
Mianda [mee-ahn-dah] My Journey, a wonderful life.   (Span)
"Mi": "My" + "Anda" [ahn-dah] "Walk."
Michima [mee-chee-mah] Beautiful True Wisdom.   (Japanese)
Midori [mih-dor-ree] Green, of the natural world.   (Japanese)
Mika [mee-kah] Beautiful Flower.   (Japanese)
Mila [mee-lah] Graced by God, a dear.   (Russian)
fr "Milo": "Favored," graced by God, kindness, a dear.
Milena [mee-lehn-nah] Graced by God, a dear.
Milenka [mee-lehnk-kah] Little Grace from God.
Milava [mee-lah-vah] A Dear, *fr* "Mila."
Milima [mih-lee-mah] Mountain.   (Swahili)

54

Mimala Win [mee-mah-lah wihn] Circle Woman.   (Sioux)
"Mimala": "Circular" (mystical circle) + "Win": "Woman."
Tatemima Win [tah-tay-mee-mah wihn] N for a shaman.
Whirlwind Woman. "Tate": "Wind" + "Mima": "Circular."
Circles (spirals) represent infinite power of universe.
Shamans survived civilization in isolated places: Himalayas,
the Americas, Celtic Isles; *see* Arianhrod, Ap2: Chakrasena.
Mir [meer] Peace, World, the world at peace.   (Russian)
The natural state of the world is without war. They know
peace begins in the home and spreads from there.
  Mirka [meer-kah] Little Peace. "Mir" + "-ka" (little).
Miraca [meer-rah-kah] Wondrous to See, a beauty.   (Latin)
fr "Miraculum," "Mira": "Wondrous," "Miraculous."
  Mirani [meer-rahn-nee] Wondrous to Behold.
  Mirabel [meer-rah-behl] Wondrous Beauty.
  "Mira": "Wondrous" + "Bellus": "Beauty."
  Mirabelle [meer-rah-behl] Behold Beauty, *fr* "Mirabel."   (Frn)
  Miralinda [meer-rah-lihn-dah] Behold Beauty.   (Span)
  "Mira": "Look" (behold) + "Linda": "Pretty" (beauty).
  Admiranda [ad-meer-rahn-dah] Admiration.   (OE)
  fr "Admiratus" = "Ad": "To" + (feel) "Mira": "Wonder."
    Admira [ad-meer-rah] *fr* "Admiranda."   (OE)
Mirembe [meer-rehm-bay] Peace.   (Ugandan)
Mirinesse [meer-rih-neess] Merry, cheerful mirth.   (ME *fr* OE)
  fr "Myrge" [meer-ree] "Merry," sounds of joy.   (OE)
  Myrge (OE) > Mirth (OE) > Merry (ME).
  Merriday [mair-rih-day] Merry Day.
Mistica [mihss-stee-kah] Mystic, a spiritual mystic.   (Span)
Mitra [mee-trah] Friend, to have compassion.   (Skt)
  Maitra [migh-trah] Friend, compassion, *fr* "Mitra."
  Sumitra [soo-mee-trah] Genuine Friend, a true friend.
  "Su": "Good" (genuine) + "Mitra": "Friend."
  Devamitra [day-vah-mee-trah] Friend of the Gods.
  "Deva": "Divine" (gods) + "Mitra": "Friend."

55

Moraika [mor-righ-kah] Angel.   (Kikuyu)

Mulan [moo-lahn] Flower in the Woods.   (Mandarin)
   "Mu": "Woods" (woodland) + "Lan": "Flowers."

Munayta [moon-nay-tah] Love, the power of love.   (Quechua)
   fr "Munay" [moon-nay] "Love."
   Munay Kusiy [moo-nay koo-see] Joyful Love.

N

Nadezhda [nah-dehj-dah] Hope, *became* **Nadia**.   (Russian)

Nadija [nah-dee-jah] River Born.   (Skt)
   "Nadi": "River" + "Ja": "Born."

Nadira [nah-deer-rah] Rare, precious.   (Hbr, Ara)

Naiya [nigh-yah] The Dreamer.   (Maya)
   fr "Nai" [nigh-ee] "Dream."
   Maya Indians believe dreams are real & reality the dream.
   In distant India they believe reality is an illusion; *see* Maya.

Najma [nahj-mah] Star Girl, *fr* "Najm": "Star."   (Ara)
   Nujaima [noo-jhigh-mah] Little Star.

Nakin [nah-keen] Life.   (Mam Maya)

Nakira [nah-keer-rah] Good for Others, Benevolent.   (Shona)

Nala [nah-lah] Plenty, Abundance.   (Zulu)

Nalani [nah-lah-nee] Calm Heaven, calm skies.   (Hwn)
   "Na": "Calm" + "Lani": "Heaven."

Nalina [nah-lee-nah] Lotus, symbol of truth.   (Skt)
   fr "Nala": "Reed" (stem of lotus), symbol of truth.
   Nalini [nah-lee-nee] Lotus, lotus woman; N for a Mystic.
   Nalika [nah-lee-kah] Little Lotus, little truth.
   "Nala": "Reed" (lotus) + "-ka" (little).

Naluri [nah-lur-ree] Good Instincts, intuition.   (Indonesian)
   fr Naluriah [nah-lur-ree-ah] Good Instincts, Intuition.

Nami [nah-mee] Wave.   (Japanese)
   Namika [nah-mee-kah] Flower of the Wave.
   "Nami": "Wave" + "Mika": "Flower."

Namiko [nah-mee-koh] Child of the Waves.
"Nami": "Wave" + "-ko" (girl), child.

Namisa [nah-mee-sah] Joy, to Rejoice. (Zulu)

Nandini [nahn-dee-nee] Joy. (Skt)
fr "Nanda": "Joy," to be delightful.
Sunanda [soo-nahn-dah] Great Joy, great delight.
"Su": "Good" (great) + "Nanda": "Joy."
Nandina [nahn-dee-nah] Joyful.
Nandika [nahn-dee-kah] Little Joy. "Nanda" + "-ka."

Nanea [nah-nay-yah] To Enjoy, to Relax. (Hwn)

Nani [nah-nee] Pretty. (Hwn)
Kanani [kah-nah-nee] The Pretty.
"Ka": "The" + "Nani": "Pretty."

Narumi [nar-roo-mee] Seed of Beauty. (Japanese)

Navarra [nah-var-rah] Navigator, sailor of the seas. (Span)

Nayana [nigh-yah-nah] Eye Pupils, to have nice eyes. (Skt)
Sunayana [soo-nigh-yah-nah] Fine Eyes, pretty eyes.
"Su": "Good" (fine) + "Nayana": "Pupils" (eyes).
Nayonika [nay-yoh-nee-kah] Expressive Eyes. (Hindi)
"Nayana": "Pupils" (eyes) + "-ka" (little).
Sunaina [soo-nigh-nah] Fine Eyes, *fr* "Sunayana." (Hindi)

Neema [nee-mah] Grace and Mercy from God. (Swahili)

Neemla [neem-lah] Waterfall. (Ixil Maya)

Neossa [nee-ohss-sah] New, new woman. (Grk)
fr "Neo" [nee-oh] "New"; *see* Genea.
Neola [nee-oh-lah] New, new little girl.
Neanika [nee-ah-nee-kah] New Victory.
"Neo": "New" + "Nike" [nee-kee] "Victory."
Neos (Grk) > Novus (Latin) > **Nouvel** (Frn) > **Nava** (Skt).
Nova [noh-vah] New, a new star is a supernova. (Latin)
Novika [noh-vee-kah] Little New One. (Russian)
Novaya [noh-vigh-yah] New, young. (Russian)
Navina [nah-vee-nah] New, Youthful. (Skt)
Novene [noh-veen] New, young girl. (ME)

Nerissa [nair-rihss-sah] Playful Nymph of the Sea.   (Grk)
fr "Nereides": "Sea Nymphs," of the Mediterranean Sea.
Neshama [neh-shah-mah] Soul.   (Hbr)
Netra [neh-trah] Eyes, nice eyes.   (Skt)
    Charunetra [char-roo-neh-trah] Beautiful Eyes.
    "Charu": "Beauty" + "Netra": "Eyes."
    Ravinetra [rah-vee-neh-trah] Sun Eyes, radiant eyes.
    "Ravi": "Sun" + "Netra": "Eyes."
    Sunetra [soo-neh-trah] Fine Eyes, pretty eyes.
    "Su": "Good" (fine) + "Netra": "Eyes."
Nicaea [nee-kay-yah] Victor, Champion.   (Grk)
fr "Nike" [nee-kee] "Victory" (champion), *became* [nigh-kee].
    Nicandra [nee-kann-drah] Victorious Woman.
    "Nike": "Victor" + "Andra": "Man," brave woman.
Nicola [neek-koh-lah] Champion of the People.   (Ital *fr* Grk)
fr "Nicholas"; *see* Ap1: Nicholas.   (Grk)
    Nicanora [neek-kah-nor-rah] Champion of the People.
Nikiqa [nee-keek-kah] Flower of the Moon.   (Mam Maya)
fr "Nikiq" [nee-keek] "Flower of the Moon."
"Nikaj" [nee-kah] "Flower" + "Iq" [eek] "Moon."
Nikiq flowers bloom every full moon on a giant tree,
and their exquisite scent will carry for miles in the night.
Nimah [nee-mah] Faith, Trust.   (Ixil Maya)
Nimla, **Neemla** [neem-lah] River, Waterfall.   (Ixil Maya)
Niwega [nee-way-gah] Thankful.   (Kikuyu)
Noella [noh-wehl-lah] Birth, the birth of Christ.   (Frn *fr* Latin)
fr "Natalis": "Birth," *became* "Noel."   (Latin)
Nur, **Noor**, **Noora** [nur, nor, nor-rah] Light, radiance.   (Ara)
    Nur Jahan [nur jah-hahn] Light of the World.
    Nujahan [nur-jah-hahn] *fr* "Nur Jahan." "Jahan": "World."
Nyana [nee-yah-nah] Baby Bird.   (Shona)
Nyasha [nee-yah-shah] Mercy.   (Shona)
Nyima [nee-mah] Sun.   (Tibetan)
    Nyima Lhamo [nee-mah lah-moh] Sun Goddess.

O

Odara [oo-dar-rah] Beauty. (Yoruba)
Odessa [oh-dehss-sah] Odyssey, a voyage. (Grk)
  Edessa [eh-dehss-sah] Odyssey, *fr* "Odessa." (ME)
  Dessa [dehss-sah] Odyssey, Nn *fr* "Odessa." (Eam)
Olenia [oh-lehn-nee-ah] Deer. (Russian)
Oluwafemi [oh-loo-wah-feh-mee] God Loves Me. (Yoruba)
  "Oluwa": "God" + "Femi": "Love."
Omaka [oh-mah-kah] Beginning, source of water. (Hwn)
Omkara [ohm-kar-rah] Sacred Sound, Nn is **Omi**. (Skt)
  N for a Shakti, the female personification of divine energy.
Omnira [ohm-neer-rah] Liberation. (Yoruba)
Onatah [oh-nah-tah] The Corn Spirit, a goddess. (Iroquois)
  Daughter of the earth who protected the crops.
Ondina [ahn-deen-nah] Mermaid. (Basque)
Onesa [oh-neh-sah] To Show, Guide. (Shona)
  To help others see things clearly, and understand them.
Onneka [ohn-neh-kah] Lucky, *fr* "Onni": "Lucky." (Finnish)
  Onnetar [oh-neh-tar] The Spirit of Luck.
  Onneleid [oh-neh-leed] Lucky Find. (Estonian)
  "Onn": "Lucky" + "Leidma": "Find."
Onwa [ohn-wah] Moon. (Igbo)
Opala, Opaline [oh-pah-lah, oh-pah-leen] Opal. (Frn *fr* Skt)
  fr "Upala": "Stone," precious stone, the opal. (Skt)
Oparia [oh-par-ree-ah] Gift. (Basque)
Orenda [or-rehn-dah] The Great Spirit, sacred power. (Iroquois)
Oriana [or-ree-ah-nah] Golden Dawn (east), the Orient. (Latin)
  fr "Aureolus": "Golden," *became* **Aurora** (dawn).
  Orovida [or-roh-vee-dah] Golden Life. (Span)
  "Oro": "Gold" + "Vida": "Life."
Orisa [or-rihss-sah] An Angelic Being. (Yoruba)
Orla [or-lah] Golden Lady. "Or": "Gold" + "Lady." (Gaelic)
Otesha [oh-tehsh-shah] Cultivate, Grow, to cherish. (Swahili)

P

Pacha [pah-chah] Earth. (Quechua)

Padma [pahd-mah] Lotus (truth), symbol of the truth. (Skt)
  Padme [pahd-may] Lotus (truth), *fr* "Padma."
  "Om Mani Padme Hum" = "Wisdom in Truth"; *see* Manika.
  Padmani [pahd-mahn-nee] Lotus, lotus woman.
  Padmaja [pahd-mah-jah] Lotus Born, born from truth.
  "Padma": "Lotus" (truth) + "Ja": "Born."
  Padmavati [pahd-mah-vah-tee] Winds of Truth.
  "Padma": "Lotus" (truth) + "Vata": "Wind."

Paiva [pigh-vah] Sun. (Finnish)

Palani [pah-lah-nee] Protector, of the truth. (Skt)

Paloma [pah-loh-mah] Dove. (Span)
  Palomita [pah-loh-mee-tah] Little Dove.

Pamoona [pah-moo-nah] Dream. (Cree)

Parama [par-rah-mah] The Best. (Skt)
  fr "Para": "Extreme" (highest degree), excellence, the best.
  Paramani [par-rah-mah-nee] Supreme Wisdom.
  "Para": "Best" + "Mani": "Jewel" (wisdom).

Parisa [par-ree-sah] Fairy, little genie with wings. (Persian)
  fr "Pari" [par-ree] "Wings," a fairy, little genie.
  Paribanu [par-ree-bah-noo] Fairy Princess.
  "Pari": "Wings" (fairy) + "Banu": "Princess."
  Parvana [par-vah-nah] Winged Being, a moth.

Parmena [par-meh-nah] Very Permanent. (Grk)
  fr "Parmenas": "Very Permanent," to be steadfast.
  "Para": "Very" + "Monimos": "Permanent."
  Paramona [par-rah-moh-nah] Permanent. (Russian)
  Parmelia [par-mehl-lee-ah] Permanent, *fr* "Parmenas." (ME)
  Parmelia, **Parmela** (ME) > Pamelia > **Pamela** (Eam).

Pavani [pah-vah-nee] Purity; N of Goddess of the Winds. (Skt)
  fr "Pava": "Purity," purified by the winds.
  Pavitra [pah-vee-trah] Purity.

60

Paxika [pah-shee-kah] Music of the Wind.   (Yucateca Maya)
  "Paxah" [pah-shah] "Music" + "Ik" [eek] "Wind."
Pejutawin [pay-joo-tah-wihn] Medicine Woman.   (Sioux)
  "Peju": "Grasses" + "Hute": "Roots" + "Win": "Woman."
○**Pema** [peh-mah] Lotus, symbol of truth.   (Tibetan)
  Pemala [peh-mah-lah] Honorable Lotus.
  "Pema": "Lotus" (truth) + "-la" (honored).
Perenna [pair-rehn-nah] Goddess of Renewal.   (Latin)
  fr "Perennis": "Perennial," blooming throughout the years.
  "Per": "Through" + "Annus": "Years," *became* Annual.
Perialla [pair-ree-ahl-lah] Exceptional; N of a prophetess.   (Grk)
  Pericaliya [pair-rih-kah-lee-yah] Exceptional Beauty.
  "Peri": "Very" (exceptional) + "Caliya": "Beauty."
Phaenna [fayn-nah] Brilliance, luminous woman.   (Grk)
  Phaedima [fay-dee-mah] Mother of Light.
  Phaedora [fay-dor-rah] Gift of Light.
  "Phaenos": "Brilliance" (light) + "Doro": "Gift."
Pherenike [fair-reh-nee-kee] Bringer of Victory.   (Grk)
  "Phere": "Bringer" + "Nike": "Victory."
  Legendary Pherenike was an athlete and fierce champion.
  Pherenike > Pherenice > **Berenice** > **Verenice** (Latin).
  Veronique [vair-rahn-neek] *fr* "Verenice."   (Frn)
Philinna [fihl-leen-nah] Love, *fr* "Phil": "Love."   (Grk)
  Philomela [fihl-loh-mehl-lah] Sweet Love; N of a princess.
  "Phil": "Love" + "Meli": "Honey" (sweet).
  Philothea [fihl-loh-thee-ah] Loving Goddess.
  "Phil": "Love" + "Thea": "Goddess."
Philyra [fihl-leer-rah] Lime Tree (linden); N of a nymph.   (Grk)
  Daughter of Oceanus, god of the river encircling the earth.
Prashanti [prah-shahn-tee] Messenger of Tranquility.   (Skt)
  "Pra" (bringer) + "Shanti": "Peace" (tranquil).
Pratima [prah-tee-mah] Image, manifestation of a goddess.   (Skt)
Pravi [prah-vee] Truth.   (Sb-Cr)
  Pravica [prah-vee-kah] Truth, truthful woman.

Prema [prehm-mah] Love, to be affectionate. (Skt)
    Premani [prehm-mah-nee] Love, loving woman.
    Premala [prehm-mah-lah] Honored Love.
    "Prema": "Love" (beloved) + "-la" (honored), venerated.
Primera [pree-mair-rah] First, leader of the way. (Latin)
    fr "Prima": "First" (leading), a leader.
    Primavera [pree-mah-vair-rah] First Green, springtime.
    Primalia [pree-mah-lee-ah] First, leader of the way. (ME)
Priya [pree-yah] Love, beloved; *see* Friyana. (Skt)
    Priyala [pree-yah-lah] Most Beloved, honored love.
    Priyanka [pree-yahnk-kah] Beloved.
    Supriya [soo-pree-yah] Great Love.
    "Su": "Good" (great) + "Priya": "Love."
    Priyasena [pree-yah-seen-nah] Warrior for Love.
    "Priya": "Love" + "Sena": "Spear" (warrior).
    Kavipriya [kah-vee-pree-yah] Love for Poetry.
    "Kavi": "Poetry" + "Priya": "Love."
Pureca [pyur-reh-kah] Pure, woman of purity. (Eam)
Purnima [pur-nee-mah] Completion, the full moon. (Skt)

Q

Qamara [kah-mar-rah] Moon, *fr* "Qamar": "Moon." (Ara)
Qinna [cheen-nah] Graceful Flower. (Mandarin)
    "Qin": "Center of Flower" + "Na": "Lithe Carriage."
Qiyana [kee-yah-nah] Clever, Crafty. (Zulu)
Qorianka [kor-ree-ahnk-kah] Golden Eagle. (Quechua)
    "Q'ori" [kor-ree] "Gold" + "Anka" [ahnk-kah] "Eagle."
    Qori Tika [kor-ree tee-kah] Golden Flower.
    "Q'ori": "Gold" + "T'ika": "Flower."
Qoya [koy-yah] Queen. (Quechua)
Quetzala [kehts-zahl-lah] Beauty; N of beautiful bird. (Nahuatl)
    N of a sacred bird of spectacular color, and a very long tail.
Qullana [koo-lah-nah] Sacredness. (Quechua)

R

Rachela [rah-kehl-lah] Merciful, *fr* "Raxum": "Merciful." (Hbr)
    Rayca [ray-kah] Merciful, Nn *fr* "Rachela."
Radeke, Radeka [rad-dee-kah] Little Counselor. (Germanic)
    "Rad": "Counselor" (wise) + "-ke" [kah] "Little."
Radha [rah-dah] Prosperity (success); N of a goddess. (Skt)
    Goddess Radha embodies divine beauty and love.
    Radhika [rah-dee-kah] Little Prosperity. "Radha" + "-ka."
Raduga [rad-doo-gah] Rainbow. (Russian)
Raika [righ-kah] Little Heaven. (Russian)
    "Rai" [righ] "Heaven" + "-ka" (little).
Rasina [rah-see-nah] Dew, *fr* "Rasa": "Dew." (Lithuanian)
Ravimani [rah-vee-dee-nah] Sun Jewel. (Skt)
    "Ravi": "Sun" + "Mani": "Jewel" (wisdom).
    Ravika [rah-vee-kah] Little Sun. "Ravi": "Sun" + "-ka."
Rayowa [righ-yoh-wah] Life. (Hausa)
Realta [rayl-tah] Star. (Gaelic)
Reliance [reh-ligh-ehnss] Reliable Girl. (Eam)
Remedy [reh-meh-dee] Remedy (medicine), the answer. (Eam)
Reyna [ray-nah] Queen. (Frn *fr* Latin)
    fr "Regno": "Reign" (ruler), *became* **Regina**. (Latin)
    Rayna [ray-nah] Queen.
    Rainelle, Raynelle [ray-nehl] Little Queen, a princess.
    Reina [ray-nah] Queen. (Span)
    Reyanna [ray-yahn-nah] Queen. (Span)
    Reinera [righ-neer-rah] Queen. (Dutch)
    Riona [ree-yoh-nah] Queen. (Gaelic)
    Rianna [ree-ahn-nah] Queen. (OE)
    Ryanna [righ-ahn-nah] Queen. (OE)
    Raji, Rajita [rah-jee, rah-jee-tah] Queen. (Skt)
    Rani [rah-nee] Queen, Nn *fr* "Raji"; *see* Amarani. (Skt)
    Riella [ree-ehl-lah] Little Queen. (Ital)
Rheia, Rhea [ree-yah] Stream of Water; N of a Titan. (Grk)

63

Richensa [rihk-kehn-sah] Ruler, *fr* "Ric": "Ruler."   (Germanic)
   Richenza [rihk-kehn-zah] Ruler.
   Rikissa [rihk-kih-sah] Ruler; N of a princess.   (Danish)
   Rixa [rihk-sah] Ruler, Nn *fr* "Rikissa."   (Danish)
   Richama [rihk-kah-mah] Ruler, *fr* "Richard."   (Eam)
Rindinya [rihn-dihn-yah] Walks Fearlessly.   (Shona)
   Rindi [rihn-dee] Walks Fearlessly, *fr* "Rindinya."
Risette [ree-seht] Little Smile.   (Frn)
   Sonrisa [sohn-ree-sah] Smile.   (Span)
   Risa [ree-sah] Laughter.   (Span)
Ristiina [rihss-stee-nah] *fr* "Kristina"; *see* Kristanna.   (Finnish)
Rita [ree-tah] Flow, cosmic order, the truth.   (Skt)
   Rituparna [ree-too-par-nah] Winged Truth.
   "Rita": "Cosmic Flow" (truth) + "Parna": "Wings."
Rodina [roh-deen-nah] Homeland.   (Russian)
Rosenda [roh-sehn-dah] Pretty Rose.   (Span)
   fr **Rosalinda** [roh-sah-lihn-dah] Pretty Rose.
   "Rosa": "Rose" + "Linda": "Pretty."
   Rosalinda > **Rosaline** > **Rosalie** (Span) > **Sally** (Eam).
   Pioneers met girls named Rosalinda living in California.
   Larrosa [lah-roh-sah] The Rose.   (Basque)
   "La": "The" + "Rosa": "Rose," representing love.
   Rozenay [roh-zeh-nay] Graced Rose, *fr* "Rosanna."   (Eam)
Roshani [roh-shawn-nee] Light, radiant girl.   (Hindi)
   fr "Roshan" [roh-shawn] "Light" (radiant).
   Roshaniya [roh-shawn-nee-yah] Light, radiant girl.
Runa [roo-nah] Secrets, sacred wisdom.   (Nor, Scand)
   ◦ *fr* "Rune": "Secret," hidden knowledge, sacred wisdom.
   Runes were carved on rowan tree wood; *see* Ap1: Rune.
   Rowan [roh-wehn] Secret Wisdom.   (OE)
   Roana [rohn-nah] Secret Wisdom.   (OE)
   Solrun [sohl-roon] Sun Wisdom.   (Scand)
   "Sol": "Sun" + "Run" (rune).
Ruva [roo-vah] Flower.   (Shona)

S

Sabine [sah-been] A Beauty Woman; N of a tribe.　　(Latin)
　The soldiers that founded Rome, stole the beautiful women
　of the Sabine tribe to populate their city in 750 BC.
　Sabina [sah-bee-nah] Beautiful as a Sabine Woman.
　Sabella [sah-behl-lah] Little Beauty.
　Sabelle [sah-behl] Little Beauty.　　(Frn)
　Sabrina [sah-bree-nah] Beautiful Woman, *fr* "Sabina."　(Eam)
　Sabrisah [sah-bree-sah] Beauty, *fr* "Sabrina."　(Eam)
Sabira [sah-beer-rah] Patience.　　(Ara)
Sachiko [sah-chee-koh] Happy Child.　　(Japanese)
Sade [shah-day] Honor of the Crown; *see* Folasade.　(Yoruba)
Safaya [sah-figh-yah] Sapphire.　　(Shona)
Sage [sayj]
　1. Wisdom, a profoundly wise person.　　(Grk)
　　fr "Sophos": "Wisdom."
　2. Safe, to be well; N of a healing plant.　　(Frn *fr* Latin)
　　fr "Salve": "Safe" (well), to be in good health.　(Latin)
Sahana [sah-hah-nah] Powerful, strong.　　(Skt)
Salila [sah-lee-lah] Water.　　(Skt)
Salima [sal-lee-mah] Safe, living in peace.　　(Ara)
　fr "Salam" [sah-lahm] "Peace" (safe).
　Shalima [shal-lee-mah] Safe, living in peace.
　Shalimar [shal-lee-mar] Peaceful; N of legendary gardens.
　The Shalimar Gardens were built by Shah Jahan, a Persian.
　Salma [sal-mah] Safe, living in peace.
　Ummisalma [oom-mee-sal-mah] Mother of Peace.
　fr **Umm Salma**, wife of Muhammad, mother of Muslims.
Samianta [sah-mee-ahn-tah] Hears God.　　(Frn *fr* Hbr)
　fr "Shimon" [shee-mohn] "Hears God," *became* Simon.　(Hbr)
　"Shmia": "Hears" (understands) + "El": "God."
　Samantha [sah-mann-thah] Hears God, *fr* "Samianta."　(ME)
　Samanda [sah-mann-dah] Hears God.　　(Span)

Samira [sah-meer-rah] Good Company, entertaining.　　(Ara)

Sananda [sah-nahn-dah] The Best Joy.　　(Skt)

　"Sa": "Best" (excellence) + "Nanda": "Joy"; *see* Nanda.

Sanning [sann-neeng] Truth.　　(Swed)

Santina [sann-teen-nah] Little Saint.　　(Frn)

Sarai [sar-ray] My Queen, *became* [sair-righ].　　(Hbr *fr* Sumerian)

　fr **Sarra** [sar-rah] Queen, *fr* "Sarrum": "King."　　(Sumerian)

　"Sarra": "Queen" + "-i" (sheli): "My" (Hbr).

　Saray [sar-ray] My Queen, *fr* "Sarai."

　Sarali [sair-rah-lee] My Queen, "Sara" + "-li" (sheli): "My."

　Sarayah [sar-ray-yah] Queen from God, *became* "Sarah."

　"Sarra": "Queen" + "Yah": "God" (Hbr).

　Sarah [sar-rah] Queen from God, *became* [sair-rah].

　fr "Sarayah": "Queen from God," Sar(ay)ah.

　Israelites wrote the Old Testament in Babylon (Sumeria).

　Sarady [sair-rah-dee] Queen From, where she lived.　　(ME)

　fr "Sarah" + "De" [day] "Of" + (where she was from).

　Sadie [say-dee] Cmpd Nn *fr* "Sarady," Sa(ra)dy.　　(ME)

　Saradella [sair-rah-dehl-lah] Little Queen, *fr* "Sarady." (Eam)

Sarama [sair-rah-mah] To be Bright, with bright eyes. (Estonian)

Sarauniya [sar-row-nee-yah] Queen.　　(Hausa)

Sarita [sar-ree-tah] River, *fr* "Sarit" [sar-reet] "River."　　(Skt)

　fr "Sari": "Cascading," "Waterfall"; N for a flowing dress.

　Sarika [sar-ree-kah] Little River.

　N of the Song Thrush, singer of cascading melodies.

Saroja [sar-roh-jah] Lake Born, a lotus flower (truth).　　(Skt)

　"Saro": "Lake" + "Ja": "Born," a lotus in the lake.

　Sarojini [sar-roh-jee-nee] Many Lotuses, profusion of truth.

　fr "Sarojin": "Many Lotus," abounding with lotuses (truth).

Sarraqa [sair-rah-kah] Rise of the Celestial Sky.　　(Amharic)

　The rising of all celestial bodies; the moon, sun, and stars.

Satomi [sah-toh-mee] The Deeper Answer.　　(Japanese)

　The profound results from a deep philosophical study.

Sayler, Saylor, Saylore [say-lur, say-lor] Sailor, navigator. (Eam)

Sedemay [seed-duh-may] Seed Maiden, symbol of plenty. (OE)
    fr "Sedemaiden" [seed-duh-may-dehn] "Seed Maiden."
    "Sede" [seed] "Seed" + "Maiden" (young woman).
    Sedemay followed the men in the fields, sowing the seed.

Selene [sehl-lee-nee] Moon; N of the Moon Goddess. (Grk)
    Selenia [sehl-lee-nee-ah] Moon Goddess, *fr* "Selene."
    Selena [sehl-lee-nah] Moon Goddess, *fr* "Selene." (Span)
    Dioselena [dee-oh-sehl-lee-nah] Moon Goddess. (Span)
    "Diosa": "Goddess" + "Selena": "Moon."

Semra [sehm-rah] Dark Beauty. (Turkish)

Sena [seen-nah] Spear, represents a warrior in action. (Skt)
    Nalasena [nah-lah-seen-nah] Lotus Warrior, for truth.
    "Nala": "Reed" (lotus) + "Sena": "Spear" (warrior).

Seraphima [sair-rah-fee-mah] Much Light, brightest angel. (Hbr)
    fr "Seraphim": "Much Light," the highest order of angels.
    "Srafe": "Fire" (light) + "Ham": "Many" (much).
    Serapia [sair-rah-pee-yah] Brightest Angel. (Ital)
    Seraphine [sair-rah-feen] Brightest Angel. (Frn)
    Seraphina [sair-rah-feen-nah] Brightest Angel. (OE)
    Serafina [sair-rah-feen-nah] Brightest Angel. (ME)
    Seraphia, Serafia [sair-rah-fee-ah] Nn *fr* "Seraphina." (Eam)

Serenita [sair-reh-nee-tah] Little Serenity, cloudless. (Latin)
    "Serenus": "Clear Up" (serene) + "-ita" (little).
    Serena [sair-ree-nah] Serenity. (Span)
    Surenea [sur-reh-nee-yah] Serenity. (Eam)

Serrana [sair-rah-nah] Mountain Girl. (Span *fr* Latin)
    fr "Serra" [sair-rah] "Saw," jagged mountain range. (Latin)
    Sierra [see-air-rah] Mountains.

Shabana [shah-bah-nah] Royal Princess. (Persian)
    "Shah": "King" (royal) + "Banu": "Princess."

Shaiyena [shigh-yehn-nah] Red Painted; N for a tribe. (Sioux)
    fr "Shaya" [shigh-yah] "Red Painted," red painted faces.
    Both Cheyenne and Sioux are Algonquin languages.
    Originally, they lived in the forests below the Great Lakes.

The Sioux described their neighbors as Shaiyena (cheyenne).

Cheyenne [shigh-yann] Red Painted, *fr* "Shaiyena." (Eam)

Cheyenna [shigh-yann-nah] *fr* "Cheyenne." (Eam)

Cheyna [shay-nah] Red Painted; N of a tribe. (Eam)

Chenoa [shay-noh-wah] N of a tribe, *fr* "Cheyna." (Eam)

Shamira [shah-meer-rah] Guardian. (Hbr)

   fr "Shmira": "Guarding" (guardian), to be protective.

   Shamara [shah-mar-rah] Guardian.

Shamisa [shah-mee-sah] Light, sunlight. (Hbr)

   fr "Shemesh" [sheh-mehsh] "Sun"; *see* Shimshon.

Shanira [shah-neer-rah] Warmed by the Sun. (Shona)

Shanta [shahn-tah] Peace, Tranquility. (Skt)

   Shantavva [shahn-tahv-vah] Peace, peaceful woman.

   Shanti [shahn-tee] Peace, Tranquility.

Shauriana [shor-ree-ah-nah] Negotiator, Counselor. (Swahili)

Shaylee [shay-lee] Fairy in the Meadow. (OE *fr* Gaelic)

   fr "Sith" [shee] "Fairy," *became* **Shay**, **Shea**. (Gaelic)

   "Sith": "Fairy" (Gaelic) + "Leah": "Meadow" (OE).

Shayna [shay-nah] Little Beauty. (Yiddish *fr* Ger)

   fr "Schoneke" [shoon-neh-kah] "Little Beauty." (Ger)

   "Schon": "Beauty" + "-ke" (little).

Shewa [shee-wah] Peace. (Tibetan)

Shima [shee-mah] True Intention. (Japanese)

Shione [shigh-oh-nay] Sound of the Ocean Waves. (Japanese)

Shira, Shara [sheer-rah, shar-rah] Singing, the singer. (Hbr)

   Sharona [shar-roh-nah] Singer; "Sharon" *for* boys.

Shivani [shee-vah-nee] Shiva Woman, a transformer. (Hindi)

   Of the Hindi gods; Brahma is the creator, Vishnu is the
   preserver, and Shiva is the destroyer or the transformer.

Shoshana [shoh-shah-nah] Lily, large beautiful flower. (Hbr)

   Sosha [soh-shah] Lily, *fr* "Shoshana."

   Susanita [soo-sah-nee-tah] Little Lily, "-ita" (little). (Span)

   Xuxana [shoo-shah-nah] Lily, Nn is **Xuxa**. (Basque)

Shulan [shoo-lahn] Kindhearted Flower. (Mandarin)

"Shu": "Kindhearted" + "Lan": "Flower."

Sidra [sigh-drah] Starry. (Latin)
   fr "Siderus": "Starry," influenced by the stars, sidereal.
Siempria [see-ehm-pree-ah] Always, *fr* "Siempre." (Span)
Sieva [see-ay-vah] Pretty. (Finnish)
Sobranna [seh-brah-nah] Friend. (Estonian)
Solara [sohl-lar-rah] Solar, Sun, a sunny girl. (Latin)
   fr "Solaris" [sohl-lar-rihss] "Sun."
    Solarisa [sohl-lar-rihss-sah] Sun, *fr* "Solaris." (Ger)
    Sola [sohl-lah] Sun. (Nor)
    Solina [sohl-lee-nah] Sunny. (Russian)
    Solenne [sohl-leen] Sunny. (Frn)
    Solana [sohl-lah-nah] Sunny Place. (Span)
    Solita [sohl-lee-tah] Little Sun. (Span)
    Sulwen [sohl-wehn] White Sun, radiant beauty. (Welsh)
    "Sul": "Sun" + "Gwen": "White."
Soleine [sohl-layn] Sun, *fr* "Soleil": "Sun." (Frn)
    Solange [sohl-lahnj] Sun Angel.
    "Soleil" [sohl-lay] "Sun" + "Ange" [ahnj] "Angel."
Solimara [soh-lee-mar-rah] Sun & Sea, sparkling waves. (Span)
    "Sol": "Sun" + "Y" [ee] "And" + "Mar": "Sea."
Solvina [sohl-vee-nah] Sun Way. (Swed)
   fr "Solveig" [sohl-vigh] "Sun Way," standing in the sun.
   "Sol": "Sun" + "Veig": "Way," the sunnyside of a fjord.
Sophia [soh-fee-yah] Wisdom, *fr* "Sophos": "Wisdom." (Grk)
    Sophronia [soh-froh-nee-yah] Wisdom, *fr* "Sophia."
    Sofronia [soh-froh-nee-yah] *fr* "Sophronia"; *see* Fronia.
    Sophrina, Sofrina [soh-freen-nah] Wisdom. (OE)
    Safronia [saf-froh-nee-yah] Wisdom, *fr* "Sophronia." (Eam)
    Sapphria [saf-free-yah] Wisdom, *fr* "Sophronia." (Eam)
Soteira, Sotira [soh-teer-rah] Savior. (Grk)
Sova [soh-vah] Owl. (Russian)
Stella [stehl-lah] Star, star woman. (Latin)
    Stellaria [stehl-lar-ree-ah] Starry, celestial, *fr* "Stellaris."

Sujala [soo-jah-lah] Sweet Water.　　　　　　　　　(Skt)
　　"Su": "Good" (sweet) + "Jala": "Water."
Sumalini [soo-mah-lee-nee] Great Flower Gardener.　　(Skt)
　　"Su": "Good" + "Malini": "Garland Grower" (gardener).
Sumaqa [soo-mah-kah] Beauty.　　　　　　　　(Quechua)
　　fr "Sumaq" [soo-mahk] "Beauty."
　　Sumaq Tika [soo-mahk tee-kah] Beautiful Flower.
　　"Sumaq": "Beauty" + "T'ika" [tee-kah] "Flower."
　　Ima Sumaq [ee-mah soo-mahk] Great Beauty.
　　Qoya Sumaqa [koy-yah soo-mah-kah] Beautiful Queen.
Sundari [soon-dar-ree] Beauty, great beauty.　　　　(Skt)
　　Sundarika [soon-dar-ree-kah] Little Beauty.
　　Sundara [soon-dar-rah] Beauty, great beauty.
　　Sundarasena [soon-dar-rah-seen-nah] Beautiful Warrior.
　　"Sundara": "Beauty" + "Sena": "Warrior."
Sunna [suhn-nah] Sunny; N of the Goddess of the Sun.　(Nor)
　　Sunneva [suhn-nee-vah] Gift from the Sun.　　　(OE)
　　"Sun" + "Giefu" [geef] "Give" (gift).
　　Sunniva [suhn-nee-vah] Gift from the Sun.
　　Saint Sunniva fled to Norway and became their first saint.
Suri [sur-ree] Learned, very wise, a Sage.　　　　　(Skt)
　　Surideva [sur-ree-day-vah] Divine Sage.
　　"Suri": "Learned" (sage) + "Deva": "Divine."
Susanna [soo-sahn-nah] Lily.　　　　　　　　(OE *fr* Hbr)
　　fr **Shoshana** [shoh-shahn-nah] Lily, a lovely flower.　(Hbr)
　　Shoshanika [shoh-shahn-nee-kah] Little Lily Flower.
　　Susande [soo-sahn-day] Lily Flower, *fr* "Susanna."　(Scand)
Sutaraka [soo-tar-rah-kah] Little Bright Star.　　　　(Skt)
　　"Su": "Good" (bright) + "Tara": "Star" + "-ka" (little).
Sutrani [soo-trah-nee] The Teachings of the Masters.　(Skt)
　　fr "Sutra": "Sew," stringing together words of the masters.
Suvi [soo-vee] Summer.　　　　　　　(Estonian, Finnish)
　　Suvine [soo-vee-nay] Summer, summer girl.
　　Suvetar [soo-veh-tar] The Spirit of Summer.　　(Finnish)

70

T

Tabara [tah-bar-rah] Prosperous. (Kikuyu)

Tadiwa [tah-dee-wah] We have been Favored. (Shona)

Tahira [tah-heer-rah] Purity. (Ara)

Taija [tay-jah] Made of Light, a splendid light being. (Skt)
    fr "Taijasa" [tay-jah-sah] "Consisting of Light."
    Teja [tay-jah] Made of Light, *fr* "Taija." (Hindi)
    Tejomaya [tay-joh-migh-yah] Magical Light. (Hindi)
    "Taijas": "Light" + "Maya": "Magic," made by magic.

Taika
    1. [tigh-kah] Peace. (Lithuanian)
    2. [tigh-ee-kah] Magic; *see* Uni. (Finnish)

Taina [tigh-ee-nah] Mystery. (Russian)

Taiva [tigh-vah] Sky. (Finnish)
    Taeva [tigh-vah] Sky. (Estonian)

Talika [tah-lee-kah] Palms (hands), to clap in celebration. (Skt)

Talora [tah-lor-rah] Dew in the Morning Light. (Hbr)
    "Tal": "Dew" + "Or": "Light," sparkling lights.
    Taliya [tah-lee-yah] Dew from God.
    "Tal": "Dew" + "Yah": "God."
    Gardens are grown in the desert by trapping the dew.

Taluma [tah-loo-mah] Endurance. (Estonian)

Tamako [tah-mah-koh] Precious Stone Child. (Japanese)
    "Tama": "Precious Stone" + "-ko" (girl), child.
    Tamane [tah-mah-nay] The Sound of Precious Stones.
    "Tama": "Precious Stone" (necklace) + "Ne": "Sound."
    The sound of her necklace means beauty approaches.

Tamayo [tah-migh-yoh] Precious Generation. (Japanese)

Tamira [tah-meer-rah] Tall and Upright in Values. (Hbr)
    fr "Tamima": "Upright," in height and values.
    Tamar, Tamara [tah-mar, tah-mar-rah] Date Palm Tree.

Tamire [tam-meer-ray] My Magic. (Amharic)
    Tamira [tah-meer-rah] The Magic, the miracle.

Tara [tar-rah]
1. Star, to sail across the cosmos, a rescuer. (Skt)
   Sutara [soo-tar-rah] Brighter Star, the better star.
   "Su": "Good" (better, brighter) + "Tara": "Star."
2. Celestial Goddesses, divine protectors. (Tibetan)
   Rescuers from the stars who protect those on earth.

Tariqah [tar-ree-kah] The Way, spiritual path of the Sufi. (Ara)
Tarkana [tar-kahn-nah] Reasoning (logic). (Skt)
    Tarkina [tar-keen-nah] Clever Thinker, logical. (Estonian)
    Tarquinia [tar-keen-nee-ah] Deep Thinker. (Latin)
Taruka, **Taruca** [tar-roo-kah] Little Deer. (Quechua)
Tashi [tah-shee] Auspicious, to have luck & success. (Tibetan)
Tashina Sapawin [tah-shee-nah sah-pah-wihn]. (Sioux)
    Black Shawl Woman. "Win": "Woman."
    "Ta": "Her" + "Shina": "Shawl" + "Sapa": "Black."
Teleia, **Telea** [tehl-lee-ah] Perfection. (Grk)
    Nicotelea [nee-koh-tehl-lee-ah] Perfect Victory.
    "Nike" [nee-kee] "Victory" + "Telea": "Perfect."
Telluria [tehl-lur-ree-ah] Daughter of the Earth. (Latin)
    fr "Telluris" [tehl-lur-rihss] "Earth."
    Telluriana [tehl-lur-ree-ah-nah] Earth Daughter.
Tembisa [tehm-bee-sah] Promise, trustable. (Zulu)
Tephania [teh-fahn-nee-ah] Goddess Voice. (OE *fr* Grk)
    fr "Theophane" [thee-oh-fahn-nee] "Goddess Voice." (Grk)
    "Theo": "God" (goddess) + "Phone" [fahn-nee] "Voice."
    Theophania > Tephania > Teffania > **Tiffany**.
    Teffania [tehf-fahn-nee-ah] Voice of the Goddess.
Terma [tur-mah] Hidden Treasure. (Tibetan)
Terra [tair-rah] Earth. (Latin)
    Terranova [tair-rah-noh-vah] New Earth.
    "Terra": "Earth" + "Nova": "New."
    Terrigena [tair-rih-jehn-nah] Born on Earth.
    "Terra": "Earth" + "Genus": "Generation" (birth), race.
    Tierra [tee-air-rah] Earth. (Span)

Tierralinda [tee-air-rah-lihn-dah] Beautiful Earth. (Span)
"Tierra": "Earth" + "Linda": "Pretty" (beauty).

Teruko [tair-roo-koh] Sunshine Child. (Japanese)

Thea [thee-ah] Goddess, *became* "Dea"; *see* Deandra. (Grk)
    Theona, Theana [thee-oh-nah, thee-ah-nah] Goddess.
    Theonia [thee-oh-nee-ah] Goddess.

Therania [theer-raw-nee-ah] Shining, brightness. (Kikuyu)

Therasia [thair-rah-see-ah] Place of Abundance. (Grk)
    fr "Thera" [thair-rah] "Harvest"; N of the Harvest Goddess.
    Goddess Thera symbolizes a good harvest and abundance.
    Teresa [tair-ree-sah] Harvest Goddess, *fr* "Therasia." (Span)
    Teresina [tair-reh-see-nah] Harvest Goddess Girl. (Ital)

Tiana, Tia [tee-ah-nah, tee-ah] Respected. (Kikuyu)
    Tianira [tee-ah-neer-rah] Respected.

Tiara [tee-ar-rah] Jeweled Crown, worn by a princess. (Latin)
    Tiarella [tee-ar-rehl-lah] Little Tiara, little princess. (Frn)

Tiesa [tee-eh-sah] Truth. (Lithuanian)

Tifara [tih-far-rah] Splendor, *fr* "Tiferet": "Splendor." (Hbr)

Tika [tee-kah] Flower, *fr* "T'ika": "Flower." (Quechua)
    Inti Tika [ihn-tee tee-kah] Sun Flower.

Tikva [teek-vah] Hope. (Hbr)

Tima, Timaea [tee-mah, tihm-may-yah] Honor. (Grk)
    Timandra [tihm-mann-drah] Honored Man.
    "Tima": "Honored" + "Andra": "Man."
    Timarete [tihm-mar-ree-tay] Honored for Bravery.
    "Tima": "Honored" + "Arete": "Valor" (brave).
    Pheretima [fair-reh-tee-mah] Bringer of Honor.
    "Phere": "Bringer" + "Tima": "Honor"; *see* Pherenike.
    Diotima [dee-oh-tee-mah] Honored Divinity.
    "Deos": "God" (divinity) + "Tima": "Honor."
    Princess of Mantineia and teacher of Socrates in 400 BC.

Tinashe [tee-nah-shay] God is With Us. (Shona)
    Tinashe > **Tinasha** > **Tinisha** > Tanesha > Taneisha.
    Tanesha, Taneisha [tah-nee-shah] *fr* "Tinashe." (Eam)

73

Tiralainn [teer-rah-lihn] Beautiful Land. (Gaelic)
   fr **Tir Alainn** [teer al-lihn] Beautiful Land.
   "Tir": "Land" + "Alainn": "Beauty."
Tivona [tihv-voh-nah] Nature, nature girl. (Hbr)
   fr "Teva" [teh-vah] "Nature" (natural), loves nature.
Tomone [toh-moh-nay] Sound of a Friend. (Japanese)
   "Tomo": "Friend" + "Ne": "Sound."
Tressa [trehss-sah] Strength. (Gaelic)
Trula, Trulee [troo-lah, troo-lee] True Love. (Eam *fr* ME)
   fr "Trulove" [troo-luhv] "True Love." (ME)
   Trufina [troo-feen-nah] Truly Fine.
Tsering [sair-reeng] Long Life. (Tibetan)
   Tseringma [sair-reeng-mah] Long Life Goddess.
Tulika [too-lee-kah] Buttercup Flower, *fr* "Tulikas." (Estonian)
Tuulia [too-lee-ah] Wind, daughter of the wind. (Finnish)
Tuvia [too-vee-ah] Goodness, to have a good heart. (Hbr)
   fr "Tuv" [toov] "Goodness," *became* "Tobias."
   Tovia [toh-vee-ah] Goodness.
   Tabitha [tab-bih-thah] Goodness, a good woman. (Grk)

U

Ucheoma [oo-chay-oh-mah] Good Will. (Igbo)
   "Uche": "Will" (intention) + "Oma": "Good."
   Uchenna [oo-chay-nah] God's Idea.
   "Uche": "Will" (idea) + "Nna": "Father" (god).
Ulla [ool-lah] Wolf Girl, *fr* "Ulv": "Wolf." (Swed)
   Ullarike, Ullarika [ool-lar-ree-kah] Wolf Ruler.
   "Ulla": "Wolf" + "Rik": "Ruler."
Uma [oo-mah] Splendor; N of a major goddess. (Skt)
   Umika [oo-mee-kah] Little Uma. "Uma" + "-ka" (little).
Umiko [oo-mee-koh] Ocean Child. (Japanese)
   "Umi": "Ocean" + "-ko" (girl), child.
Umita [oo-mee-tah] Hope. (Turkish)

Umoja [oo-moh-jah] Unity. (Swahili)

Uni [oo-nee] Dream. (Finnish)

    Uni Taika [oo-nee tigh-ee-kah] Dream-spell.

    "Uni": "Dream" + "Taika": "Magic" = Magical Dream.

Unita [yoo-nee-tah] Oneness, Unity. (Latin)

Ursinda [ur-sihn-dah] Bear, *fr* "Ursa": "Bear." (Latin)

Usha [oo-shah] Dawn; N of the Dawn Goddess. (Skt)

    Usha Kirana [oo-shah keer-rah-nah] Rays of Dawn.

    "Usha": "Dawn" + "Kirana": "Ray" (light).

V

Vajrani [vahj-rah-nee] Thunderbolt, symbol of the truth. (Skt)

    fr "Vajra": "Hardest" (diamond), "Mightiest" (thunderbolt).
    Truth is the mightiest force in the universe, like lightning,
    which cannot be stopped from illuminating the world.

Valentia [val-lehn-tee-ah] Strong, to be Valiant (brave). (Latin)

    Valenza [val-lehn-zah] Strong, to be Valiant.

    Valencia [vah-lehn-see-ah] Valiant, Brave. (Span)

    Valera [vahl-leer-rah] Valiant, Brave. (Frn)

    Valerian [val-lair-ree-ehn] Valiant, Brave. (Ger, Scand)

    Valeska [val-lehss-skah] Little Brave One. (Ger)

    Valora [val-lor-rah] Valiant, Brave, *fr* "Valerian." (ME)

    Velura [vehl-lur-rah] Valiant, Brave, *fr* "Valora." (Eam)

Valossa [val-loh-sah] Light, *fr* "Valo": " Light." (Finnish)

    Valosade [vah-loh-shah-day] Rain of Light, beams of light.

    "Valo": "Light" + "Sade" [shah-day] "Rain," beaming.

Vasanti [vah-sahn-tee] Springtime Woman; *see* Basanti. (Skt)

    fr "Vasanta": "Brilliant Season" (spring), as the sun returns.

    Vasantasena [vah-sahn-tah-seen-nah] Spring Warrior.

    "Vasanta": "Springtime" + "Sena": "Warrior."

Vasara [vah-sar-rah] Summer. (Lithuanian)

Veda [vay-dah] Knowledge; N for hymns (scriptures). (Skt)

    Vedas are sacred verses that date back to 3,000 BC.

Vedanta [vay-dahn-tah] Complete Knowledge.

Vela [vehl-lah] Candlelight, the light. (Span)

Verania [vair-rah-nee-ah] Truth, truthful woman. (Latin)
    fr "Veritas" [veer-ree-tahss] "Truth."
    Verena [vair-reh-nah] Truth; N of a saint in the 3rd century.
    Verina [vair-ree-nah] Truth, truthful woman.
    Verity [vair-rih-tee] Truth. (ME)

Viana [vee-ah-nah] Journey, down a good road. (Span)
    fr "Via": "Way," "Road," journey, traveling through life.
    Vialinda [vee-ah-lihn-dah] Beautiful Journey.
    "Via": "Road" (journey) + "Linda": "Pretty" (beautiful).

Vida [vee-dah] Life. (Span)
    Vidaluz [vee-dah-looz] Light of my Life.
    "Vida": "Life" (living) + "Luz": "Light."

Vimala [veem-mah-lah] Spotless, Stainless, pure. (Skt)
    To be stainless and pure in both heart and mind.
    Suvimala [soo-vee-mah-lah] Very Pure. (Skt)
    "Su": "Good" (very) + "Vimala": "Spotless" (pure).
    Vimla [veem-lah] Purity, cmpd Nn *fr* "Vimala." (Hindi)

Vinita [vih-nee-tah] Disciplined Master. (Skt)
    fr "Vin": "Disciplined," practice makes the master (teacher).
    Vinetra [vih-neh-trah] Eyes of the Disciplined Master.
    "Vin": "Disciplined" (master) + "Netra": "Eyes."
    Vineeta [vih-nee-tah] Disciplined Master, *fr* "Vinita." (Hindi)

Viola [vee-oh-lah] Purple Flower, *became* **Violet**. (Latin *fr* Grk)
    fr "Io" [i-oh] "Purple"; *see* Yolande. (Grk)
    Veola [vee-oh-lah] Purple Flower, *fr* "Viola." (Frn)

Virani [veer-rah-nee] Brave (hero), heroic woman. (Skt)
    Viramati [veer-rah-mah-tee] Spiritual Hero.
    "Vira": "Hero" + "Mati": "Prayer" (devotion), spiritual.
    Virasena [veer-rah-seen-nah] Heroic Warrior.
    "Vira": "Brave" (hero) + "Sena": "Spear" (warrior).

Viva, Vivana [vee-vah, vee-vah-nah] Lively, full of life. (Latin)
    fr "Vivacitas": "Long Life" (lively), vivacious.

W

Wailani [wigh-lah-nee] Water from Heaven. (Hwn)
"Wai": "Water" + "Lani": "Heaven."

Wakanhdi Win [wah-kahn-dee wihn] Lightning Woman. (Sioux)
"Wakan": "Sacred" + "Ide" [ee-day] "Blaze" = Lightning.
Tiwakan Win [tee-wah-kahn wihn] Holy Lodge Woman.
"Ti": "Tipi" (lodge) + "Wakan": "Sacred" + "Win."
Wiyaka Wakan Win [wee-yah-kah wah-kahn wihn].
Sacred Feather Woman. "Wiyaka": "Feather."

Wamani [wah-mah-nee] Sacred Mountain Peak. (Quechua)

Wanahca Win [wah-nahk-chah wihn] Flower Woman. (Sioux)
Wanaca [wah-nah-kah] Flower, *fr* "Wanahca." (Eam)

Wayanay [wigh-yah-nigh] Swallow, a songbird. (Quechua)

Wendela [wehn-dehl-lah] Wandering Hunter. (OE *fr* Germanic)
fr "Wandalar": "Wanderer," wanders far to hunt. (Germanic)
King Wandalar of the Ostrogoths was born in 395 AD.

Wenya [wehn-yah] Polite Elegance. (Mandarin)

Wihopa Win [wee-hohp-pah wihn] Astonishing Woman. (Sioux)
"Wihopa": "Astonishing" + "Win": "Woman."

Winaya [wih-nigh-yah] Forever. (Aymara)

Winfrey [wihn-free] Friend of Peace, loves peace. (ME *fr* OE)
fr "Winifred" = "Wine": "Friend" + "Fred": "Peace." (OE)

Winona [wih-noh-nah] Nourisher, a mother. (Algonquin)
Mother of the legendary Hiawatha, unifier of the Iroquois.
Winora [wih-nor-rah] Nourisher, *fr* "Winona." (Eam)

Witena [wih-tehn-nah] One Who Knows, a wise man. (OE)
fr "Wit": "To Know" (wise); *see* Ap1: Rune.

Wren, Wrenna [rehn, rehn-nah] Wren, a small bird. (OE)
Wrenneta [rehn-neh-tah] Little Wren. (Eam)
Amberwren [am-bur-rehn] Amber Wren. (Eam)

Wyndream [wihn-dreem] Jubilation, very joyful, delighted. (OE)
"Wynn" [wihn] "Joy" + "Dream": "Joy."
Wynsome [wihn-suhm] Delightful, winsome, *fr* "Wynsum."

X

Xamurra [shah-mur-rah] Gentleness. (Basque)

Xanay [shah-nay] Walker, walks upon the earth. (Ixil Maya)
  Chimala Xanay [chee-mah-lah shah-nay] Beauty Walks.

Xenia [zee-nee-ah] Hospitable Farm Woman, kindness. (Grk)
  fr **Xena** [zee-nah] Farmer (hospitable), kind farm woman.
  When travelers passed by farmhouses, the women would
  always be remarkably kind and hospitable to them.
  Callixena [kal-lee-zee-nah] Beautiful Hospitality.
  "Kallia": "Beauty" + "Xena": "Farmer" (hospitable).

Xochi [soh-chee] Flower. (Nahuatl)
  fr "Xochitl" [soh-chee-tuhl] "Flower."

Xristina [krihss-stee-nah] Anointed, a Christian. (Grk)
  fr "Chrizo": "Anoint" (consecrate), to declare sacred.
  "Xristo" is the orig spelling of "Christ"; *see* Christiana.

Xylina [zigh-lee-nah] Forest Woman. (Grk)

Y

Yachana [yah-chah-nah] Wise, to know much. (Quechua)
  fr "Yachay" [yah-chay] "To Know" (wisdom).

Yafa, Yaffa [yah-fah] Pretty, *fr* "Yafe": "Pretty." (Hbr)

Yakira [yah-keer-rah] Dearest, Darling, *fr* "Yakir": "Dear." (Hbr)

Yalina [yah-leen-nah] Fir Tree. (Russian)

Yamuna [yah-moon-nah] Crystal Clear Water. (Skt)
  The source of the Yamuna River is a glacier lake on top
  of Mt Kalinda. In mythology, she's the daughter of the sun.

Yardena [yar-dehn-nah] River, *became* the Jordan River. (Hbr)
  fr "Yarden" [yar-dehn] "Descending," like a river.
  Jordana [jor-dahn-nah] River. (Grk)
  Jordania [jor-dahn-nee-ah] River. (OE)

Yasmin [yahz-meen] Jasmine, fragrant flower. (Ara *fr* Persian)
  fr "Yasaman" [yah-sah-mahn] "Jessamine" (jasmine). (Persian)

Yasaman > **Yasamin** (Ara) > **Jasmin** (Frn), **Jasmine**.
Yasmina, Yazmina [yaz-meen-nah] Jasmine.
Jasma, Jazzma [jaz-mah] Nn *fr* "Jasmine."   (Eam)
Yavina [yah-vee-nah] God Knows, he has knowledge.   (Hbr)
   "Yah": "God" + "Vin" [veen] "Knowledge."
Yaxeka [yahsh-shee-kah] New Star.   (Yucateco Maya)
   "Yax" [yahsh] "New" + "Ika" [ee-kah] "Star."
   Yaxkin [yahsh-keen] New Sun.
   "Yax": "New" + "Kin": "Sun."

Yejide [yeh-jee-day] The Image of her Mother.   (Yoruba)
Yemoja, Ymoja [yay-moh-jah] N of River Goddess.   (Yoruba)
   Yemaya [yay-migh-yah] The River Goddess, *fr* "Yemoja."
Yemura [yeh-mur-rah] Admired, Appreciated.   (Shona)
Yetimwork [yeh-teem-wurk] Wherever Gold.   (Amharic)
   "Yetim": "Wherever" + "Work": "Gold."
   Wherever she goes, turns to gold.
Yimei [yee-may] Beautiful as a Rose.   (Mandarin)
   "Yi": "Rose" + "Mei": "Beauty."
Yoella [yoh-wehl-lah] The Lord is God.   (Hbr)
   "Yehu" (yah): "God" (lord) + "El": "God."
   Joella [joh-wehl-lah] The Lord is God.   (Grk)
Yolande [yoh-lahn-day] Purple Flower.   (Frn *fr* Grk)
   fr "Iolanthe" [i-oh-lahn-thay] "Purple Flower."   (Grk)
   "Io": "Purple" (violet) + "Anthea": "Flower"; *see* Ione.
   Yolante, Yolene [yoh-lahn-tay, yoh-leh-nay] Purple Flower.
   Yolanda [yoh-lahn-dah] Purple Flower.   (Span)
Yonina [yoh-nee-nah] Little Dove, symbol of peace.   (Hbr)
   fr "Yonah" [yoh-nah] "Dove"; *see* Ap1: Jonah.
   Jonina [joh-nee-nah] Dove.   (Grk)
Yoshiko [yoh-shee-koh] Good Luck Child.   (Japanese)
   "Yoshi": "Good Luck" + "-ko" (girl), child.
Yucala [yoo-kah-lah] Hope.   (Mam Maya)
Yumeko [yoo-may-koh] Dream Child.   (Japanese)
   "Yume" [yoo-may] "Dream" + "-ko" (girl), child.

Z

Zafara [zah-far-rah] Singer, *became* **Zaphara**.   (Hbr)

Zahara [zah-har-rah] Many Flowers, much beauty.   (Ara)
    fr "Azhara" [ah-zar-rah] "Flower," a beauty.

Zahiya [zah-hee-yah] Shining Beauty.   (Ara)
    fr "Zahiy": "Clear," to be shining, radiant beauty.

Zalika [zah-lee-kah] Born into the world.   (Swahili)

Zalisha [zah-lee-shah] Enrich & Cultivate the Land.   (Swahili)

Zamina [zah-mee-nah] Earth.   (Russian)

Zamira [zah-meer-rah] Singer.   (Hbr)
    fr "Zamar" [zah-mar] "Singer."

    Zemara [zeh-mar-rah] Singing, chanting.   (Amharic)

    Zema [zay-mah] Hymn.   (Amharic)

Zaria, Zariya [zar-ree-yah] Goddess of the Dawn.   (Russian)
    fr "Zarya" [zar-ree-yah] "Dawn."

    Zorya [zor-ree-yah] Dawn; Slavic Goddess of the Dawn.

    Zora [zor-rah] Dawn.   (Sb-Cr)

    Zorica [zor-ree-kah] Dawn, dawn woman.   (Sb-Cr)

    Zorana [zor-rah-nah] Dawn, dawn woman.   (Sb-Cr)

Zawadi [zah-wah-dee] A Gift.   (Swahili)

Zaya [zigh-yah] Victory.   (Tibetan)

Zeina [zayn-nah] Beauty.   (Ara)

Zema [zay-mah] Music.   (Amharic)

Zerrin [zair-rihn] Golden.   (Turkish)

Zhivana [jhih-vahn-nah] Life; the Goddess of Life.   (Russian)
    fr "Zhivan" [jhih-vahn] "Life."

Zinka [zeenk-kah] Little Bird.   (Eam *fr* Sioux)
    fr "Zintkala" [zeent-kah-lah] "Small Bird."   (Sioux)

Zoe [zoh-wee] Life.   (Grk)

    Zoelia [zoh-wehl-lee-ah] Life, lively, *fr* "Zoe."   (Frn)

    Zoya [zoy-yah] Life, *fr* "Zoe."   (Russian)

Zoriona [zor-ree-ah-nah] Happiness.   (Basque)

Zuwena [zoo-wehn-nah] A Good One.   (Swahili)

Boy Names

A

Aarre [ar-ray] Treasure. (Finnish)

Abram [ay-bruhm] Father. (Hbr *fr* Sumerian)
   fr "Abum": "Father." (Sumerian)
    Abraham [ay-brah-hahm] Father of Many.
    "Abram": "Father" + "Ham": "Many."
    Israelites in Babylon (Sumeria) were freed by Persians from
    538-323 BC, and wrote the Old Testament; *see* Shimshon.
    Avram, Avrom [ay-vruhm] Father, *fr* "Abram."
    Bram [bram] Father, Nn *fr* "Abram." (Ger)
    Ebram [ee-brahm] *fr* "Ebrahim" (Abraham). (Amharic)

Ace, Aece [ayss] Number One, the best. (ME *fr* Grk)
   fr "Asos" [ay-sohss] "One," number one, the best. (Grk)

Ademar [ad-deh-mar] Famous Nobleman. (Germanic)
   "Aedel": "Noble" + "Mar": "Fame."
    Adhemar [ad-deh-mar] Famous Nobleman, *fr* "Ademar."
    Adamir [ad-dah-meer] Noble Fame, *fr* "Adhemar." (Span)

Adestan [ah-dehss-stehn] Adam's Stone Mansion. (OE)
   "Adam" + "Stan": "Stone" (mansion); *see* Ap1: Adam.
   Adamstein (Ger) > Adamstan (OE) > Adastan > Adestan.

Adiron [ah-deer-ruhn] Mighty Joyful Song. (Hbr)
   "Adir": "Mighty" + "Oneg": "Delight" (joy), singing.

Aedan [ay-dehn] Sparks, superior warrior. (Gaelic)
   fr "Aedh": "Sparks" (fire), superior sword, superior warrior.
   Superior swords were made by creating many sparks,
   imbued with power by the Govan for the superior warrior.
    Aidan [ay-dehn] Sparks, superior warrior, *fr* "Aedan."
    Caidan [kay-dehn] Superior Warrior's Son.
    fr "MacAidan" [mak-kay-dehn] "Superior Warrior's Son."
    "Mac": "Son" + "Aidan": "Sparks," superior warrior.
    Aodhan [ay-dehn] Sparks, superior warrior. (Scottish-Gaelic)
    Eagan [ee-guhn] Young Warrior. (Scottish-Gaelic)
    "Eagan" is *fr* "Aodhagan": "Young Warrior."

Aedh > Aodh > Aodhagan > **Aogan** > Eagan > **Egan**.
"Aodhagan" = "Aodh": "Sparks" + "Ogan": "Youth."
Ceegan [kee-guhn] Lineage of Warriors.   (Scottish-Gaelic)
fr "MacEagan" [mak-kee-guhn] "Warrior's Son."
"Mac": "Son" + "Eagan": "Son of Sparks," son of a warrior.
MacAodhagan > MacEagan > Mac(k)eagan > Keegan.
Keegan, Keigan [kee-guhn] Warrior's Son.   (Scottish-Gaelic)
fr "MacEagen" [mak-kee-guhn] "Son of Eagan."
"Mac": "Son" + "Eagen": "Son of Sparks," a warrior.
Ajkin [ah-keen] Sun Man, *fr* "Kin" [keen] "Sun."   (Mam Maya)
The man who is one with the sun is the holy man (ajkin).
Akin [ah-keen] Bravery, Hero.   (Yoruba)
    Akinade [ah-keen-nah-day] Heroic King.
    "Akin": "Brave" (hero) + "Ade" [ah-day] "Crown" (king).
    Akintunde [ah-keen-toon-day] Our Hero Returns.
    "Akin": "Hero" + "Tunde": "Returns," reincarnates.
Akira [ah-keer-rah] Light.   (Japanese)
Alaric [ah-lar-rihk] Ruler of All.   (Germanic)
"Al": "All" (everything) + "Rik": "Ruler."
King Alaric ruled the Visigoth tribe in 395 AD.
    Alarich, Alarik [ah-lar-rihk] Ruler of All, *fr* "Alaric."
Alerion [al-leer-ree-ahn] Eagle, winged warrior.   (OE *fr* Latin)
fr "Ala": "Wing," of an eagle, of the military.
Alexin [al-lehks-zihn] Defender of Men.   (Grk)
fr **Alexander** [al-lehks-zann-dur] Defender of Men.
"Alex": "Defender" + (of) "Ander": "Men."
Legendary conqueror whose name spread across Europe.
    Alexion [ah-lehks-zee-ahn] Defender of Men.
Alexander > Alessander (Frn) > Aleister (ME), Ales(an)der.
    Alexe, Aleksei [al-lehks-see] *fr* "Alexander."   (Russian)
    Sander, Zander [sann-dur, zann-dur] *fr* "Alexander."   (Frn)
    Xander [zann-dur] Defender of Men, *fr* "Alexander."   (ME)
    Aleister [al-lehss-stur] *fr* "Alessander," Aless(an)der.   (ME)
    Alister, Allister [al-lihss-stur] *fr* "Alexander."   (ME)

Amador [ah-mah-dor] Loved by God. (Span *fr* Latin)
fr **Amadeus** [ah-mah-day-uhss] Loved by God. (Latin)
"Amor": "Love" (beloved) + "Deus": "God."
Ambrose [am-brohz] Immortal, like the gods. (Latin *fr* Grk)
fr "Ambrosia": "Immortality"; N of a nectar. (Grk)
The gods were immortal because they sipped ambrosia
from goblets, which became the idea for the Holy Grail.
Ambroz [am-brohz] Immortal. (Span)
Ambrus [ahm-bruhss] Immortal. (Russian)
Embre [ehm-bray] Immortal, *fr* "Ambrose." (Frn)
Ember [ehm-bur] Immortal, *fr* "Embre." (ME)
Amir [ah-meer] Prince. (Ara)
◦ **Anden** [ann-dehn] The Courage of the Spirited. (Nor, Scand)
fr "Anda": "Spirit" (spirited, courage) + "En": "The."
Andhun [ann-duhn] Spirited and Courageous, *fr* "Anden."
Viking King Andhun ruled Sussex of Britain in 684 AD.
Andreas [ann-dray-uhss] Manly, brave. (Grk)
fr "Ander" [ann-dur] "Man" (manly), men are brave.
Andraemon [ann-dray-muhn] Manly, Brave.
Andre [awn-dray] Manly, Brave, *fr* "Andreas." (Frn)
Ondrej, Ondre [awn-dray] *fr* "Andre"; *see* Ondreian. (Czech)
Andrew [ann-droo] Manly, Nn is **Drew.** (OE)
Kendrew [kehn-droo] Son of a Brave Man. (Scottish-Gaelic)
fr **Mcandrew** [mihk-ann-droo] Son of a Brave Man.
"Mac": "Son" + "Andrew" (manly) = Mc(k)andrew.
Andrey [ahn-dray] Manly, Brave, *fr* "Andreas." (ME)
Deandre [dee-ahn-dray] From a Brave Man, the son. (ME)
"De": "Of" (from) + "Andre": "Man" (brave man).
Andrez [ann-drehz] Brave Man, *fr* "Andreas." (Eam)
Aragon [air-rah-gahn] Noble Warrior. (Germanic)
fr "Arnegund" [arn-neh-guhnd] "Noble Warrior."
"Arn": "Noble" + "Gund": "Battle" (warrior).
Daragon [dair-rah-gehn] Of Noble Warriors. (Span)
fr "D'Aragon" [dah-air-rah-gahn] "Of Noble Warriors."

Aramde [ar-rahm-day] The Walker. (Amharic)
The one whom helps you walk further and progress.

Arcadius [ar-kay-dee-uhss] Bear, great strength. (Grk)
fr "Arkada" [ar-kay-dah] "Bear," symbol of great strength.
The Greeks were an early major influence across Europe.
Arcady [ar-kah-dee] Bear, great strength. (Frn)
Arkady [ar-kah-dee] Bear, great strength. (Russian)
Artan [ar-tahn] Bear, great strength. (Welsh)
Artur, Arthur [ar-tur, ar-thur] Bear, great strength. (Welsh)
Celtic King Artur (Arthur) and Wizard Emrys (Merlin) took
a last stand against the invaders of the 6th century.
Artagan [ar-tah-guhn] Young Bear, son of Arthur. (Welsh)
"Art": "Bear" + "Ogan" [oh-guhn] "Youth" (son).
Artair [ar-tair] Bear, strength, *fr* "Arthur." (Scottish-Gaelic)
Arthur > Arthern > Ardern > **Arderen** > Ardren > Arden.
● **Arden** [ar-dehn] Bear, great strength, *fr* "Arderen." (ME)

Archon [ark-kahn] Leader. (Grk)
fr "Archios" [ark-kee-ohss] "First" (leader), leads the way.
Archinus [ark-kihn-nuhss] The Leader.
Archander [ark-kann-dur] Leader of Men.
"Arch": "First" (leader) + "Ander": "Men" (manly).
Archelus [ark-keh-luhss] Leader of the People.
fr "Archilaus" = "Arch": "First" + "Laos": "People."
Arkhip [ar-kihp] Leading Horseman. (Russian)
fr "Archippus": "Leading Horseman," leading warrior.
"Arch": "Leader" + "Hippos": "Horse."
Archange [ark-kahnj] Leading Angel, Archangel. (Frn)
"Arch": "First" (leading) + "Ange": "Angel."

● **Ari, Arie** [ar-ree] Lion, to be strong and fearless. (Hbr)
fr "Arye" [ar-yeh] "Image of a Lion."
Ariel [ar-ree-ehl] God is like a Lion.
"Arye": "Image of a Lion" + "El": "God."
Ariav [ar-ree-ahv] God is like a Lion.
"Arye": "Image of a Lion" + "Avi": "Father" (God).

85

Arion [ar-ree-ahn] Excellence, a master of the arts.   (Grk)
    fr "Aristos": "Excellence," to have an excellent life.
    He grew up by the sea and played his lyra for the dolphins,
    and won first prize for being the best musician in the land.
Arjun [ar-joon] White; N of Charioteer of the Sun.   (Hindi *fr* Skt)
    fr **Arjuna** [ar-joon-nah] White, day (sun).   (Skt)
Arneken, Arnekin [arn-neh-kihn] Noble King.   (Germanic)
    "Arn" (aryan): "Noble" (eagle) + "Kindins": "King."
    The Indo-European symbol of nobility is the eagle.
    Arien > Ariaantje > **Ariaante** (Dutch) > **Arinn** (Swed).
    Arvid [ar-vihd] is *fr* **Arnvid** [arn-vihd] Great Eagle.   (Nor)
    "Orn": "Eagle" (noble) + "Vid": "Wide" (great).
Atavus [ah-tay-vuhss] Ancestral Father, the grandfathers.   (Latin)
    Ataveus [ah-tay-vee-uhss] Father of the Great Grandfathers.
Attericus [at-teer-rih-kuhss] Ruling Father.   (Germanic)
    "Atta": "Father" + "Rik": "Ruler" (powerful).
₀ **Aubrey** [awe-bray] King of the Elves.   (Frn *fr* Germanic)
    fr **Alberich** [al-bur-rihk] Elf King.   (Germanic)
    "Alv" (alb): "Elves" + "Rik": "Ruler" (king).
    Alberich > **Auberich** (Ger) > **Aubery** > Aubrey > **Aubry.**
    Auberon [awe-bur-rahn] Elf King, *fr* "Auberich."   (ME)
    Aubryn [awe-brihn] Elf King, *fr* "Auberon."   (ME)
    Avery [ay-vur-ree] Elf King, *fr* "Aubery."   (ME)
Avatar [av-vah-tar] Descent from Heaven, celestial being.   (Skt)
    A celestial being who descended from heaven to earth.
Avidan [ah-vee-dahn] God is my Judge.   (Hbr)
    "Avi": "Father" (god) + "Dan": "Judge."
    Avinatan [ah-vee-nah-tahn] God Gave to Us; *see* Jonatan.
    "Avi": "Father" (god) + "Natan": "Gave," gave this child.
Avion [av-vee-ahn] Jet.   (Frn)
Avishua [ah-vee-shoo-wah] Father is my Savior.   (Hbr)
    "Avi": "Father" + "Yeshua": "Savior."
Azarel [ahz-zar-rehl] Help from God.   (Hbr)
    "Ezer": "Helps" + "El": "God."

B

Bach [bahk] Brook, stream, *became* **Beck**. (Ger)
Baishan [bigh-shahn] Tall Mountain. (Mandarin)
Baisong [bigh-sawng] Tall Pine. (Mandarin)
Barak, Barack [bar-rahk] Lightning Bolt. (Hbr)
Baruch [bar-rook] Blessed. (Hbr)
Bazzel [baz-zehl] King. (ME *fr* Grk)
   fr "Basilias" [baz-zihl-lee-uhss] "King," *became* **Basil**. (Grk)
   Basil (Grk) > Basile (Frn) > **Bassil** > Bazzel (ME).
Benajah [behn-nah-jah] Building for God. (Eam *fr* Hbr)
   fr "Benaiah" [behn-nay-yah] "Builder for God." (Hbr)
   "Banay": "Builder" (establishes) + "Yah": "God."
Bhuvan [buh-vahn] Earth Man, *fr* "Bhuvana": "Earth." (Skt)
   Bhuvanesh [buh-vahn-nehsh] Lord of the Earth.
Binyamin [bihn-yah-meen] Son to the Right of God. (Hbr)
   "Ben": "Son" + "Yah": "God" + "Min": "Right" (side).
   Binyamin (Hbr) > **Benjamin** (Grk) > **Benjamyn** (Ger).
   Benjham [behnj-juhm] Son to the Right of God. (ME)
Bion [bigh-ahn] Great Force, a powerful man. (Grk)
   fr "Bia" [bee-ah] "Force" (power), the power of force.
Bjorn [bee-yorn] Bear. (Nor, Swed, Scand)
   Biorn [bee-yorn] Bear. (Danish)
   Torbiorn [tor-bee-yorn] Thunder Bear. (Danish)
   "Tor": "Thunder" + "Biorn": "Bear."
   Torben [tor-behn] Thunder Bear, *fr* "Torbiorn." (Danish)
   Tarben [tar-behn] Thunder Bear, *fr* "Torben." (Danish)
Blaan [blayn] Blossom; N of a legendary Saint. (Scottish-Gaelic)
   fr "Blathan" [blay-hahn] "Blossom."
   Blane [blayn] Blossom, *fr* "Blaan." (OE)
   Blaine [blayn] Blossom, *fr* "Blane." (ME)
Boddhri [boh-dree] Perceives, understands; N for a Seer. (Skt)
Boden [boh-dehn] Messenger, to be prophetic. (OE)
   Bodian [boh-dee-ehn] Messenger, to foretell.

Bode [boh-dee] Messenger, the royal messenger. (ME)

Bodiam [boh-dee-ehm] Royal Messenger's Home. (ME *fr* OE)

fr "Bodeham": "Royal Messenger's Home." (OE)

"Bode" [bohd] "Messenger" + "Ham": "Home."

Bodwyn [bohd-wihn] Victorious Knight. (Welsh)

"Buddugol": "Victory" + "Gwyn": "White" (shiny), armor.

The white knight in shining armor is victorious.

Bogen [boh-gehn] Bow, bow of an archer. (Ger)

  Bowman [boh-mihn] Bow Man, an archer, a warrior. (OE)

  "Boga": "Bow" (weapon) + "Mann": "Man."

Bolade [boh-lah-day] Honor Comes. (Yoruba)

Bozhin [boh-zihn] Divine. (Russian)

Braco [brahk-koh] Brother. (Sb-Cr)

Braedon, Braeden [bray-dehn] Broad, to be muscular. (OE)

  Braddock [brad-duhk] Broad Oak.

  "Brad": "Broad" + "Aecen" [ay-kihn] "Oak."

  He lives down the road by the broad oak tree.

  Brayden, Bray [bray-dehn, bray] Broad, *fr* "Braeden." (ME)

Brand [brannd] Burning (fire), superior sword. (Germanic)

  Fire forms a sword in the hands of the blacksmith (govan),

  who makes a superior sword for the superior warrior.

  Brand was grandson of Woden, first Viking King of Britain.

  Branden [brann-dehn] Fire, superior sword.

  Brandis [brannd-dihss] Fire, superior sword. (Dutch)

  Brandon [brann-duhn] Fire, superior sword. (OE)

  Branyon, Branion [brann-nee-yuhn] *fr* "Brandon." (OE)

  Brandell [brann-dehl] Fire, superior sword, *fr* "Brand." (ME)

  Branston [brann-stuhn] Fire Stone, Brimstone. (ME)

  "Brand": "Burning" + "Ston": "Stone" = Brimstone.

  Brandeston > **Brandston** > **Brynston** > **Brinston**.

Brann [brann] Raven, a clever bird. (Welsh)

  Brannoc [brann-nahk] Raven.

  Branwyn [brann-wehn] White Raven.

  "Brann": "Raven" + "Gwyn" [gwehn] "White."

Branigan [brann-nih-guhn] Young Raven.
"Bran": "Raven" + "Ogan" [oh-guhn] "Youth."

Braven, Bravin [bray-vihn] Brave.   (ME *fr* Frn)
fr "Brave" [brayv] "Brave."   (Frn)

Brec, Brecc [brehk] Freckled.   (Gaelic)
fr "Breac" [brehk] "Speckled" (freckled).

    Brychan [brigh-kehn] Freckled; N of a Celtic king.   (Welsh)
    Famous King Brychan ruled Wales in 440 AD.

    Brechan [brehk-kahn] Freckled Man, *fr* "Brychan."   (OE)

    Breccan, Brecon [brehk-kehn] *fr* "Brechan."   (OE)

    Brecken, Breck [brehk-kehn, brehk] Freckled Man.   (ME)

Brehane [bray-hahn-nay] Light.   (Amharic)

Brenin [brehn-nihn] King.   (Welsh)

    Brennan [brehn-nehn] King, *fr* "Brenin."   (Gaelic)

    Brendan [brehn-dehn] King, *fr* "Brennan."   (Gaelic)

    Briant [brigh-ehnt] King, *fr* "Brenin," Bre(n)in.   (OE)

    Brian, Brion [brigh-ehn] King, pron N *fr* "Briant."   (ME)

Brocc [brawk] Badger.   (Gaelic)

    Broccan [brawk-kehn] Badger, badger man.

    Brock [brawk] Badger, *fr* "Brocc."   (ME)

Brodric [brawd-drihk] Wide Ruler.   (OE)
"Brad": "Broad" (wide) + "Ric": "Ruler."

    Brodrick [brawd-drihk] Wide Ruler.   (ME)

Bromley [brahm-lee] Meadow in the Thicket.   (OE)
"Brom": "Brush-wood" + "Leah" [lee] "Meadow."

Bronik [brawn-nihk] Armored Warrior, battle ready.   (Russian)
fr "Bron": "Armor," armored & ready for battle, a warrior.

    Bronius [brawn-nee-uhss] Warrior, armored.   (Lithuanian)

Bronte [brawn-tay] Thunder.   (Grk)

Brunn [broon] Spring of Water, a well.   (Swed)

Bryn [brihn] Hill.   (Welsh)

Budhan [boo-dahn] Awake, to be Enlightened.   (Skt)
    fr "Budh": "Awake" (enlightened), *became* "Buddha."
Buddha was born Prince Siddhartha in 563 BC to Mayadeva.

"Siddhartha": "Accomplished," "Complete," "Perfected."

Bodhi [boh-dee] Enlightened, like a buddha.

Buddha became enlightened under a Bodhi tree (fig tree).

The next Buddha will be Maitreya, the compassionate one.

Bodh [bohd] Enlightened, *fr* "Bodhi."

Bodhan [boh-dahn] Enlightened.

Budan [boo-dahn] Enlightened. (Sb-Cr, Russian)

Budimir [boo-dih-meer] Enlightened Peace. (Sb-Cr, Russian)

"Budan": "Awake" (enlightened) + "Mir": "Peace."

Byram [bigh-ruhm] Homestead with a Barn, a farm. (OE)

"Byre": "Barn" + "Ham": "Home," for growing gardens.

Byram > **Byrom** (OE) > **Byron** > Byran (ME).

C

Cadarian [kad-dar-ree-yehn] Silver Knight, in armor. (Welsh)

"Cad": "Battle" (warrior) + "Arian": "Silver" (shiny).

White knight in shining armor.

Cadwyn [kad-wihn] White Knight.

"Cad": "Battle" (knight) + "Gwyn": "White" (shiny).

White knight in shining armor.

Caddaric [kad-dar-rihk] Knight. (Welsh)

fr "Cad" [kad] "Battle" (warrior), knight.

Cadigan [kad-dih-guhn] Young Knight.

fr **Cadogan** [kad-doh-guhn] Young Knight.

"Cad": "Battle" (knight) + "Ogan": "Youth" (son).

Caderyn [kad-dair-rihn] Battle King; N of a Celtic king. (Welsh)

"Cad": "Battle" + "Rhyan" (rhi): "King."

Cadmus [kad-muhss] Brings Order to Chaos. (Grk)

fr "Xaodes" [kay-oh-deez] "Chaos"; N of an ancient king.

Cadoc [kad-dawk] Knight. (Welsh)

fr "Cadog" [kad-dawk] "Battle" (warrior), knight.

King Cadog was famous for being a saint in 500 AD.

Cadog > Cadoc > **Caddoc** (OE) > **Caddock** (ME).

Caedmon [kayd-muhn] The Moon Knight. (OE)
"Cad": "Battle" (knight) + "Mona" [moh-nah] "Moon."
Poet Saint Caedmon was inspired by his dreams at night.
    Caedon, Caeden [kayd-dehn] Knight, *fr* "Cadoc." (OE)
    Cade, Kade [kayd] Knight, *fr* "Caeden." (ME)
Cadwallon [kad-wahl-lawn] Exits the Battle, survives. (Welsh)
"Cad": "Battle" + "Allan": "Exit."
The greatest warriors exit their battles alive.
    Cadellin [kad-dehl-lihn] Exits Battle, *fr* "Cadwallon." (OE)
    Cadell [kad-dehl] Exits the Battle, survives. (OE)
• **Caelian** [kigh-lee-ehn] Celestial, heavenly sky. (Latin)
fr "Caelum" [kighl-luhm] "Celestial" (heaven), sky.
    Caelinus [kigh-lihn-nuhss] Celestial, heavenly sky.
    Caelus [kigh-luhss] Celestial.
Cain [kayn] Fighter, warrior. (Gaelic)
fr "Cathain" [kay-hihn] "Battle" (fighter), warrior.
"Cath" [kay] "Battle" + "-ain," common ending for a LN.
    Caine [kayn] Warrior, *fr* "Cain." (OE)
    Kane [kayn] Warrior, *fr* "Caine." (ME)
Calem [kay-luhm] Dreamer. (Hbr)
fr "Chalom" [kay-luhm] "Dream."
Callidus [kahl-lee-duhss] Clever Expert. (Latin)
Cambrin [kaym-brihn] Welsh; N of Celtic tribe. (Latin *fr* Welsh)
fr "Cymru" [koom-ree] "Welsh" (people), tribe. (Welsh)
Cymru (Welsh) > Cumbria (Latin) > **Cambrian** (OE).
The Cambrian Mountains are in the country of Wales.
    Kember [kehm-bur] Welsh Tribe, *fr* "Cambrian." (ME)
Cante, Chante [chahn-tay] Heart. (Sioux)
    Micante, Michante [mee-chahn-tay] My Heart.
"Mi": "My" + "Cante" [chahn-tay] "Heart."
    Chante Peta [chahn-tay pay-tah] Fire Heart.
    Chante Pejuta [chahn-tay pay-joo-tah] Medicine Heart.
Casan [kah-sahn] Path, the way. (Gaelic)
Cavan [keh-vahn] Kindness. (OE *fr* Gaelic)

91

fr "Caomhin" [kee-fahn] "Kindness."   (Gaelic)
Keevan [kee-vahn] Kindness, pron N *fr* "Cavan."   (ME)
Kevan, Keven [keh-vehn] Kindness, *fr* "Cavan."   (ME)
Kevin [keh-vihn] Kindness, *fr* "Cavan."   (ME)
Cedar [see-dur] Cedar Tree.   (Frn)
Cemp [kehmp] Warrior.   (OE *fr* Ger)
   fr "Kemper": "Warrior," *became* **Champ**, Champion.   (Ger)
   Cemper [kehmp-pur] Warrior.
   Kemp (Ger) > Cemp > Camp > Champion (OE).
   An encampment is where the cemp (warriors) camp out.
   Cemp > Camp > Campeden > Camden; *see* Kemper.
   Camden [kam-dehn] Valley where Champions Battle.
   fr "Campeden" [kamp-dehn] "Champion Valley."
   "Champions" + (in the) "Denu" [deen] "Valley."
   Champeon [cham-pee-ahn] Warrior, *fr* "Champion."   (Eam)
Cetan, Chetan [chay-tahn] Hawk.   (Sioux)
   Chetan Maza [chay-tahn mah-zah] Iron Hawk.
   "Maza": "Iron," hardest element, to be impenetrable.
   Chetan Ona [chay-tahn oh-nah] Prairie Fire Hawk.
   Chetan Wakinyan [chay-tahn wah-keen-yahn].
   Thunder Hawk. "Wakinyan": "Thunder"; *see* Kinyan.
   Lifelong band member of Crazy Horse, *see* Ap3: Tashunka.
Chace [chayss] The Pursuer, the hunter.   (ME *fr* Frn)
   fr "Chasse": "Chase" (pursue), to hunt; N of a hunter.   (Frn)
Chadrel [chah-drehl] Free from Work, having fun.   (Tibetan)
   "Cha": "Activity" (work) + "Drel": "Free."
Chakrin [chah-krihn] Mystical Wheel; N of powerful Sage.   (Skt)
   fr "Chakra": "Wheel" (spinning), the mystical power of spin.
   Ancient shamans knew about the power of spinning;
   now they're in India, Ireland, and the Americas; *see* Arian.
Chaman [chah-mahn] Garden.   (Skt)
Chavan [chah-vahn] Earth, *fr* "Chava": "Earth."   (Ixil Maya)
Chelem [kay-lehm] Dream.   (Hbr)
   Calem [kay-lehm] Dream, *fr* "Chelem."

92

Chenre [chehn-ray] Eyes Looking with Compassion.   (Tibetan)
  fr "Chenrezi" [chehn-ray-zee] "Eye Looking."
  "Chen": "Eye" + "Zi" : "Looking."
  A being who looks at others with great compassion.
Chenzin [chehn-zihn] Holder of Great Power.   (Tibetan)
  "Chen": "Greatness" + "Zin": "To Hold."
Chetan [chay-tahn] Consciousness, a sentient being.   (Skt)
  fr "Chaitanya" [chigh-tahn-yah] "Consciousness."
  Excellent Intelligence, to be distinguished and noble.
  Chaitan [chigh-tahn] Consciousness, *fr* "Chaitanya."
Chevalier [sheh-vah-leer] Horseman, knight.   (Frn)
  fr "Cheval" [sheh-vahl] "Horse."
  Chevance [sheh-vahnss] Horseman, knight.
  Chevy [cheh-vee] Knight, Nn *fr* "Chevalier."   (ME)
Chiwen [chee-wehn] Persistent, Steady.   (Mandarin)
Chodron [choh-druhn] Truth Light. "Cho" + "Dron." (Tibetan)
  Choden [choh-dehn] Dharma Truth.
  "Cho": "Dharma" (teachings) + "Denpa": "Truth."
Choje [choh-jay] Lord of the Dharma.   (Tibetan)
  "Cho": "Dharma" (teachings) + "Rje": "King" (lord).
  "Rje" is *fr* "Raja" [rah-jah] "King" (Skt).
Chomdende [chohm-dehn-day] Overtakes Negativity.   (Tibetan)
  A Buddha who can overcome negativity.
Chotanka, Cotanka [choh-tahn-kah] Sacred Flute.   (Sioux)
  "Co" [choh] "Core" + "Tanka": "Great"; N for a flute.
Chrishaun [krih-shawn] Anointed, *fr* "Christian."   (ME *fr* Grk)
  "Christ" is *fr* "Chrizo": "Anointed," to be baptised.   (Grk)
  "Jesus Christ" is the "Anointed Savior"; *see* Yeshua.
• **Cian** [kee-uhn] Long Time (ancient), wise elder.   (Gaelic)
  Cianan [kee-ah-nuhn] Ancient Wisdom, *fr* "Cian."
  Saint Cianan lived in 500 AD, *became* "Saint Kenan."
  Kenan, Keenan [kee-nuhn] Wise Elder, *fr* "Cianan."   (ME)
  Keane, Kean [keen] Wise Elder, *fr* "Kenan."   (ME)
Cion [kee-on] Love.   (Gaelic)

Clermont [klair-mahnt] Mountain of Light. (Frn)
"Clair": "Bright" (light) + "Montagne": "Mountain."

Cogan [koh-guhn] Justice, just and fair man. (Manx-Gaelic)
fr "Cagadhan" [koh-guhn] "Justice."

Concord [kahnk-kord] Harmony (agreement). (Latin)

Connery [kahn-nur-ree] Guard Dog. (Gaelic)
fr "Conaire" [kahn-neer-roo] "Hounds" (guard dogs).
"Cun": "Hounds" + "Aire": "Attentive" (watching).
The greater the wealth, the more dogs needed to protect it.
Connor, Conor [kahn-nur] Guard Dog.

Corbus [kor-buhss] Raven. (Latin)
fr "Corvus" [kor-vuhss] "Raven."
Corbin [kor-bihn] Raven, *fr* "Corbus."

Corran [kor-rehn] Warrior. (Gaelic)
"Cor": "Barb," "Spear," carried by warriors.
The spear means the presence of a warrior, the protector.
Corey, Correy [kor-ree] Warrior, *fr* "Corran."
Corrigan [kor-rih-guhn] Young Warrior.
"Cor": "Spear" (warrior) + "Ogan": "Youth" (son).
Corgan [kor-guhn] Young Warrior, *fr* "Corrigan."
Cormac [kor-mak] Son of a Warrior.
"Cor": "Spear" (warrior) + "Mac": "Son."
Cormick [kor-mihk] Warrior's Son, *fr* "Cormac." (ME)

Courtland [kort-lehnd] Hidden Land, a hidden estate. (ME)
"Court": "Hidden" + "Land," an estate.
Cortland [kort-lehnd] Hidden Estate, *fr* "Courtland."
Corky [kor-kee] Hidden Estate, Nn *fr* "Cortland." (Eam)
Cortlan, Cortlin [kort-lihn] *fr* "Cortland." (Eam)

Culligan [kuhl-lih-guhn] Young Holy Tree. (Gaelic)
"Cuileann": "Holly" (holy) + "Ogan": "Youth."
Cuileann > Cuileagan > Culligan > Colligan > Colgan.
Colligan [kohl-lih-guhn] Young Holy Tree.
Colgan [kohl-guhn] Cmpd Nn *fr* "Colligan."

◦ **Curran** [kur-rehn] Hero, *fr* "Curaidh": "Hero" (courage). (Gaelic)

94

Cynan [kihn-nehn] King. (OE)

   fr "Cyning" [kihn-neeg] "King," *became* Cing (king), C(yn)ing.

   Koning (Ger) > Cyning (OE) > Kynge (ME) > King.

   Cynnard [kihn-nard] Tough King, *became* **Kennard**.

   "Cyning": "King" + "Hard" (tough).

   Cynestan [kihn-nehss-stehn] King's Stone Mansion.

   "Cyning": "King" + "Stan": "Stone" (mansion), his castle.

   Kynestan, Kynaston [kihn-neh-stuhn] *fr* "Cynestan." (ME)

   Kyngston [keeng-stuhn] King's Stone Mansion. (ME)

   "Kynge": "King" (king's) + "Ston": "Stone" (mansion).

   Cynestan > Kynastan (1200 AD) > **Kynstan** > Kingston.

   Kingston [keeng-stuhn] *fr* "Kyngston" by 1700 AD. (ME)

Cyrus [sigh-ruhss] Throne, throne of a king. (Grk *fr* Persian)

   fr "Kyros" is *fr* "Kurush" (kurshi): "Throne" (king). (Persian)

   Persian King Cyrus freed the Israelites in Babylon.

D

Dachen [day-chehn] Great Joy. (Tibetan)

Daeland [day-lahnd] Land in the Valley. (OE)

   "Dael" [dayl] "Valley" + "Land," *became* **Dale, Dayle**.

   Daelan [day-lihn] Valley Land, Nn *fr* "Daeland."

   Deland [day-lahnd] Valley Land. (ME)

   Daylan [day-lihn] Valley Land, *fr* "Daeland." (ME)

Daggry [dahg-gree] Day Grows, daybreak, dawn. (Nor)

   "Dag": "Day" + "Gro": "Grow."

   Daeg, Daegan [dayg, day-gehn] Day. (OE)

   Daevin [day-vihn] Fair as Day, bright blonde. (OE)

   "Daeg" [day] "Day" (bright) + "Finn": "Fair" (blonde).

   Dayvin, Davin [day-vihn] Fair as Day, *fr* "Daevin." (ME)

Daitan [digh-tahn] Daring, Bold. (Japanese)

Dakoda [dah-koh-dah] Friend, an ally. (Dakota Sioux)

   fr "Koda": "Friend" (ally); "Dakoda" is RN of the Sioux.

   Cody [koh-dee] Friend, Nn *fr* "Dakoda." (Eam)

Dakota [dah-koh-tah] Friend, *fr* "Dakoda." (Eam)

Dandin [dahn-dihn] Staff Bearer, a powerful man. (Skt)
fr "Danda": "Staff" (scepter), to be holding great power.

Danian [dann-nee-yihn] God is my Judge. (OE *fr* Hbr)
fr "Daniah" [dahn-nee-yah] "God is my Judge." (Hbr)
"Dan": "Judge" + "Yah": "God."

Danion, Dannion [dann-nee-yuhn] *fr* "Danian."

Dargo [dar-goh] Red; N of a fearless Druid. (OE *fr* Gaelic)
fr "Dearg": "Red," red-haired and complexioned. (Gaelic)

Darshan [dar-shawn] Holy Manifestation, to be perceived. (Skt)
fr "Darsha": "See," "Perceive," to be seen, become visible.
A darshan master can manifest himself anywhere.

Darshin [dar-sheen] Holy Manifestation.

Daveren [dah-vur-rehn] Thunder. (Dutch)

Deacon [dee-kuhn] Servant of God. (Grk)
fr "Diakonos": "Serving God."

Deakon [dee-kuhn] Servant of God, *fr* "Deacon." (ME)

Deke [deek] Servant of God, Nn *fr* "Deakon." (ME)

Declan [dehk-lann] Excellent Purity, pure for God. (Gaelic)
fr "Deaglan" [dehk-lann] "Excellent Purity."
"Deagh": "Good," "Excellence" + "Glan": "Purity."
Saint Declan was a miracle worker in the 5th century.

Dedan [deh-dahn] Having Happiness. (Tibetan)

Deemer [deem-mur] Of the Sea, from the sea. (ME)
"De": "Of" + "Mer": "Sea."

Degan [day-gahn] Two Rivers Flowing Together. (Iroquois)
fr **Deganawidah** [day-gahn-nah-wee-dah].
Deganawidah and Hiawatha united the Iroquois nation, by
using their arrows to show how strong they become when
united together. This concept was adopted into America's
official seal, where an eagle clutches a bundle of arrows.

Deion [day-ahn] God. (Grk)

Dele [day-lay] Back Home. (Yoruba)

Bamidele [bah-mee-day-lay] Return Back Home.

96

Delion, Delyon [dehl-lee-ahn] From a Lion, born fearless. (Frn)
"De": "Of" (from) + "Lion," from the strong and fearless.

Dendron [dehn-drahn] Tree Man, of the forest. (Grk)
fr "Dendro": "Tree" (forest), *became* "Druid"; *see* Druian.

   Dendreon [dehn-dree-ahn] Tree Man, of the forest.

Denpa [dehn-pah] Truth. (Tibetan)

   Denzin [dehn-zihn] Upholder of the Truth.
   "Denpa": "Truth" + "Zin": "To Hold"; *see* Tenzin.

Destan [deh-stahn] Legend. (Turkish)

Devan [day-vahn] Little God, divine man. (Skt)
fr "Deva" [day-vah] "Divine," divine being, a little god.

   Dewan [day-wahn] Little God, *fr* "Devan." (Hindi)

   Diwan [dee-wahn] Little God, *fr* "Dewan." (Hindi)

Devananda [day-vah-nahn-dah] Delight of the Gods. (Skt)
"Deva": "Divinities" (gods) + "Ananda": "Joy" (delight).

   Devinder [day-vihn-dur] Divine Conqueror.
   "Deva": "Divine" + "Indra": "Conquering."

   Davinder [dahv-vihn-dur] *fr* "Devinder." (Hindi)

Devrim [dehv-rihm] Revolution, generation. (Turkish)

Dex [dehks] Skillful, to have dexterity. (Grk)
fr "Dexter" [dehks-stur] "Right" (right-handed), skillful.

   Dax [daks] Skillful Man, *fr* "Dexter." (OE)

Dhanvi [dahn-vee] Bow Man, Archer, achiever of his goal. (Skt)

Dharman [dar-mehn] Teachings of Buddha, the truth. (Skt)
fr "Dharma": "Justice" (truth), the teachings.
Teaching how to wake up to the truth, and be enlightened.

   Dharminder [dar-mihn-dur] Victorious Teachings.
   "Dharma": "Teachings" + "Indra": "Conquering" (victor).

   Dharmin [dar-mihn] Teachings, the truth. (Hindi)

Dhruva [droo-vah] Stable, Constant; N of the Polar Star. (Skt)

Diomedes [dee-oh-meh-deez] Guardian of the Gods. (Grk)
"Deos" (dio): "God" + "Medeon": "Guardian."

   Diogenes [dee-oh-jeh-neez] God's Child.
   "Deos": "God" + "Genia": "Generation" (progeny), child.

Diogo [dee-oh-goh] God's Child, *fr* "Diogenes." (Portuguese)

Diego [dee-ay-goh] God's Child, *fr* "Diogenes." (Span)

Dobrin [doh-brihn] Good Man, *fr* "Dobro": "Good." (Russian)

   Dobrik [doh-brihk] Good Man.

Dolen [dohl-lehn] Wanderer. (Dutch)

Donden [dahn-dehn] Deep Meaning. (Tibetan)

   Tonden [tahn-dehn] Deep Meaning, *fr* "Donden."

Doran, Doron [dor-rehn] Gift, *fr* "Doro": "Gift." (Grk)

Dorje [dor-jay] Lord of the Thunderbolt, the truth. (Tibetan)

   "Do": "Stone" (diamond) + "Rje": "King" (lord); *see* Vajrin.

   The diamond represents the mightiest force, the lightning.

   Buddhist symbol for the indestructibility of the truth,

   cutting through the darkness to illuminate the world.

   Pema Dorje [pay-mah dor-jay] Lightning Truth Lotus.

   "Pema": "Lotus" (truth) + "Dorje": "Thunderbolt" (truth).

   Truth blossoms from purity; birth N of first Dalai Lama.

Doruk [dor-rook] Mountain Peak. (Turkish)

Dostan [doh-stuhn] Friend, *fr* "Dost": "Friend." (Turkish)

Dowan [doh-wahn] Singer. (Dakota Sioux)

   Mato Dowanse [mah-toh doh-wahn-say] Singing Bear.

   "Dowan" in Dakota; "Lowan" in Lakota.

Drayton [dray-tuhn] Estate Protected by Dragons. (OE *fr* Grk)

   fr "Drakos": "Dragon," *became* **Drake**. (Grk)

   "Draca" [drah-kah] "Dragon" + "Tun": "Estate."

   Dragon images were placed over doorways for protection.

   Drayce [drayss] Dragon, *fr* "Draca." (ME)

   Drayson [drayss-suhn] Dragon, *fr* "Drayce." (ME)

Drazhan [drah-zahn] Precious, a dear. (Russian)

   fr "Drago" [drah-goh] "Treasure," "Precious," a dear.

   Drazhek, Drazek [drah-zehk] Precious.

   Drazko [drahz-koh] Little Precious. "Drago" + "-ko."

   Drazen [drah-zehn] Precious. (Sb-Cr)

Drenpa [drehn-pah] Liberator. (Tibetan)

Dromen [droh-mehn] Dreamer. (Dutch)

Dromeus [droh-may-uhss] Runner; N of an Olympian.   (Grk)
fr "Dromeas": "Runner" (athlete), a fast runner.

Druian [droo-ehn] Druid.   (Grk)
fr "Druinos" [droo-ee-nohss] "Oak Trees," *became* "Druid."
Greeks were amazed how the druids vanished in the trees.
   Dryden [drigh-dehn] Druid, *fr* "Dry": "Magician."   (OE)

Drupchen [druhp-chehn] Very Perfect.   (Tibetan)
"Drup": "Perfect" + "Chen": "Great" (very).
   Dondrup [dahn-druhp] Perfect Meaning, perfect wisdom.
   "Don": "Meaning" + "Drup": "Perfect."
   Gendun Drup [gehn-duhn druhp] Perfect Pure Intention.
   N the monks gave to the first Dalai Lama, born 1391 AD.

Dryhten [drigh-tehn] Lord, Ruler, *became* **Drighten**.   (OE)

Dugan, Duggan [doo-guhn] Dark Haired Youth.   (Gaelic)
"Dubh": "Black" + "Ogan": "Youth" (son).

Durante [dur-rahn-tay] Tough, Enduring, strong.   (Ital *fr* Latin)
fr "Duro": "Hardness" (tough), enduring strength.   (Latin)
   Dante [dahn-tay] Cmpd Nn *fr* "Durante," D(ur)ante.   (Frn)
   Duren [dur-rehn] Enduring, Tough.   (Dutch)

Durjay [dur-jay] Difficult to Conquer, invincible.   (Skt)
fr "Durjaya" [dur-jigh-yah] "Difficult to Conquer."
"Dur": "Difficult" + (to) "Jaya" [jigh-yah] "Conquer."

Durven [dur-vehn] Daring, boldness.   (Dutch)

Dwani [dwah-nee] Sound of Thunder.   (Hindi *fr* Skt)
fr "Dhvani" [dhuh-vah-nee] "Loud Noise" (thunder).   (Skt)

Dyrkan [dur-kahn] Worship, worthy of worship.   (Swed)

E

🌼 **Eamon** [ay-muhn] Protector of our Prosperity.   (Welsh *fr* OE)
fr **Edmund** [ehd-muhnd] Protector of Prosperity.   (OE)
"Ead": "Prosperity" (wealth) + "Mund": "Hand" (trust).
A handshake means trust, and represents a protector.
Eamonn [ay-muhn] Protector of our Prosperity.

Edric, Edrich [ehd-drihk] Wealthy Ruler.   (Germanic)
"Ead": "Prosperous" (wealthy) + "Rik": "Ruler."
Ehren [air-rehn] To be Honored, *fr* "Ehre": "Honor."   (Ger)
   Ehrengard [air-rehn-gard] Spear of Honor.
Ehsan [ay-sahn] Excellence, to be good and powerful.   (Persian)
   fr "Ahsan" [ay-sahn] "Excellence," all things excellent.
Eilon, Elon [ay-lawn] Oak Tree.   (Hbr)
   fr "Alon" [ay-lawn] "Oak Tree."
Einar [i-nar] One Man Army; N for superior warrior. (Germanic)
"Ein": "One" + "Heer": "Army"; to be equal to an army.
   Ejnar [i-nar] Superior Warrior, *fr* "Einar."   (Scand)
   Ejwind [i-wihnd] Wind Warrior, *fr* "Ein" + "Vind." (Finnish)
   Einion [i-nee-yuhn] Superior Warrior, *fr* "Einar."   (OE)
   Eynon [i-nuhn] Superior Warrior, *fr* "Einion."   (Welsh)
Eitan, Eytan [ay-tahn] Strong, a muscular man.   (Hbr)
   Ethan [ee-thihn] Strong Man, *fr* "Eitan."   (OE)
Ekundayo [ay-koon-day-yoh] Sorrow becomes Joy.   (Yoruba)
"Ekun" (sorrow) + "Dayo": "Joy."
Elan [ay-lahn] Life Force, to be inspired, spirited.   (Frn)
   Elan Vital [ay-lahn vee-tal] Vital Life Force.
Elazar [ehl-lah-zar] God Helps; N of Moses's brother.   (Hbr)
"El": "God" + "Ezer": "Helps."
Eldan [ehl-dehn] God is my Judge.   (Hbr)
"El": "God" + "Dan": "Judge."
   Daniel [dann-nee-yehl] Judged by God; "Eldan" in reverse.
Eldric, Eldrich [ehl-drihk] Elder King, wise old king.   (OE)
   fr "Ealdric" [ehl-drihk] "Elder King," more experienced.
"Ealdor": "Elder" (authority) + "Rik": "Ruler" (king).
   Eldridge [ehl-drihdj] Elder King, *fr* "Eldrich."   (ME)
Eldrinn, Eldrin [ehl-drihn] The Fire.   (Nor)
"Eld": "Fire" + "En": "The."
Eliam [el-lee-uhm] God's People, nation of God.   (Hbr)
"El": "God" + "Am": "Nation" (people).
Elic [ehl-lihk] Godly, *fr* "El" [ehl] "God."   (Hbr)

100

Eliyahu [ehl-lee-yah-hoo] God is the Lord.

"El": "God" + "Yehu" (yah): "God" (Jehovah), lord.

Elijah [ehl-ligh-jah] God is the Lord; Nn is **Eli**.   (Grk)

Elias [ehl-ligh-uhss] God is the Lord, *fr* "Elijah."   (Grk)

Eliot [ehl-lee-aht] God is the Lord, *fr* "Elijah."   (Welsh)

⚜ **Elion** [ehl-lee-ahn] Sun God, *fr* "Helios": "Sun."   (Grk)

The sun was central to the religion of the Hellenic culture.

Elior [ehl-lee-or] God is my Light.   (Hbr)

"El": "God" + "Or": "Light."

Eliron [ehl-leer-rahn] Singing Joyfully to God.   (Hbr)

"El": "God" + "Ron": "Joy," "Song," singing joyfully.

Emek [ehm-mehk] Valley.   (Hbr)

Emerich [ehm-mur-rihk] Ruler of the Homeland.   (Germanic)

fr "Heimerich" [highm-mur-rihk] "Homeland Ruler."

"Heim": "Home" + "Rik": "Ruler"; *see* Ap1: Hendrix.

Emeric, Emerick [ehm-mur-rihk] Homeland Ruler.

Emyric [ehm-mur-rihk] Homeland Ruler.   (OE)

Aimeric [aym-mur-rihk] *fr* "Heimerich."   (Frn)

Aimeric was popular Frankish N in Medieval Europe.

Aymer [ay-mur] Homeland Ruler, *fr* "Aimeric."   (Frn)

Emric [ehm-rihk] Homeland Ruler, *fr* "Emerich."   (OE)

Emerton [ehm-mur-tuhn] Emerich's Estate.   (OE)

"Emerich": "Homeland Ruler" + "Tun": "Estate" (town).

Emerson [ehm-mur-suhn] Emerich's Son.   (OE)

Emrick [ehm-rihk] Homeland Ruler, *fr* "Emerick."   (ME)

Emery, Emory [ehm-mur-ree] *fr* "Emerich."   (ME)

Emerit [ehm-mur-riht] Gaining Merit, deserving honor.   (Latin)

fr "Emeritus": "Merit" (deserving).

Merit, Merritt [mair-riht] Gaining Merit.   (OE)

Emet [ehm-meht] Truth.   (Hbr)

Emin [ehm-mihn] Safe, to be safe.   (Turkish)

Emman [ehm-mehn] God is With Us.   (OE *fr* Hbr)

fr "Emmanuel" is *fr* "Immanuel" [ee-mahn-noo-wehl].   (Hbr)

"Im": "With" + "El": "God."

101

Emlen [ehm-lehn] God is With Us, *fr* "Emmanuel."   (ME)

    Emon, **Emen** [eh-muhn] *fr* "Emman."   (Eam)

Emnet [ehm-neht] Trust.   (Amharic)

Emre [ehm-ray] Mango; N of a legendary bard.   (Turkish *fr* Skt)

    fr "Amra": "Mango," beloved fruit brought from India.   (Skt)

Emrys [ehm-rihss] Immortal; orig N of Merlin.   (Welsh *fr* Grk)

    fr "Ambrosia": "Immortality" (nectar).   (Grk)

    The nectar of the Gods that gave them immortality.

    Emrys (Merlin) was an ancient Indo-European god

    who manifested as a wizard to save the Celts; *see* Merlin.

    Emryn [ehm-rihn] Immortal, *fr* "Emrys"; *see* Ambrose.

Endre [ehn-drah] Harmony, *became* [ehn-dray].   (Nor)

Ennius [ehn-nee-uhss] Sword, warrior.   (Latin)

    fr "Ensis": "Sword," symbol of a warrior.

Eppy [ehp-pee] Fruitful Abundance.   (Hbr)

    fr **Ephraim** [ehf-fruhm] Fruitful, *fr* "Pri": "Fruit."

    Evron [ehv-vrahn] Fruitful, producing abundance.

Erben [ur-behn] Inherit.   (Ger)

Erden [air-dehn] Of the Earth, *fr* "Erde": "Earth."   (Ger)

Ergun [air-guhn] Sun Man.   (Turkish)

    "Er": "Man" + "Gun": "Day" (solar), sun, daylight.

Errol [air-rohl] Nobleman's Land, Nn *fr* **Erland**.   (OE)

    "Earl": "Nobleman" + "Land."

Etkin [eht-kihn] Effective, Active, a doer.   (Turkish)

Evan [eh-vehn] Good Angel.   (OE *fr* Grk)

    fr "Evangelos": "Good Angel," to be evangelical.   (Grk)

Evander [ehv-vann-dur] Good Man, with a good heart.   (Grk)

    "Eu" (ev): "Good" + "Ander": "Man."

    Evandy [eh-vahn-dee] Good Man, *fr* "Evander."   (Span)

Even [eh-vehn] Stone (tablet), sacred tablet.   (Hbr)

    Eben [eh-behn] Helpful Stone, carved with holy text.

    fr **Ebenezer** [eh-beh-nee-zur] Helpful Stone.

    "Even": "Stone" (tablet) + "Ezer": "Helps."

    Ebban, **Eban** [eh-behn] Helpful Stone, *fr* "Ebenezer."   (OE)

Everich [ehv-vur-rihk] Boar Ruler, strong ruler. (Ger)
    fr "Eberich" [ehb-bur-rihk] "Boar Ruler," a strong ruler.
    "Eber": "Boar" (strength) + "Rik": "Ruler."
    Evrich, Evric, Evrick [ehv-rihk] Boar Ruler, *fr* "Everich."
Evred [ehv-rehd] Boar, symbol of great strength. (Germanic)
    fr "Eberhardt": "Hard Boar," tough, very strong.
    "Eber": "Boar" (strength) + "Hardt": "Hard" (tough).
    Eberhardt > Everard > Evred > Everett > **Evrett**.
    Images of boars were put over doorways for protection.
    Everett [eh-vur-reht] Tough Boar, great strength. (OE)
    Everley [ehv-vur-lee] Meadow protected by Boars. (OE)
    "Eber": "Boar" + "Leah" [lee] "Meadow," *became* "Ley."
    Everton [eh-vur-tuhn] Estate protected by the Boar. (OE)
    "Eber": "Boar" + "Tun": "Estate."
    Evett [eh-veht] Boar; Cmpd Nn *fr* "Everett." (OE)
Evren [ehv-rehn] The Universe. (Turkish)
Ezrah [ehz-rah] Helper, *fr* "Ezra": "Help." (Hbr)

F

Fallon, Phalen [fal-luhn] Wolf, *fr* "Faol": "Wolf." (Gaelic)
Fenji [fehn-jee] Not Afraid to Go Forward. (Mandarin)
    "Fen": "Look Forward," "Get Braced," to have courage.
Fordel [for-dehl] Advantage, to have the advantage. (Swed)
Forester [for-rehss-stur] Ranger of the Forest. (ME)
    Foster [fahss-stur] Cmpd Nn *fr* "Forester," Fo(re)ster.
    Deforest [deh-for-rehst] Of the Forest. "De": "Of."
Fortrend [for-trehn] Fortress, a stronghold. (OE *fr* Latin)
    fr "Fort": "Strong," to fortify and protect. (Latin)
    Fortren [for-trehn] Great Strength. (ME)
Freland [free-lehnd] Free Land, *fr* **Freeland**. (ME)
Fynn, Finn [fihn] Fair, blonde, from Finland. (Gaelic)
    fr "Fionn" [feehn] "White" (fair), to be blonde.
    Phineas, Phinneas [fihn-nee-uhss] Fair, blonde. (OE)

G

Gadel [gah-dehl] A Wonderful Surprise from God.   (Amharic)

Gaderen [gah-dair-rehn] Gatherer, reaper of abundance.   (OE)

    fr "Gader": "Gather," gatherer of the harvest.

      Gadren [gah-drehn] Gatherer, cmpd Nn *fr* "Gaderen."

Gage [gayj] Pledge, promise.   (Frn)

    Gaige [gayj] Pledge, promise.   (ME)

Gaian [gigh-yahn] Earth, to understand the earth.   (Grk)

    fr "Gaia" [gigh-yah] "Earth," to have a Gaian mind.

    Gaia > Gaian (Grk) > **Gaius** > Caius (Latin) > Cai (OE).

    Cai [kigh] Earth; popular N *fr* "Caius Julius Caesar."   (Latin)

    Cajus [kigh-juhss] Earth Man, *fr* "Caius."   (Latin)

Gainde [gighn-day] Lion.   (Wolof)

Gaiseric [gigh-sair-rihk] Warrior Ruler.   (Germanic)

    "Gais": "Spear" (warrior) + "Ric": "Ruler."

Galdor, Galdore [gal-dor] Magic Chants, a wizard.   (OE)

    fr "Galdor": "Song" (chant), magic incantations.

    Galdren [gal-drehn] Wizard, chanter of incantations.

    fr "Galdre" [gal-dray] "Magician" (wizard).

Galen [gay-lehn] Singer, *fr* "Gale" [gayl] "Singer."   (ME)

    The Nightingale is "Night-in-Gale," singing in the night.

Galorian [gah-lor-ree-ihn] Abundance.   (OE *fr* Gaelic)

    fr "Guleoir": "To Have Enough," an abundance.   (Gaelic)

    "Gu": "To" + "Leor" is *fr* "Leoir": "Enough" (plenty).

Gandar [gann-dar] Magical Staff, a wizard.   (Nor, Scand)

    fr "Gandr": "Staff," magical staff for wizards.

    Gandre [gann-dray] Magical Staff, wizard.

    Gandalf [gann-dawlf] Elf Wizard; *see* Ap1: Gandalf.

Ganden [gahn-dehn] Joy, blissful place, paradise.   (Tibetan)

Ganel [gahn-nehl] God's Garden.   (Hbr)

    "Gan": "Garden" + "El": "God."

    Ganeden [gahn-ee-dehn] Garden of Eden.

    "Gan": "Garden" + "Eden": "Fertile Plain" (Sumerian).

Garriden [gair-rih-dehn] Spear Protected Area, a garden.   (OE)
"Gar": "Spear" (warrior) + "Denn": "Enclosure" (fenced).
An enclosed area protected by warriors with spears.
A garden is a "Guarded Den" (spear protected); *see* Garron.
Garriden > **Garridan** > **Gairden** > Gardener > Gardner.
Gardner [gard-nur] Cmpd Nn *fr* "Gardener."   (ME)
Garron, Garren [gair-rehn] Spear Warrior.   (OE)
fr "Gar": "Spear," weapon of a warrior, *became* **Garth**.
Garrison [gair-rih-suhn] Many Spears, many warriors.
Jarren, Jaryn [jair-rehn] Spear Warrior, *fr* "Garren."   (ME)
Gateward [gayt-wurd] Gate Keeper.   (ME *fr* OE)
fr "Geatweard" = "Geat": "Gate" + "Weard": "Ward." (OE)
Gaverik [gah-vair-rihk] Generous Ruler.   (Nor)
"Gave" [gah-vay] "Gives" (generous) + "Rik": "Ruler."
Gavran [gahv-rahn] Raven.   (Sb-Cr)
Gavri [gahv-vree] God is my Strength.   (Hbr)
fr **Gavriel** [gahv-vree-ehl] God is my Strength.
"Gav" [gahv] "Strong" (strength) + "El": "God."
Gabriel [gayb-bree-ehl] *fr* "Gavriel."   (Grk)
Gebriel [gehb-bree-ehl] *fr* "Gabriel" (gavriel).   (Amharic)
Jibril [jihb-brihl] God is my Strength, *fr* "Gabriel."   (Ara)
Gavrii, Gavril [gahv-ree, gahv-rihl] *fr* "Gabriel."   (Russian)
Gabrius [gayb-bree-uhss] *fr* "Gabriel."   (Latin)
Gabrien [gayb-bree-ehn] God's Strength, *fr* "Gabriel."   (Frn)
Gabe [gayb] God is my Strength, *fr* "Gabriel."   (Ger)
Gaxan [gah-shahn] Grateful for God's Grace.   (Basque *fr* Span)
fr "Gracias" [grah-see-uhss] "Graced," grateful.   (Span)
Geir, Geirr [geer] Spear, the presence of a warrior.   (Swed, Nor)
Geirny [geer-nee] New Spear, young warrior.
"Geir": "Spear" (warrior) + "Ny" [nee] "New."
Geirbrand [geer-brehn] Warrior of the Superior Sword.
"Geir": "Spear" (warrior) + "Brand": "Burn" (sword).
Geirsson, Geirson [geer-suhn] Geir's Son, warrior son.
Garrett [gair-reht] Little Warrior.   (OE)

Jarrett, Jarret [jair-reht] Little Warrior, *fr* "Garrett."   (ME)

Gendun [gehn-duhn] Pure Intention; N for the Sangha. (Tibetan)
"Gen": "Virtue" (pure) + "Dun": "Intention."
The Sangha is a group of students studying Buddhism.
Gedun, Gedhun [geh-duhn] Pure Intention.
Gendhun [gehn-duhn] Pure Intention.

Geraent [geer-raynt] Ruling Warrior, warrior king.   (Nor)
"Geir": "Spear" (warrior) + "Raent": "Ruler" (king).
Geraent (Nor) > **Geraint** (OE) > Gerant.
Gerant [gair-rehnt] Ruling Warrior, *fr* "Geraint."   (OE)

Gervis [gur-vihss] Wise Warrior.   (Nor, Scand)
"Ger": "Spear" (warrior) + "Vis": "Wise."
Weise (Ger) > Vis (Scand) > Wis (OE); *see* Harvin.
Gervaise, Gervais [gur-vayss] Wise Warrior.   (Frn)
Jervis [jur-vihss] Wise Warrior, *fr* "Gervaise."   (ME)
Jarvis [jar-vihss] Wise Warrior, *fr* "Jervis."   (ME)
Jarvin [jar-vihn] Wise Warrior, *fr* "Jarvis."   (ME)

Gevan [geh-vuhn] Generous, one who has given.   (OE)
fr "Giefan" [gihf-fuhn] "Given" (generous).

Gianni [jee-ahn-nee] Pron N *fr* "Johnny"; *see* Jonatan.   (Ital)

Gidron [ghee-drahn] Wren, a songbird.   (Hbr)

Giedrius [ghee-dree-yuhss] Calm Man.   (Lithuanian)
fr "Giedre" [ghee-drah] "Calm."

Gitan [jee-tahn] Gypsy.   (Frn)

Givon [ghee-vawn] Hill, eminence, *fr* "Giva": "Hill."   (Hbr)

Gobez [goh-behz] Courage.   (Amharic)

Godfrey [gahd-free] God's Peace; an old saying.   (Germanic)
fr "Godfrid" = "God" + "Frid": "Peace," to travel in peace.

Goran [gor-rehn] Mountain Man.   (Sb-Cr)

Govan [goh-vahn] Magical Blacksmith.   (OE *fr* Gaelic)
fr "Gobhann" [goh-vahn] "Blacksmith," alchemist.   (Gaelic)
Blacksmiths were the first alchemists, masters of a magical
craft, creating swords from molten metal with by fire.
Gawain [gah-wayn] Magic Blacksmith, *fr* "Govan."   (Welsh)

106

Gavin [gav-vihn] Magical Blacksmith, *fr* "Govan."   (ME)

Gavan [gav-vehn] Magic Blacksmith, *fr* "Govan."   (ME)

Grandis [grann-dihss] Greatness.   (Latin)

Gramercy [gram-mur-see] Great Thanks.   (Frn)

"Grand": "Great" + "Merci": "Thanks," to God.

Grant [grannt] Great, a great man, *fr* "Grand."   (ME)

Grandison [grannd-dih-suhn] Son of Greatness.   (ME)

Grian [gree-yihn] The Sun.   (Gaelic)

°**Griffin** [grih-fehn] An Eagle & Lion Hybrid, a protector.   (Latin)

A fabled creature combining the best of the eagle and lion.

Gunder [guhn-dur] Army Warrior, *became* **Gunther**.   (Germanic)

fr "Gund": "Battle" (warrior) + "Heer": "Army."

Gunder > **Gunnar** (Scand) > Gunther (OE).

Gunderic [guhn-dair-rihk] Ruling Warrior.

"Gund": "Battle" (warrior) + "Rik": "Ruler."

Gundram [guhn-druhm] Warrior Raven.

"Gund": "Battle" (warrior) + "Ram": "Raven."

Gwydion [gwih-dee-uhn] Knight in Shining Armor.   (Welsh)

fr "Gwyndolyn": "Shining Armor"; *see* Ap1: Gwyndolyn.

H

Haakon, Hakon [hah-kuhn] Supreme King.   (Nor)

"Hoy" [high] "High" (supreme) + "Konge": "King."

Hagen [hah-gehn] Supreme King.   (Danish)

Hucksley [huhks-lee] Supreme King's Meadow.   (OE)

"Hakon": "High King" + "Leah" [lee] "Meadow."

Huxley [huhks-lee] Supreme King, *fr* "Hucksley."   (OE)

Hadrian [hay-dree-ihn] Wide, Stout (muscular).   (Grk)

Adrian [ay-dree-ihn] Muscular Man, *fr* "Hadrian."

"The Wide Adriatic Sea" means "The Wide Wide Sea."

Hady [hah-dee] The Guide, who shows the way.   (Ara)

Haelan [hay-lehn] Healer.   (OE)

Harbour [har-bur] Saved by the Army, sheltered.   (Scand)

"Haer": "Army" + "Bergen": "Saves."

Harvin [har-vihn] Wise Soldier, army captain. (OE)
  "Here": "Army" (soldier) + "Wis": "Wise."
  Herewis > **Harvey** > Harvin > Harbin.
  Harbin [har-bihn] Army Captain, *fr* "Harvin."

Harvinder [har-vihn-dur] Absorbed in God. (Skt)
  "Hari": "Remover" (a God) + "Vinda": "Gain" (absorbing).
  Harbinder [har-bihn-dur] *fr* "Harvinder."
  Harkiran [har-keer-rehn] Ray's of God's Light.
  "Hari": "Remover" (a God) + "Kiran": "Rays" (light).

Hesten [hehsst-tehn] Horse, *fr* "Hest": "Horse." (Nor)

Hieron [heer-ruhn] Holy, *fr* "Hiera": "Holy." (Grk)

Holden [hohl-dehn] Deep Valley. (OE)
  "Hol": "Hollow" (deep) + "Denu" [deen] "Valley."

I

Iasion, Iason [yah-see-uhn, yah-suhn] Comforter, healer. (Grk)
  Son of Star Goddess Electra and Zeus; *see* Jason.

Icante, Ichante [ee-chahn-tay] From My Heart. (Sioux)
  "I" (my) + "Cante" [chahn-tay] "Heart."

Ihsan [ee-sahn] Kindness. (Turkish)

Ije [i-jay] Road, Journey, symbolic of life. (Igbo)
  Ijezie [i-jay-zay] Smooth Journey.

Ikeno [ee-keh-noh] Joy. (Kikuyu)

Imbi [ihm-bee] Singing Together. (Swahili)
  fr **Imbiana** [ihm-bee-ahn-nah] Singing Together.

Ionathan [i-ahn-nah-thehn] Gift from God. (Grk *fr* Hbr)
  fr "Yonatan": "Gift from God"; *see* Jonatan. (Hbr)

Ishan, Eshan [ee-shahn] Sunlight, a luminous being. (Skt)
  fr "Ishana": "Light," "Splendor," sunlight.

Itanchan Ki [ee-tahn-chahn kee] The Chief. (Sioux)
  "Itancan" [ee-tahn-chahn] "Chief" + "Ki": "The."

Iyabo [ee-yah-boh] Devotion. (Yoruba)

J

Jacobae [jah-koh-bay] To Hold the Heel. (Latin *fr* Hbr)
 fr "Yakov" [yah-kohv] "To Hold the Heel." (Hbr)
 "Ye" (Le): "To" (hold) + "Akev": "Heel" = Ya'akov.
 At birth, newborn Yakov grabbed his brother's ankle.
 Yakov (Hbr) > **Jacob** (Grk) > Jacobae (Latin) > Jacobe.
 Jacobe [jah-koh-bay] To Hold the Heel. (Basque)
 Jackson, Jaxon [jak-suhn] Son of Jacob (Jack). (OE)
 Jax [jaks] Son of Jacob, *fr* "Jaxon." (OE)
 Jacomus [jak-koh-muhss] Jacob's Man, *fr* "Jacob." (Latin)
 James [jaymz] Jacob's Man, cmpd Nn *fr* "Jacomus." (OE)
 Jemerson [jehm-mur-suhn] James's Son. (ME)
 Jemson [jehm-suhn] James's Son, *fr* "Jemerson." (ME)
 Jachery, Jacory [jak-kur-ree] Nn *fr* "Jacob." (Eam)
Jaday, Jadd [jah-day, jahd] Magical Man. (Hindi *fr* Skt)
 fr "Jadu" [jah-doo] "Magic." (Skt)
Jadi, Jadian [jah-dee, jah-dee-ihn] Creation. (Malaysian)
Jadon [jay-duhn] He will Judge Me. (Grk *fr* Hbr)
 fr "Yadon" [yah-duhn] "He will Judge," God will. (Hbr)
 "Ye": "He" (God) + "Dan": "Judge."
Jahan [jah-hahn] The Universe, World. (Persian)
 Shah Jahan built the Shalimar Gardens; *see* Salima.
Jai, Jaya [jigh, jigh-yah] Victory. (Skt)
 Jaitra, Jaitran [jigh-trah, jigh-trahn] Victorious.
 Jaiveer [jigh-veer] Victorious. (Hindi)
 Jaideep [jigh-deep] Victory of the Light. (Hindi)
 "Jai": "Victory" + "Deep": "Light."
 Jetavan [jeh-tah-vehn] Forest of Victory. (Hindi)
 "Jeta" is *fr* "Jaitra": "Victory" + "Vana": "Forest."
Jakin [jah-keen] To Know, having great knowledge. (Basque)
Jamba [jahm-bah] Hero. (Kikuyu)
Jampa, Jhampa [jahm-pah] Love. (Tibetan)
Jamphel, Jampel [jahm-pehl] Supreme Splendor. (Tibetan)

Jamphel Shenyon [jahm-pehl shehn-yuhn].
Supreme Splendor of Gentleness.
Jamphel Gyatso (supreme ocean) was Eighth Dalai Lama.

Jared [jair-rehd] Descending River. (Grk *fr* Hbr)
   fr "Yored": "Descending," like a river. (Hbr)
   Yored > Yered > **Yarden** > Jordan > **Jordin, Jordyn**.
   Jordan [jor-dehn] Descending; N for the Yarden River.

Jasan [jah-sahn] Endurance, man with endurance. (Basque)
Jasar [jah-sar] Bold. (Ara)
   Jasir [jah-seer] Bold. (Swahili)
Jasim [jah-seem] Thickness, muscular, to be tremendous. (Ara)
Jason [jay-suhn] Comforting, the healer. (Grk)
   fr "Iason" [yah-suhn] "Comforts" (heals), a healer.
   Jase [jayss] Comforting, the healer, *fr* "Jason." (Eam)
   Jacen, Jaycen [jay-sehn] The Healer, *fr* "Jason." (Eam)
   Jace, Jayce [jayss] The Healer, *fr* "Jason." (Eam)
Jator [jah-tor] Loyal, a genuinely good person. (Basque)
Javid [juh-veed] Immortal. (Persian)
   fr **Javedan** [juh-veh-duhn] Immortal.
   Javed [jah-vehd] Immortal. (Hindi)
Jayade [jigh-yah-day] Victorious God, *fr* "Jayadeva." (Skt)
   Jayadeva [jigh-yah-day-vah] Victorious God.
   "Jaya": "Victorious" + "Deva": "Divine," a god.
   Jayakiran [jigh-yah-keer-rahn] Victorious Rays of Light.
   "Jaya": "Victory" + "Kiran": "Rays of Light."
Jebran [jeh-brahn] Mighty, powerful. (Ara)
   fr "Jabran" [jah-brahn] "Force," to be mighty.
   Gibran [gih-brahn] Mighty; N of poet Khalil Gibran. (Eam)
Jedediah [jeh-deh-digh-ah] Friend of God. (Grk *fr* Hbr)
   fr "Yedidiah" [yeh-deed-dee-yah] "Friend of God." (Hbr)
   "Yadid": "Friend" + "Yah": "God."
   Jeduah [jeh-doo-wah] Friend of God, Nn *fr* "Jedediah."
   Jeddie, Jeddy, Jedy [jeh-dee] Cmpd Nn *fr* "Jedediah." (ME)
   Jedian [jeh-dee-uhn] Friend of God. (ME)

Jedeon [jeh-dee-uhn] Friend of God, *fr* "Jedian."   (Eam)

Jedock [jeh-dawk] Friend of God, *fr* "Jedediah."   (Eam)

Jeet [jeet] Lord of Conquerors.   (Hindi *fr* Skt)

    fr **Jitendra** [jeet-tehn-drah] Conquering Victor.   (Skt)

    "Jit" is *fr* "Jaitra": "Victor" + "Indra": "Conqueror."

    Jeetendra [jeet-tehn-drah] Conquering Victor.

Jenner [jehn-nur] Engineer.   (ME)

    fr "Geonor" [jehn-nur] "Engineer."

Jeremian [jair-reh-migh-ehn] Uplifted by God.   (Eam *fr* Hbr)

    fr "Yermiyahu" [yair-mee-yah-hoo] "God Uplifts."   (Hbr)

    "Yermi" is "Le'harim": "Uplifts" + "Yehu" (yah): "God."

    Yermiyahu (Hbr) > **Jeremiah** (Grk) > **Jeremy**.

    Jerian [jair-righ-ehn] Uplifted by God, *fr* "Jeremian."

Jesse [jehss-see] My Present from God.   (Grk *fr* Hbr)

    fr **Yishai** [yee-shay] My Present from God.   (Hbr)

    "Yishai" = "Shay": "Present" + "-i" (sheli): "My."

    Jesse Root Grant was the father of Ulysses S. Grant.

    Jessce [jehss-see] My Present from God, *fr* "Jesse."   (Eam)

Jet [jeht] Rocket, to hurl into space.   (Frn)

    fr "Jeter" [jeht-tur] "Throw" (sling), to hurl into space.

Jetsun [jeht-suhn] Venerable Master.   (Tibetan)

    Jetsun Jampa [jeht-suhn jahm-pah] Master of Compassion.

    "Jetsun": "Venerable Master" + "Jampa": "Love."

Jide Obi [jee-day oh-bee] Unite the Family.   (Igbo)

    "Jide": "Hold On" (unite) + "Obi": "Heart" (family).

Jivan [jee-vahn] Life, full of life, *fr* "Jiva": "Live."   (Skt)

    Jeevan [jee-vahn] Life.   (Hindi)

    Jiwan [jee-wahn] Life.   (Modern Hindi)

Jixin [jee-sheen] New Miracle.   (Mandarin)

Jodha, Joddha [joh-dah] Warrior, *became* "Jedi."   (Hindi *fr* Skt)

    fr "Yoddha" [yoh-dah] "Warrior"; *see* Yodi.   (Skt)

    Ancient warriors (yoda) became the wise old teachers

    of the younger generation of warriors, the Jedi (Jodha).

    Jodhan [joh-dahn] Warrior.

Jedi [jeh-digh] Warrior, young warrior, cadet, *fr* "Jodha."

Joffrey, **Joffre** [jaw-free] God's Gift of Peace. (ME *fr* OE)

fr "Geoffrey" (geoffrid): "God's Gift of Peace." (OE)

"Gief" [geef] "Gift" + "Frid" [freed] "Peace," from God.

Geoffrid > **Geoffrey** (OE) > Joffrey > **Jeffrey** (ME).

Javaris [jah-var-rihss] Gift of Peace, *fr* "Joffrey." (ME)

Javaron [jah-var-ruhn] Gift of Peace, *fr* "Joffrey." (ME)

Jevington [jehv-veeng-tuhn] God's Peaceful Estate. (ME)

fr "Geoffrey" (jeving): "Gift of Peace" + "Tun": "Estate."

Jogan [joh-gehn] Yogi, a mystic master. (Hindi *fr* Skt)

fr "Yogan" [yoh-gehn] "Yogi," a mystic master. (Skt)

Joji [joh-jee] Strong Physical Constitution. (Japanese)

Jonatan [joh-nah-tahn] Gift from God. (Grk *fr* Hbr)

fr "Yonatan" is *fr* "Yehonatan," Y(eh)onatan. (Hbr)

"Yehu" (yah): "God" + "Natan": "Gift."

Jonam [joh-nahm] Gift from God, *fr* "Jonatan."

Yonatan > Jonatan > **Jonathan** > Johnathan > John.

John [jawn] God's Gift, *fr* "Johnathan"; *see* Yonatan.

"Iohnes" [yoh-neess] (OE), *became* "Johnes" (Jones). (ME)

Preachers made "Iohnes" (Jones) their LN in 1100 AD,

chosen because the "Book of John" was very popular.

Gian [jee-ahn] God's Gift, *fr* "John." (Ital)

Ian [ee-ihn] Gift from God, *fr* "John." (Scottish-Gaelic)

Ewen [ee-wehn] Gift from God, *fr* "Ian." (Welsh-Gaelic)

Evan [eh-vehn] Gift from God, *fr* "Ewen." (OE)

Sean [shawn] Pron N *fr* "John"; *see* Sean. (Irish-Gaelic)

Eoin [ee-ehn] Gift from God, *fr* "John." (Scottish-Gaelic)

Maceon [mak-kee-on] Son of Eoin. (Scottish-Gaelic)

fr "MacEoin" [mak-kee-on] "Son of Eoin."

Mackeon [mihk-kee-on] Son of Eoin, *fr* "Maceon." (ME)

Keon [kee-yahn] Son of Eoin, Nn *fr* "Mackeon." (ME)

Mckewen [mihk-kew-wehn] Son of Ewen (eoin). (Welsh)

"Mac": "Son" + "Ewen" (eoin): "Gift from God."

MacEwen > Mac(k)ewen > Mckewen > Kewen > **Keyon**.

Kewen [kew-wehn] Son of Ewen, *fr* "MacEwen."   (ME)

Jori, Jorion [jor-ree, jor-ree-on] Abundance.   (Basque)

Jory, Jorey [jor-ree] Farmer.   (ME *fr* Grk)

    fr "Georgos": "Farmer," *became* **George**.   (Grk)

Josef [joh-sehf] Storyteller of God; *see* Yosi.   (Grk *fr* Hbr)

    fr "Yosef" is cmpd Nn *fr* "Yehosef," Y(eh)osef.   (Hbr)

    "Yehu" (yah): "God" + "Sipur": "Storyteller."

    Yosef > Josef > **Joseph** (Grk) > Josuph > Jessup > Jessop.

    Jessup, Jessop [jehss-suhp] *fr* "Joseph."   (ME)

Josseran [jahss-sur-rehn] Shield of Joseph.   (Germanic)

    fr "Josserand": "Joseph's Shield,"

    "Josse" is *fr* "Joseph" + "Rand": "Shield."

    Josse, Joss [jahss] Nn *fr* "Joseph," Jos(s)eph.   (ME)

Jotai [joh-tigh] Sincerity and Truth.   (Japanese)

Jumel [joo-mehl] Twin.   (Frn)

K

Kachen [kah-chehn] Upholder and Uplifter.   (Tibetan)

Kai [kigh] Sea.   (Hwn)

    Kaishiro [kigh-sheer-roh] Ocean Boy.

    Kainoa [kigh-noh-wah] The Wide Open Sea.

    "Kai": "Sea" + "Noa": "Unrestricted" (wide open).

Kaitan [kigh-tahn] Open and Develop.   (Mandarin)

    To progress straight ahead with one's development.

Kaizan [kigh-zahn] Ocean Mountain, *fr* "Kai": "Sea."   (Japanese)

Kalden [kal-dehn] Fortunate, to be worthy.   (Tibetan)

Kaleb, Caleb [kay-lehb] Dog, trustworthy, *fr* "Kelev."   (Hbr)

Kallio [kal-lee-oh] Rock (stable), solid foundation.   (Finnish)

Kallion [kal-lee-ahn] Beauty, handsome man.   (Grk)

    fr "Kallos" [kah-lohss] "Beauty" (good-looking), handsome.

    Kalliden [kal-lee-dehn] Place of Beautiful Trees.

    fr "Kallidendros" [kal-lee-dehn-drohss] "Beautiful Trees."

    "Kallos": "Beauty" + "Dendro": "Trees" (branches).

Kanah [kahn-nah] Reed (support). (Hbr)

    Kaniel [kahn-nee-ehl] God is my Support.

    "Kanah": "Reed" (support) + "El": "God."

Kanan [kah-nahn] Forest, *fr* "Kanana": "Forest." (Hindi)

Kane [kah-nay] Man, the creator of mankind. (Hwn)

Kangi [kahng-ghee] Crow. (Sioux)

    Kangi Wanagi [kahng-ghee wah-nah-ghee] Crow Spirit.

    Kangi Wakita [kahng-ghee wah-kee-tah] Watching Crow.

    "Wakita": "To Look" (seek), he is watching.

Kanichiro [kah-nee-cheer-roh] Perfect, Admirable. (Japanese)

Kanoa [kah-noh-wah] The Unrestrained, total freedom. (Hwn)

    "Ka": "The" + "Noa": "Unrestrained" (freedom).

Kanzen [kahn-zehn] Complete, Perfect. (Japanese)

Karl [karl] Man, fellow man. (Swed, Ger)

    Karl (Ger) > Carl > **Charles** (Frn) > Chez > Chas.

    Chez [chay] Man, *fr* "Charles." (Frn)

    Chay [chay] Man, *fr* "Chez." (Span)

    Chas, Chase [chaz, chayss] Man. (ME)

    Chalion [chal-lee-uhn] Lion Man, to be fearless. (ME)

    "Charles": "Man" + "Lion."

    Chaylen [chay-lehn] Lion Man, *fr* "Chalion." (ME)

Kasai [kah-sigh] Fire. (Japanese)

Kavin [kah-veen] Poet, one who is gifted with insight. (Skt)

    fr "Kavi": "Insightful" (poet), deep thinker, wise man.

Kawinge [kah-weeng-gay] He Came Back, reincarnated. (Sioux)

    "Kawinge": "To Turn Around."

Kayode [kay-yoh-day] He Brings Joy. (Yoruba)

    "K" + "Ayo": "Joy" + "De": "Arrives" (brings).

Kazuhiro [kah-zoo-heer-roh] Widespread Unity. (Japanese)

    "Kazu": "One" (unity) + "Hiro": "Wide."

Keanu [kay-ah-noo] The Cold, the cool breeze. (Hwn)

    "Ke": "The" + "Anu": "Cold," refreshing coolness.

Keb [kehb] Heavy with Values, full of values. (Amharic)

    fr **Kebede** [keh-beh-day] Heavy, with many values.

Keen, Kene [keen] Bold Man. (ME *fr* OE)

  fr "Cene" [keen] "Bold Man." (OE)

Keeton [keet-tuhn] Cottage Home, for horses. (ME *fr* OE)

  fr "Chatham": "Cottage Home," home for horses. (OE)

  "Cyte" [keet] "Cottage" (horse shed) + "Ham": "Home."

  Keaton [keet-tuhn] Cottage Home, *fr* "Keeton."

  Keate, Kyte [keet] Cottage Home, *fr* "Keeton."

Kei [kigh] Boulder, symbol of stability & strength. (Dutch)

Keiran [keer-rehn] Dark-haired. (ME *fr* Gaelic)

  fr "Ciaran" [kee-ur-rehn] "Darker," a swarthy man. (Gaelic)

  "Ciar" [kee-ur] "Darker," dark complexion or hair.

  Kerron, Kyran [keer-ruhn] Dark-haired, *fr* "Keiran." (ME)

  Keir, Kerr, Keer [keer] Dark-haired, *fr* "Keiran." (ME)

  "Kier" *is* "Christian" (Scand); "Keir" *is* "Darker" (Gaelic).

Keizo [kay-zoh] Blessing Man. (Japanese)

Kemon [kehm-muhn] Rain. (Cree)

Kemper [kehmp-pur] Warrior. (Ger)

  Kemp > **Cemp** (OE) > Camp > Champ; *see* Camden.

  "Camp": "Combat" (warrior) = **Champion.** (OE)

  Kempton [kehmp-tuhn] Warrior Town. (ME)

  Kemton [kehm-tuhn] Warrior Town, *fr* "Kempton." (ME)

Kendian [kehn-dee-ihn] Sincere Truth. (Mandarin)

Kenji [kehn-jee] Wisdom Boy. (Japanese)

  Kenzo [kehn-zoh] Wisdom Boy, healthy boy.

  Kentaro [kehn-tar-roh] Wisdom Boy, healthy boy.

  Kenichi [kehn-nee-chee] Wisdom from Insight.

Kenner [kehn-nur] Knowledge, an expert. (Ger)

  fr "Kennen" [kehn-nehn] "Know," knowledgeable expert.

  Kennis [kehn-nihss] Knowledgeable, an expert. (Dutch)

  Kennan, Kennon [kehn-nuhn] *fr* "Kennen." (OE)

Kennett, Kenet [kehn-neht] Good Leader. (Welsh)

  fr "Cunedda" [kahn-nehth-thah] "Good Leader."

  "Cyn": "Leader" + "Da": "Good."

  Cunedda > Kunedda > **Kenneth** > **Kenith** > **Kynith.**

115

Kenric [kehn-rihk] Ruling King.   (Germanic)
   "Cyning": "King" + "Ric": "Ruler."
   Kenrick, **Kendrick** [kehn-rihk, kehn-drihk] *fr* "Kenric."
   Cynric [kihn-rihk] Ruling King, *fr* "Kenric."   (OE)
   King Cynric ruled Saxon settlements in the 6th century.
   Cyneric [kihn-nur-rihk] Ruling King, *fr* "Cynric."   (OE)
   Kinrick [kihn-rihk] Ruling King, *fr* "Cynric."   (ME)
   Kedrick, **Kedric** [kehd-drihk] Cmpd Nn *fr* "Kendrick." (ME)
Keshen [kuh-shehn] Deeply Profound.   (Mandarin)
Kester [kehss-tur] Castle.   (ME *fr* OE)
   fr "Chaester": "Castle," *became* **Chester** > **Chet**.   (OE)
   Keston [kehss-tuhn] Castle Estate, castle town.
   "Chaester": "Castle" + "Tun": "Estate" (town).
   Every king had many serfs living around their castles,
   and the populations of these estates often became towns.
Keter [keh-tur] Crown.   (Hbr)
Kevad [kay-vahd] Springtime.   (Estonian)
Kevalin [keh-vahl-lihn] Seeker of the Absolute.   (Skt)
   fr "Kevala": "Absolute," the absolute truth.
Khasar [kah-sar] Sky Glider, sky-gliding buddha.   (Tibetan)
   Khasarpana [kah-sar-pah-nah] Sky Glider.
   "Kha": "Sky" + "Sarpa": "Gliding."
   A bodhisattva of compassion in the form of a sky glider.
Khenchen [kehn-chehn] Great Learned One.   (Tibetan)
   "Khenpo": "Learned One" + "Chen": "Great."
Kibo [kee-boh] Hope.   (Japanese)
Kinay [keen-nay] Sun Child, *fr* "Kin": "Sun."   (Mam Maya)
Kincaid [kihn-kayd] Top Mountain Pass.   (Scottish-Gaelic)
   fr **Cincaid** [kihn-kayd] Top Mountain Pass.
   "Cin": "Increase" (height) + "Cadha": "Pass," narrow pass.
   Kincade [kihn-kayd] Top Mountain Pass, *fr* "Kincaid." (ME)
Kinyan, **Kinye** [keen-yahn, keen-yay] Flying.   (Sioux)
   Kinyan Mani [keen-yahn mah-nee] Flying Walker.
   "Kinyan": "Flying" + "Mani": "Walker," man who can fly.

Wakinyan [wah-keen-yahn] Sacred Flight, the Thunderbird.
"Wakan": "Sacred" (Great Spirit) + "Kinyan": "Flying."
Thunder is the booming sound of the Thunderbird's wings.
    Wakinye [wah-keen-yay] Thunderbird; *see* Wakan.

Kinyo [keen-yoh] *fr* **Morakinyo** [mor-rah-keen-yoh].   (Yoruba)
    My hero is here, so I am happy.

Kiran [keer-rahn] Ray of Light.   (Skt)
    fr "Kirana": "Particles of Light" (rays), radiant, luminous.
    Ravikiran [rah-veek-keer-rahn] Sun Rays, sunbeams.
    "Ravi": "Sun" + "Kiran": "Rays."

Kirk [kurk] Church, *fr* "Kirche" [kurk] "Church."   (Ger)
    Kerk [kurk] Church.   (Dutch)
    Kyrk, Kyrke [kurk] Church.   (ME)
    Kirkland, Kirklan [kurk-lihn] Church Land.   (ME)
    Kirkley [kurk-lee] Meadow with a Church.   (ME)
    "Kirk": "Church" + "Leah" [lee] "Meadow."

Kitane [kee-tahn-nay] Big River.   (Lenape)
Kito [kee-toh] Precious Stone, rare gem.   (Swahili)
Kivinen [kee-vee-nehn] Stone, to be stable and strong. (Finnish)
Kiyo [kee-yoh] Purity.   (Japanese)
Koa [koh-wah] Brave.   (Hwn)
    Nakoa [nah-koh-wah] Very Brave.
    Makoa [mah-koh-wah] Oath of the Brave, a hero.
Kobe [koh-bay] Turtle.   (Swahili)
Koda [koh-dah] Friend; *see* Dakoda.   (Sioux)
Kogan [koh-gehn] Priest.   (Russian *fr* Hbr)
    fr **Kohen** [koh-hehn] Priest.   (Hbr)
    Kagan [kay-gehn] Priest, *fr* "Kogan."
Koji [koh-jee] Good Organization Skills.   (Japanese)
    Lights the Way.
Konane [koh-nah-nay] Brightness.   (Hwn)
Koren [kor-rehn]
    1. Root.   (Russian)
    2. Beam of Light, *fr* "Keren": "Beam" (of light).   (Hbr)

Kosan [koh-sahn] Leader. (Zulu)

Kotaro [koh-tar-roh] Happy Boy. (Japanese)
   Kitaro [kih-tar-roh] Happy Boy.

Kovanen [koh-vah-nehn] Tough, very strong man. (Finnish)
   fr "Kova": "Hard," "Harsh," tough and very strong.
   Kuvan [koo-vahn] Tough, *fr* "Kuva": "Hard." (Estonian)

Kudret [koo-dreht] Power. (Turkish)

Kuende [kwehn-day] Fast Grower, evolutionary. (Swahili)

Kumbi [koom-bee] Ask God for It. (Shona)
   fr **Kumbirai** [koom-beer-righ] Ask for It, ask God.

Kundun [koon-doon] He's in Front of us, his presence. (Tibetan)
   "Kun": "Body" (incarnation) + "Dun": "In Front."
   A title given to every incarnation of the Dalai Lama.
   Kundun Drup "Perfect Presence" was the very first one.

Kurt [kurt]
   1. Wolf. (Turkish)
   2. Cmpd Nn *fr* **Konrad** [kahn-rad] Bold Counselor. (Ger)
      "Kuhn": "Bold" + "Rad": "Decree," a counselor.
      Konrad > Kurt > **Conrad** > **Curt** > **Curtis.**

Kuutamo [koo-tah-moh] Moonlight, *fr* "Kuu" (moon). (Finnish)

Kyle [kighl] Slender, an isthmus of land. (Gaelic)
   fr "Caol" [kayl] "Slender," narrow strip of land.
   Kyleakin [kighl-lah-kihn] Isthmus of the King.
   "Caol": "Slender" + "Hakon": "Supreme King" (Nor).

Kyler [kigh-lur] Archer, a bowman. (Dutch)
   fr "Keilen" [kigh-lehn] "Fling," shoot arrows with a bow.

L

Landeric [lann-dair-rihk] Ruler of the Land. (Germanic)
   "Land" + "Ric": "Ruler."
   Landric, Landrick [lannd-drihk] *fr* "Landeric."

Lasan [lah-sahn] The Spark. (Gaelic)

Lazer [lay-zur] Helper of God, Nn *fr* "Elazar"; *see* Elazar. (Hbr)

Leigh [lee] Healer, doctor. (Gaelic)

Leland [lee-lehnd] Meadow Land. (OE)
    "Leah" [lee] "Open space" (meadow) + "Land."
    Leeland [lee-lehnd] Meadow Land, *fr* "Leland."

Lemont [leh-mahnt] The Mountain. (Frn)
    "Le": "The" + "Mont" (montagne): "Mountain."
    Lamont [lah-mahnt] The Mountain, *fr* "Lemont." (ME)

• **Leomar** [lay-oh-mar] Lion by the Sea. (Span)
    "Leo" [lay-oh] "Lion" + "Mar": "Sea."

Leoric [lee-or-rihk] Beloved Ruler. (OE)
    fr "Leofric" [leef-rihk] "Loved Ruler."
    "Leof" [leef] "Love" (beloved) + "Ric": "Ruler."

Lev [lehv] Lion. (Russian)
    Levon [lehv-vawn] Lion, lion man.
    Levko [lehv-koh] Little Lion. "Lev" + "-ko" (little).

Leven [leh-vehn] Smooth, as the waters of a river. (OE *fr* Welsh)
    fr "Llyfn" [leh-vehn] "Smooth"; the N of a river. (Welsh)

Levi [leh-vee] Heart; N of a tribe with many priests. (Hbr)
    fr "Lev" [lehv] "Heart" (love).
    Levias [leh-vigh-uhss] Heart, *became* "Levi" [lee-vigh]. (Grk)

Lewin [lee-wihn] Beloved Friend. (OE)
    fr "Leofwin" [leef-wihn] "Beloved Friend."
    "Leof" [leef] "Love" + "Wine" [wihn] "Friend."

Lochene [lahk-keen] Little Lake. (Gaelic)
    fr "Loch" [lahk] "Lake."
    Lachlann [lahk-luhn] Land of Lakes. (Scottish-Gaelic)
    "Loch": "Lake" + "Lann": "Land."
    Lachlan [lahk-luhn] *fr* "Lachlann." (Scottish-Gaelic)

Loomis [loo-mihss] Holy Lake, sacred pool. (ME *fr* OE)
    fr "Lumhalghs" = "Luh": "Lake" + "Halig": "Holy." (OE)

Lorgan [lor-gehn] Warrior, the spear of the warrior. (Gaelic)
    fr "Lorg" [lorg] "Shank of Spear" (warrior), ready to defend.
    Talorgan [tal-lor-gehn] Warrior Ready with Weapons.
    "Tal": "Axe" (steel) + "Lorg": "Spear."

Talorcan [tal-lor-kehn] *fr* "Talorgan"; *see* Talorc.　　(OE)
Logan [loh-gehn] Warrior; cmpd Nn *fr* "Lorgan."
Lorcan [lor-kehn] Warrior, *fr* "Lorgan."　　　　　　(OE)
Larkin, Larken [lar-kehn] Warrior, *fr* "Lorcan."　　(ME)
Lowan [loh-wahn] Singer.　　　　　　　　(Lakota Sioux)
　　Mahto Lowanse [mah-toh loh-wahn-say] Singing Bear.
　　Life-long band member of Crazy Horse; *see* Ap3: Tashunka.
Lucinus [loo-kihn-nuhss] Light, man of light.　　　　(Latin)
　　fr "Lucis" [loo-kihss] "Light," *became* **Lucas**.
　　Lucian [loo-kee-ehn] Light, man of light, *fr* "Lucinus."
　　Lucan [loo-kehn] Light; N of a knight of King Arthur.

M

Maccon [mak-kuhn] Son of the Watch Dogs, of wealth.　(Gaelic)
　　"Mac": "Son" + "Con": "Hounds," watch dogs.
　　The greater the wealth, the more dogs needed to watch it.
　　Machyn [mak-keen] Son of Wealthy Man, *fr* "Maccon." (OE)
Machaon [mahk-kay-ahn] The Fighter.　　　　　　　(Grk)
　　fr "Mache" [mahk-kay] "Fighter," warrior, the defender.
　　Machemon [mahk-kay-muhn] The Fighter.
Madoc [mad-dahk] Fortunate Man.　　　　　　　(Welsh)
　　fr "Madog": "Fortunate Man," deserving luck.
　　"Mad" [mad] "Fortunate," for being a good soul.
　　Famous Prince Madog was born in Wales in 1140 AD.
　　Madog > Madoc > Maddox > Maddocks > Maddock.
　　Maddox [mad-dahks] Fortunate Man.　　　　　　(OE)
　　Maddock [mad-duhk] Fortunate Man, *fr* "Maddox."　(ME)
Maitreya [migh-tray-yah] Compassionate One.　　　(Skt)
　　Maitreya the Buddha of Compassion will be the next
　　buddha to be born into the world; *see* Budhan, Sanjay.
Majorian [may-jor-ree-ihn] The Greater Man.　　　(Latin)
　　fr "Major" [may-jor] "Greater," to be greater.
　　Majo [may-joh] The Greater Man, Nn *fr* "Majorian."　(Ital)

Makan Nahon [mah-kahn nah-hohn] Hears the Earth.　(Sioux)
　　"Maka": "Earth" + "Nah'on": "Hears" (understands).
　　Makan Mani [mah-kah mah-nee] Earth Walker.
Makani [mah-kahn-nee] Wind.　(Hwn)
Makor [mah-kor] Source, the root.　(Hbr)
Malachi [mal-lah-kee] My Angel, messenger from God.　(Hbr)
　　"Malak": "Angel" (messenger) + "-i" *fr* "Sheli": "My."
　　Melak [mahl-lahk] Angel.　(Amharic)
Mandar [mann-dar] Mystical Flower of Buddha.　(Skt)
　　fr "Mandara": "Mystical Flower," dancing in the sky.
　　Mystical flowers fall slowly from Buddha's heaven,
　　as if dancing in the sky; N for a mystical Sky Dancer.
Mandel [mann-dehl] Almond.　(Swed)
Mandron [mann-druhn] Commander, *fr* "Mando."　(Latin)
Mantius [mann-tee-uhss] A Visionary, a Seer.　(Grk)
　　fr "Mantis": "Seer" (visionary), one who has insight.
　　Mantineus [mann-tihn-nee-uhss] Visionary, a Seer.
　　Mantrin [mann-trihn] Insightful Counselor.　(Hindi)
Marvel, Marvell [mar-vehl] Marvelous.　(ME *fr* Frn)
　　fr "Marvaile" (merveille): "Marvel."　(Frn)
　　Marven, Marvin [mar-vihn] Marvelous, *fr* "Marvel."
Matan [mah-tahn] Gift.　(Hbr)
　　Mattaniah [mah-tahn-nee-ah] Gift from God.
　　"Matan": "Gift" + (from) "Yah": "God."
　　Mattan [mah-tahn] Gift from God, *fr* "Mattaniah."
　　Matthew [math-thew] God's Gift, *fr* "Mattaniah."　(Grk)
　　Mathanias [mah-thahn-nee-uhss] *fr* "Mattaniah."　(Grk)
　　Matthias [mah-thigh-uhss] Cmpd Nn *fr* "Mathanias."　(Grk)
　　Mathan [mah-thahn] Gift from God, *fr* "Mathanias."　(OE)
　　Matteo [mat-tay-yoh] Gift from God, *fr* "Matthias."　(Ital)
　　Mattei [mat-tigh] Gift from God, *fr* "Matthew."　(Frn)
　　Matthewson > **Mattheson** > **Mathissen** > **Matteson**.
　　Mattson [mat-suhn] Son of God's Gift, *fr* "Matteson."　(OE)
Matar [mah-tar] Rain.　(Hbr)

121

Matin [mah-teen] Morning. (Frn)

Mato, Mahto [mah-toh] Bear. (Sioux)

   Mato Otanka [mah-toh oh-tanhk-kah] Great Bear.
   "Mato": "Bear" + "Tanka": "Great."

   Mato Chante [mah-toh chahn-tay] Bear Heart.

   Mato Wakan [mah-toh wah-kahn] Sacred Bear.

Mavrik [mav-rihk] Intelligent. (Hbr)

Maynard [mayn-nard] Very Mighty. (OE)

   "Maegen" [mayn] "Mighty" + "Hard": "Tough."

Maza Mani [mah-zah mah-nee] Walking Iron. (Sioux)

   "Maza": "Iron" (impenetrable) + "Mani": "Walks."

   Maza Ojan [mah-zah oh-jahn] Shining Steel, in the sun.

   "Maza": "Iron" + "Aojanjan": "Light," reflecting sunlight.

Mazin [mah-zeen] Water Increase, blessed rain. (Ara)

   "Ma": "Water" + "Ziada": "Increase."

Medeon [meh-dee-ahn] Guardian. (Grk)

Mendi [mehn-dee] Mountain. (Basque)

Merlin [mur-lihn] Little Falcon. (Frn)

   Merlin's RN was "Emrys Myrddin" (Welsh), but author
   Sir Geoffrey changed "Myrddin" for sounding like "Merde."
   Emrys was an ancient, omnipotent god who manifested as
   a wizard to save the Celtic people; *see* Ambrose, Emrys.

Metin [meh-teen] Solid (strong), big muscles. (Turkish)

Micah [mee-kah] Similar, to be like someone divine. (Hbr)

   Micaiah [mee-kigh-yah] Who's like God, man like God.

   "Micah": "Who is like" + "Yah": "God."

   Micaijah [mee-kigh-jah] *fr* "Micaiah." (Grk)

   Micai [mee-kigh] Man like God, *fr* "Micaijah." (Eam)

   Micajay [mee-kah-jay] Man like God, *fr* "Micajah." (Eam)

   Micojah [mee-koh-jah] *fr* "Micajah," Nn is **Mico**. (Eam)

Micha [mee-kah] Similar, just like someone divine. (Hbr)

   Michael [mee-kah-ehl] Who's Like God, *became* [migh-kehl].

   "Micha": "Like" (similar) + "El": "God."

   Micheas [mihk-kay-uhss] *fr* "Michael." (Grk)

Mykolas [mee-koh-lahss] *fr* "Michael." (Lithuanian)
Michael > Michall > Michell (OE) > **Mitchell** > **Mitch**.
    Micol, Mycal [migh-kuhl] Pron N *fr* "Michael." (Eam)
Mikio [mee-kee-oh] Big Tree. The Future. (Jpn)
Milam [mee-lahm] Dream. (Tibetan)
Mipam [mee-pawm] Never Defeated. (Tibetan)
Mirkan [meer-kehn] Peaceful, man of peace. (Russian)
    fr "Mir": "Peace," "World," a peaceful world.
    They believe that a peaceful world begins at home.
    Mirko [meer-koh] Little Peace, making the world peaceful.
    "Mir": "Peace" + "-ko" (little).
    Umir [oom-meer] To Bring Peace.
    Temir [tehm-meer] This World, this World at Peace.
    "Te": "This" + "Mir": "Peace," "World," peaceful world.
    Branimir [brawn-nih-meer] Warrior to bring Peace.
    "Brania": "Armor" (warrior) + "Mir": "Peace."
Mishan [mee-shahn] Supportive, like a staff. (Hbr)
    fr "Mishenet": "Support" (staff), supportive & strong.
Mitran [mee-trahn] Friend, to be compassionate. (Skt)
    fr "Mitra": "Friend," compassionate.
    Mitravin [mih-trah-vihn] Gains Friends, has many.
    fr "Mitravinda" = "Mitra" + "Vinda": "Gains."
Monte [mahn-tay] Mountain. (Ital)
    Montel [mahn-tehl] Lion on the Mountain.
    fr "Monteleone" [mahn-tay-lee-ohn-nay] "Mountain Lion."
    "Monte": "Mountain" + "Leon": "Lion."
Morcan [mor-kuhn] Larger Herd, obvious wealth. (Welsh)
    "Mawr": "More" (larger) + "Cant": "Hundred" (herd).
    Morcant (600 AD) > **Morgant** (1200 AD) > Morgan.
    Morgan [mor-guhn] Larger Herd, *fr* "Morcant." (ME)
Morgen [mor-gehn] Morning. (Ger)
Morito [mor-ree-toh] Guardian of the Forest. (Mandarin)
    Men go to him for his special wisdom.
Mshauri [mah-shor-ree] Advisor, Counselor. (Swahili)

123

Mshindi [mah-shihn-dee] Victor, Conqueror. (Swahili)

Munderic [moon-dair-rihk] Trusted Ruler. (Germanic)

"Mund": "Hand" (trusted) + "Ric": "Ruler."

People trust him with their lives, he is their protector.

Geirmund [geer-moond] Trusted Warrior.

"Geir": "Spear" (warrior) + "Mund": "Hand" (trusted).

Thurman [thur-mihn] Thor's Protection. (OE)

fr "Thormund" = "Thor" + "Mund": "Hand" (trust).

Muroti [mur-roh-tee] The Dreamer, a shaman. (Shona)

N

Nader [nay-dur] Unique, *fr* "Nadir": "Rare." (Ara)

Nahshon [nah-shawn] Wave, man of the wave. (Hbr)

fr "Nahshol" [nah-shohl] "Wave."

The first man to cross the Red Sea when it parted.

Naizak [nigh-zak] Shooting Star. (Ara)

Najin [nah-jihn] Stands. (Sioux)

Mato Najin [mah-toh nah-jihn] Standing Bear.

Makatonajin [mah-kah-toh-nah-jihn] Stands on Blue Earth.

"Maka": "Earth" + "To": "Blue" + "Najin": "Stands."

Nakin [nah-keen] Life. (Mam Maya)

Namdren [nahm-drehn] Liberator. (Tibetan)

Namiid [nah-meed] Star Dancer. (Chippewa)

fr "Niimi'idi" [nih-mee-dee] "Dancing," dancing to drums.

Ceremonial drumming and dancing are medicinal.

Namio [nah-mee-oh] Wave Man. (Japanese)

fr "Nami": "Wave," surf of the sea.

Nandin [nahn-dihn] Bliss. (Skt)

fr "Ananda" [ah-nahn-dah] "Bliss," ultimate happiness.

Anandan [ah-nahn-dehn] Bliss.

Nandan Kanan [nahn-dahn kah-nahn] Blissful Forest.

Natan [nah-tahn] Gift, *became* **Nathan**. (Hbr)

Nataniel [nah-tahn-nee-yehl] Gift from God.

"Natan": "Gift" + "El": "God."

Nathian, Nathion [nay-thee-yehn] *fr* "Nathaniel." (Eam)

Navin [nah-veen] New, new man, *fr* "Nava": "New." (Skt)

Naveen [nah-veen] New, new man. (Hindi)

Navon [nah-vohn] Sharp Wits. (Hbr)

To be wise in the ways of the world.

Nebi [neh-bee] Holy, prophet. (Ara)

Neeve [neev] Holy Spirit. (Gaelic)

fr "Niamh" [neev] "Holy Spirit."

"Naomha" [nay-vah] "Holy," *became* pron N "Nevin."

Nevin [neh-vihn] Holy Man; a N given to saints. (OE)

Nevyn [neh-vihn] Holy Man, *fr* "Nevin." (Welsh)

Nevan, Nevian [neh-vehn, neh-vee-ihn] *fr* "Nevin." (OE)

Nen [nehn] Deep Hope. (Japanese)

Neo [nee-oh] New. (Grk)

Neotheus [nee-oh-thee-uhss] New God.

"Neos": "New" + "Theos": "God."

Neote [nee-oh-tay] New God, *fr* "Neotheus."

Novan [noh-vehn] New, *fr* "Novus": "New." (Latin)

Nuvan [noo-vahn] New Man, *fr* "Nuevo": "New." (Span)

Novian [noh-vee-ehn] New, new man. (Russian)

Neos (Grk) > Novus (Latin) > **Nouvel** (Frn) > Nava (Skt).

Netran [neh-trahn] Eyes, a guide and teacher. (Skt)

fr "Netra": "Eyes," trained eyes, guidance, a guide.

Ravinetra [rah-vee-neh-trah] Sun Eye, sun guidance.

"Ravi": "Sun" + "Netra": "Eye" (guidance), a teacher.

Nikitas [nee-kee-tahss] Victor, the champion. (Grk)

fr "Nike" [nee-kee] "Victory," *became* pron [nigh-kee].

Nicos, Nikos [nee-kohss] Victor, Nn *fr* "Nikitas."

Nicander [nee-kann-dur] Victorious Man, the champion.

"Nike" [nee-kee] "Victory" + "Ander": "Man" (brave).

Nikanor [nee-kah-nor] Victory Man, *fr* "Nicander." (Russian)

Nikko [neek-koh] Sun. (Japanese)

Nimet [nee-meht] Blessing. (Turkish)

Njere [nah-jeer-ree] Cleverness, great mental abilities.   (Shona)

Noam [noh-uhm] Pleasant, *fr* "Naim": "Pleasant."   (Hbr)

Nomeus [noh-may-uhss] Shepard.   (Grk)

Nychas [nee-kuhss] Champion of the People.   (Russian *fr* Grk)

   fr **Nicholas** [nee-koh-lahss] Champion of People.   (Grk)

   "Nike" [nee-kee] "Victory" + "Laos": "People."

   Saint Nicholas was a generous old man from Turkey,

   who lived in a Greek colony, back in 270 AD.

   Nicholas (Grk) > **Nielsson** (Swed) > **Nilsson** > **Nelson**.

   Niel [neel] Champion of the People, *fr* "Nicholas."   (Swed)

   Nielsen [neel-suhn] Niel's Son, *fr* "Nielsson."   (Swed)

   Neeson [nee-suhn] Cmpd Nn *fr* "Nielsson."   (OE)

   Nicholas (Grk) > Niel (Swed) > Niall > **Neal** (OE).

   Nealand [neel-lehnd] Land of the Champion.   (OE)

   fr "Nieland" = "Niel": "Champion" + "Land."

   Niall, **Niallan** [nee-yahl, nee-yal-luhn] Champion.   (Gaelic)

   Nyall [nee-yahl] Champion, *fr* "Niel."   (Welsh)

   Nyle [nighl] Champion, pron N *fr* "Nyall."   (OE)

Nylander [nee-lann-dur] New Landowner.   (Swed)

   "Ny" [nee] "New" + "Lander": "Landowner."

O

Ojo [oh-joh] Rain.   (Yoruba)

Okoro [oh-kor-roh] A Fine Boy.   (Igbo)

Olowan [oh-loh-wahn] Song, the singer.   (Lakota Sioux)

Omar [ohm-mar] Life, *became* **Omarion**.   (Persian *fr* Ara)

   fr "Umr" [oo-mur] "Life."   (Ara)

   Omar Khayyam advanced mathematics in the 2nd century.

Omid [ohm-mihd] Hope, *fr* "Omed": "Hope."   (Persian)

Omri [ohm-ree] Grain, harvesting an abundance.   (Hbr)

   fr "Omer": "Sheath" (grain), for a good harvest.

Ondreian [ahn-dray-ihn] *fr* "Andrei"; *see* Andreas.   (Russian)

P

Palden [pal-dehn] Glorious. (Tibetan)

Parmenas [par-mehn-nuhss] Permanent. (ME *fr* Grk)
  fr "Parmenas": "Very Permanent," very steadfast. (Grk)
  "Para": "Very" + "Monimos": "Permanent" (steadfast).
  Parmenion [par-mehn-nee-uhn] Very Permanent.
  Parmen [par-mehn] Very Permanent, *fr* "Parmenas." (OE)
  Parmenio [par-mehn-nee-oh] *fr* "Parmenas." (Span)

Pavan [pah-vahn] Purity, purified by the wind. (Skt)
  N of the God of the Winds, the great purifier.
  Pavitran [pah-vee-trehn] Purifier, by the wind.

Pax [paks] Peace. (Latin)
  Pace [payss] Peace, *fr* "Pax." (Ital)
  Pascal, Pasqual [pass-skal] Peace, *fr* "Paix": "Peace." (Frn)
  Paxton [paks-tuhn] Peaceful Estate. "Pax" + "Tun." (OE)

Pemba [pehm-bah] Lotus, symbol of truth. (Tibetan)
  Pemba Rinchen [pehm-bah rihn-chihn] Lotus Jewel.

Penden [pehn-dehn] Lotus Throne. (Tibetan)

Prashant [prah-shahnt] Bringer of Peace. (Skt)
  "Pra": "Fulfiller" (brings) + "Shanti": "Peace" (tranquility).

Pravdin [prahv-dihn] Truth, *fr* "Prav": "Truth." (Russian)

Preman [prehm-muhn] Beloved, *fr* "Prema": "Love." (Hindi)

Prentice [prehn-tihss] Apprentice, Student. (ME)

Princeton [prihn-stuhn] Estate of the Prince. (ME)
  "Prince": "First" (Frn) + "Tun": "Estate" (town).

Q

Qamar [kah-mar] Moon. (Ara)

Qawe [kah-way] Brave. (Zulu)

Qiniso [kee-nee-soh] Truth, Nn is **Qin** [keen]. (Zulu)

Quetzal [kehts-zal] Sacred Bird, of magnificent color. (Toltec)

Qullan [kool-lahn] Sacredness, *fr* "Qullana" (sacred). (Quechua)

R

Radegun [rad-deh-guhn] Battle Advisor.   (Germanic)
    fr **Radegund** [rad-deh-goond] Battle Advisor.
    "Rad": "Opinion" (advisor) + "Gund": "Battle."
    "Rad" is an opinion that becomes a decree, an order.
    Radegan [rad-deh-gehn] Battle Advisor, *fr* "Radegund."
    Radigan [rad-dih-gehn] Battle Advisor, *fr* "Radegan."
    Radman [rad-mehn] Council Man, an advisor.
Radin [rad-dihn] Joy, *fr* "Rad": "Joy."   (Russian)
    Radik [rad-dihk] Joy.
    Radko [rad-koh] Little Joy. "Rad" + "-ko" (little).
    Radikon [rad-dih-kuhn] Joy.
    Radzin [rad-zihn] Joyful, *fr* "Radin."
    Radomir [rad-doh-meer] Joyful Peace.
    "Rad": "Joy" + "Mir": "Peace."
    Radimir [rad-dih-meer] Joyful Peace, *fr* "Radomir."
    Radovan [rad-doh-vehn] Joy, joyful man.   (Sb-Cr)
Rahmet [rah-meht] Mercy.   (Turkish)
Rainer [ray-nur] Commander of the Army.   (Germanic)
    fr "Ragnar" [ray-nar] "Commander of the Army."
    "Ragin": "Mighty" (decree) + "Heer": "Army."
    Ragnar, Ragner > Regner > Regnier > Reynier > **Reiner**.
    Reynier [ray-neer] Mighty Army.   (Dutch)
    Raynier, **Rayner** [ray-neer, ray-nur] Mighty Army.   (Frn)
    Rainier [ray-neer] Mighty Army, *fr* "Rayner."   (Frn)
Rajan [rah-jahn] King, *fr* "Raja."   (Skt)
    Rajinder [rah-jihn-dur] Conquering King, mighty king.
    "Raja": "King" + "Indra": "Conquering"; N of a god.
    Rajen [rah-jehn] King, *fr* "Rajan."   (Hindi)
Rami [rah-mee] High Up, to be supreme.   (Hbr)
    Ramiel [rah-mee-ehl] God is Supreme. "Rami" + "El."
Rangzen [rahn-zehn] Freedom, *became* **Ranzen**.   (Tibetan)
Rannikko [rahn-neek-koh] Coast, the ocean shore.   (Finnish)

Ravi [rah-vee] Sun. (Skt)

    Ravinder [rah-vihn-dur] Sun Prince.

    "Ravi": "Sun" + "Indra," a god (lord), prince.

Raviro [rah-veer-roh] Gift from God. (Shona)

Razo [rah-zoh] King, *fr* **Roi** [roy] King, Royal; *see* Rian. (Frn)

Razum [rah-zuhm] Reason. (Sb-Cr)

Reason [ree-zuhn] Reason, to be logical & intelligent. (Eam)

    Reason Wells [ree-zuhn wehlz] Reason Wells.

Reikan [righ-kehn] Ruler, *fr* "Reiks": "Ruler." (Germanic)

    Alareiks [al-lar-rihks] Ruler of All.

    "All": "All" + "Reiks": "Ruler."

    Alaric [al-lar-rihk] Ruler of All, *fr* "Alareiks."

    Legendary King Alaric ruled the Visigoths in 5th century.

    Riland, Ryland [righ-lehnd] King's Land. (OE)

    "Ri" [righ] "King" + "Land."

    Riley [righ-lee] Meadow belonging to the King. (OE)

    "Ri": "King" + "Leah" [lee] "Meadow," *became* "Ley."

    Ryley [righ-lee] King's Meadow, *fr* "Riley." (OE)

    Reighly [righ-lee] French spelling for "Riley." (ME)

    Righly [righ-lee] King's Land, *fr* "Reighly." (ME)

    Rylund [righ-luhnd] King's Land, *fr* "Ryland." (Eam)

Remi [reh-mee] Consoling, one who is comforting. (Yoruba)

    Oluremi [oh-lur-reh-mee] God Consoles Me.

    "Remi": "Consoling" + "Olu": "God."

Remington [rehm-meeng-tuhn] Coastline Estate. (OE)

    fr "Rimington" = "Rim": "Coast" (border) + "Tun" (estate).

Remy [rehm-mee] Swift Oarsman. (Frn)

    fr "Remigius": "To Row" (oarsman); N of a saint.

Rene [rehn-nay] Reborn. (Frn)

    fr "Renaissance" [rehn-nah-sahnss] "Rebirth."

    Renay [rehn-nay] Reborn, *fr* "Rene." (Span)

    Renan [rehn-nahn] Reborn, *fr* "Renay." (Span)

Renshan [rehn-shawn] Kind High Ideals. (Mandarin)

    One with high ideals will always show kindness.

Renzo [rehn-zoh] Champion, Victor. (Ital)
    fr "Lorenzo": "Champion"; *see* Ap1: Laurence.

Rey [ray] King. (Span)
    Monterey [mahnt-tur-ray] Wilderness of the King.
    "Monte": "Wilderness" (mountainous) + "Rey": "King."

Rezin [reh-zehn] Strong Willed. (Hbr)
    fr "Ratson" [rehts-zehn] "Willful," to be strong willed.
    Reeson, Reasin [ree-zihn] Strong Willed, *fr* "Rezin." (Eam)

Rhidian [rihd-dee-ihn] Free Man, *fr* "Rhyd": "Free." (Welsh)

Rian [righ-yehn] The King, *fr* "Riaghan" [righ-yehn]. (Gaelic)
    "Righ": "King" + "-an."
    Rhyan [righ-yehn] King, *fr* "Rhi" [righ] "King." (Welsh)
    Tegryn [teeg-grihn] Handsome King. (Welsh)
    "Teg": "Fair" (good-looking) + "Rhyan" (ryan): "King."
    Rhys [reess] King, *fr* "Rhi." (Welsh)
    Ryan, **Rion** [righ-yuhn] King. (OE)
    Reese [reess] King, *fr* "Rhys." (OE)
    Reece [reess] King, *fr* "Reese." (ME)
    Rion [righ-yahn] King, *fr* "Rian." (ME)
    Derian, Derrien [dair-ree-ehn] Of the King. (ME)
    "De": "Of" (from) + "Rian": "King," place of the king.
    Darien [dair-ree-ehn] Of the King, *fr* "Derian." (ME)

Riggo [ree-goh] Little King, a prince. (Ital *fr* Latin)
    fr "Regulus" = "Regis" (rex): "King" + "-ula" (little). (Latin)

Rinchen [rihn-chehn] Great Value, precious jewel. (Tibetan)
    "Rin": "Value" + "Chen": "Great."
    Precious jewel of wisdom, symbol of great clarity.

Rio [ree-oh] River. (Span)

Rishon [ree-shohn] First, the first one. (Hbr)

Rochan [roh-kahn] Radiant, bringer of light. (Skt)
    fr "Roca" [roh-kah] "Shining," "Radiant."
    Rowshan [roh-shahn] Radiant, bringer of light. (Persian)
    Roshan [roh-shahn] Radiant, bringer of light. (Hindi)

Rodan [roh-dahn] The Earth. (Sb-Cr)

Roderic [rahd-dur-rihk] Red Ruler.   (Germanic)
   "Rod": "Red" + "Rik": "Ruler"; *see* Ap1: Robert.
   Roderic the Great was first king of the Britons in 820 AD.
   Rhodri [roh-dree] Red Ruler, *fr* "Roderic."   (Welsh)
Rohan [roh-hahn] Ascends the Throne, a king.   (Skt)
   fr "Ruh": "Red" (sunrise), ascension, a king.
   Like the sunrise, he ascends the throne to become king.
Rommel [rahm-mehl] A Spiritual Pilgrim.   (Latin)
   The word "Roaming" came from spiritual pilgrims whom
   were always migrating to the religious capitol of "Rome."
   Romel [rahm-mehl] A Spiritual Pilgrim, *fr* "Rommel." (Span)
Ronan [roh-nehn] Little Seal, a seal of the Sea.   (Gaelic)
   fr "Ron": "Seal" + "-an" (little).
Ronel [rahn-nehl] Delight of God, God's joyful song.   (Hbr)
   "Ron" is *fr* "Oneg": "Delight" (joyful song) + "El": "God."
   Ronen [rahn-nehn] God's Delight, *fr* "Ronel."   (New Hbr)
Ronn [rohn] Red, Rune, the rune tree; *see* Ap1: Rune. (Swed)
   The Mountain Ash Tree (rowan) was named for it's red
   berries, and has a very hard wood used for carving runes.
   Ancient mystical wisdom was expressed by runic script.
   Rune [roon] Secret Writing, mystical meaning.   (Scand)
   Runi [roon-nee] Wise Man of the Runes.   (Scand)
   Runere [roon-neer] Wise Man of the Runes.   (OE)
   Runian [roo-nee-ihn] Wise Man of the Runes.   (OE)
   Roan [rohn] Rune Tree, the tree of wisdom.   (ME)
Rooney [roon-nee] Heroic.   (OE *fr* Gaelic)
   fr "Ruanaid": "Heroic," to be firm and fierce.   (Gaelic)
Ruadan [roo-dahn] Red Man, to have red hair.   (Gaelic)
   fr "Ruadh" [roo] "Red"; *see* Rohan.
   Rogan, Roghan [roh-guhn] Young Red.
   fr "Ruadhagan" [roo-guhn] "Young Red," red-haired boy.
   "Ruadh" [roo] "Red" + "Ogan" [oh-guhn] "Youth."
Rydell [righ-dehl] Valley of the King; *see* Rian.   (OE)
   "Ri": "King" + "Dael": "Valley."

131

Ryder [righ-dur] Rider, horse rider, *fr* "Reider." (OE *fr* Nor)

    Reider [righ-dur] Rider, horse rider, soldier or knight. (Nor)

    Ridley [rihd-lee] Riding Horses across a Meadow.

    "Ridda": "Rider" + "Leah" [lee] "Meadow," *became* "Ley."

    Ryden [righ-dehn] Rider, horse rider, *fr* "Ryder."

Rytis [ree-tihss] Morning. (Lithuanian)

S

Saeborn [say-burn] Sea Hero, *fr* "Saebeorn." (OE)

    "Sae" [say] "Sea" + "Beorn": "Hero."

    Sebron [say-bruhn] Sea Hero, *fr* "Saeborn." (ME)

Sagus [say-guhss] Prophetic Speech, a Sage (wise). (Latin)

    Sagen [say-gehn] "Say" (saga), storyteller. (Ger)

    Saywell [say-wehl] Say Well, to speak the truth. (Eam)

Saige [sayj] Wisdom, *fr* "Sage" [sayj] "Wisdom." (Frn)

Sajan [sah-jahn] Sweetheart. (Hindi)

Sajeevan [sah-jee-vahn] Possessing Life, *fr* "Jiva": "Life. (Hindi)

Samten [sahm-tehn] Meditation, transcendence. (Tibetan)

Sanjay [sann-jay] Bestower of Victory; a N for Buddha. (Skt)

    fr **Sanjaya** [sann-jigh-yah] Bestower of Victory.

    "San": "Gains" (bestows) + "Jaya": "Victory."

    Sanjeev [sann-jeev] Full of Life. (Hindi)

    "San": "Gains" (filled) + "Jiva": "Life."

Santino [sann-tee-noh] Saint. (Ital)

Sardion [sar-dee-ahn] Carnelian Stone, a red chalcedony. (Grk)

Sarjan [sar-jahn] Scholar, scientist. (Indonesian)

Saul [sawl] Asked For, asked for a favor by god. (Hbr)

    fr "Nishal" [nee-shawl] "Asked For," asking for a favor.

    Savel [sah-vehl] Asked by God, pron N *fr* "Saul." (Russian)

Savene, Savenay [sah-veh-nay] Place of the Savior. (Frn)

    fr "Sauveur": "Saviour," *became* **Savier** > **Xavier** (Span).

    Saveny [sah-veh-nee] Savior's Place, *fr* "Savenay." (ME)

    Savion [sav-vee-ahn] Savior's Place, *fr* "Savenay." (Eam)

Sean

    1. [shann] Ancient, the wisdom of an elder.   (Gaelic)

      Seanan [shann-nuhn] Ancient, wise elder.

      Shannon [shann-nuhn] Pron N *fr* "Seanan."   (OE)

    2. [shawn] Gift from God.   (Gaelic *fr* Hbr)

      "Sean" is pron N *fr* "John" [jawn]; *see* Jonatan.   (Hbr)

      Shawn [shawn] God's Gift, pron N *fr* "Sean" (John). (OE)

      Deshawn [day-shawn] Of Shawn (John).   (ME)

      "De": "Of" + "Shawn": "God's Gift."

      Shane [shayn] Gift from God, *fr* "Shawn."   (ME)

      Zane [zayn] Gift from God, *fr* "Shane."   (Eam)

Sebiorn [say-bee-yorn] Victorious Bear.   (Swed, Nor)

    fr "Sigbjorn" [sihg-bee-yorn] "Victorious Bear."

    "Sig": "Victory" + "Bjorn" [bee-yorn] "Bear."

Seijin [say-jihn] To Grow Up, an adult.   (Japanese)

Sejati [seh-jah-tee] True, Genuine.   (Indonesian)

Sengchen [sehng-chehn] Great Lion.   (Tibetan)

    "Senge" [sehng-gay] "Lion" + "Chen": "Great."

Shahin [shah-heen] Falcon.   (Persian)

Shain [shayn] Handsome.   (Yiddish *fr* Ger)

    fr "Schon" [shoon] "Beauty," handsome.   (Ger)

Shantaram [shahnt-tar-ruhm] Delightful Peace.   (Skt)

    "Shanta": "Peace" (tranquil) + "Ram": "Delight."

Shay [shay] Present, a gift; *see* Jesse.   (Hbr)

    Shai [shay] My Present, given by God, *became* [shigh].

    "Shay": "Present" + "-i" (sheli): "My."

    Shilo, Shiloh [shigh-loh] My Present from Him, from God.

    "Shai" [shay] "My Present" + "-lo" (shelo): "His."

Shea, Shay [shay] Supernatural Being, a fairy.   (OE *fr* Gaelic)

    fr "Sith" [shee] "Supernatural," magical being, fairy. (Gaelic)

Shenden [shehn-dehn] To Benefit Others.   (Tibetan)

Sheridan [shair-rih-dehn] Valley of the Sheriff.   (OE)

    fr **Sheriden** [shair-reh-dehn] Valley of the Sheriff.

    "Sheriff": "Shire-man" (overseer) + "Denu": "Valley."

Shimon [shee-mohn] He Hears God, he understands him.   (Hbr)
   fr **Shemaiah** [sheh-migh-yah] He Hears God.
   "Shmia": "Hears" (listening) + "Yah": "God."
   Shimuel [shihm-mew-wehl] He Hears God.
   "Shmia": "Hears" (listens) + "El": God."
   Samuel [sam-mew-wehl] He Hears God, *fr* "Shimuel."   (Grk)
   Shemaiah > Shimon > **Simon** (Grk) > **Simeon** (Latin).
Shimshon [shihm-shawn] Sun.   (Hbr *fr* Sumerian)
   fr "Shemesh" [sheh-mehsh] "Sun," very powerful. (Sumerian)
   Mighty Samson was a Nazir monk (nazirene), who did not
   cut their hair in order to accumulate great personal power.
   Shimshai [shihm-shay] My Sun, *became* [shihm-shigh].
   "Shimshon": "Sun" (power) + "-i" (sheli): "My."
   Samson [sam-suhn] Sun, *fr* "Shimshon."   (Grk)
   Sampson [samp-suhn] Sun, *fr* "Samson."   (OE)
Shomron [shohm-rahn] Guardian.   (Hbr)
   fr "Shomer": "Guardian" (protector).
   Shimron [shihm-rahn] Guardian, a protector.
   Shimri [shihm-ree] Guardian, *fr* "Shimron."
Sidon [sigh-duhn] Star Man.   (Latin)
   fr "Sidus" [sigh-duhss] "Starry," influenced by the stars.
   Sidran [sigh-druhn] Star Man.
Siebrand [see-brannd] Victorious Warrior.   (Ger)
   fr "Siegbrand": "Victorious Warrior"; *see* Brand.
   "Sieg" [seeg] "Victor" + "Brand": "Fire" (sword), warrior.
   Sigbrandt > Siegbrand > Siebrand > Sybrand > Sybran.
   Sybrant [sigh-brannt] Victorious Warrior.
   Sybrand [sigh-brannd] *fr* "Siegbrand."   (Dutch)
   Sybran, Sy [sigh-brehn, sigh] *fr* "Sybrand."   (ME)
Sigur [seeg-gur] Victor, *fr* "Sig" [seeg] "Victor."   (Germanic)
   Siggo [seeg-goh] Victor, Champion.
   Siegen [seeg-gehn] Victor, the Champion.
   "Sieg" [seeg] "Victor" (champion) + "En": "The."
   Sieger, Siegler [seeg-gur, seeg-lur] Victor, Champion.

Sieger > Siegler > **Ziegler** > Zieler > Zyler.

Zieler [zigh-lur] Victor, champion, *fr* "Ziegler."

Zyler [zigh-lur] Victor, pron N *fr* "Zieler."   (OE)

Sieffre [sigh-free] Peaceful Victory.   (Welsh)

    fr "Siegfrid" [sihg-freed] "Peaceful Victory."

Skye [skigh] Cloud, misty clouds.   (Swed)

    The Isle of Skye is always covered with mist.

Skyler [skigh-lur] Scholar, to be highly educated.   (Dutch)

    fr "Schuyler" [skigh-lur] "Scholar," learned, educated.

    Skylar [skigh-lar] Scholar, *fr* "Skyler."

Sojiro [soh-jeer-roh] Wise Boy.   (Japanese)

Solaris [sohl-lar-rihss] Sun, of the sun.   (Latin)

    Soleone [sohl-lay-own-nay] Sun Lion.

    "Sol": "Sun" + "Leon" [lay-own] "Lion."

    Solen [sohl-lehn] The Sun. "Sol" + "-en": "The."   (Swed)

Solomon [sahl-loh-muhn] His Peace, as in God's peace.   (Hbr)

    fr "Shlomo" = "Shalom": "Peace" + "-o" *fr* "Shelo": "His."

    King Solomon's extraordinary wisdom was legendary.

    Solon [sohl-lahn] N of a wise statesman, *fr* "Solomon."   (Grk)

Somerton [suhm-mur-tuhn] Summer Farm.   (OE *fr* Nor)

    "Sommer": "Summer" + "Tun": "Estate" (farm).   (Nor)

    The southern farm used during the summer months.

Sonam [soh-nahm] Merit, deserving honors.   (Tibetan)

    Sonam Gyatso [soh-nahm jaht-soh] Ocean of Merit.

    N the monks gave to the Third Dalai Lama, born 1543.

Sovin [soh-vihn] Owl.   (Russian)

Sovrano [soh-vrahn-noh] Supreme Ruler.   (Latin)

    "Super": "Above" (supreme) + "Regno": "To Reign."

    Souverain (Frn) > Sovereign (ME) > **Sovern** > Seven.

    Sovran [sahv-rehn] Supreme, *fr* "Sovrano.

    Seven [seh-vehn] Nn *fr* "Severin": "Sovereign."   (ME)

Stavros [stahv-rohss] Cross, *fr* "Stauros": "Cross."   (Grk)

Steen [steen] Stone.   (Dutch *fr* Ger)

    fr "Stein" [stighn] "Stone," a stable foundation.   (Ger)

Stanton [stann-tuhn] Stone Estate, a mansion.   (OE)
    "Stan": "Stone" + "Tun": "Estate" (town).

Striden [strigh-dehn] Warrior.   (Nor)
    fr "Strid" [strighd] "Combat" (combatant), a warrior.

Sujay [soo-jay] Great Victory.   (Skt)
    fr "Sujaya" [soo-jigh-yah] "Great Victory."
    "Su": "Good" (great) + "Jaya": "Victory."

Sulwyn [sohl-wehn] White Sun, radiant man.   (Welsh)
    "Sul": "Sun" + "Gwyn": "White."

Summit [suhm-miht] Top, top of the mountain.   (Latin)

Sundar [suhnd-dar] Handsome.   (Skt)

    Sunder [suhnd-dur] Handsome, *fr* "Sundar."   (Hindi)

Surin [sur-rihn] Sage, wise man.   (Skt)
    fr **Suri** [sur-ree] Sage (wise), to be educated.
    Surinder [sur-rihn-dur] Lord of Wisdom.
    "Suri": "Wise" + "Indra": "Conquering," a god (lord).

Symmachus [sihm-mahk-kuhss] Similar to a Warrior.   (Grk)
    "Sym": "Similar" + "Mache" [mahk-kay] "Warrior."

T

Tachante [tah-chahn-tay] Buffalo Heart.   (Sioux)
    "Tatanka" [tah-tahnk-kah] "Buffalo" + "Chante": "Heart."

Tage [tayj] Day (sunlight), a sunny disposition.   (Danish)
    Taggert, Taggart [tay-gurt] Bright Sunny Day.   (OE)
    fr "Tagbert" = "Tage": "Day" + "Bert": "Bright."

Tai [tigh] Supreme.   (Mandarin)
    Taishan [tigh-shahn] Supreme Height, like a mountain.
    "Tai": "Supreme" (great) + "Shan": "Good" (tall).
    Taibei [tigh-bay] High Mountain; N for the North Star.

Taigen [tigh-gehn] Great Ambition.   (Japanese)
    Taishiro [tigh-sheer-roh] Ambitious Boy.

Taivas [tigh-vuhss] Sky, Heaven.   (Finnish)
    Taevas [tigh-vuhss] Sky, Heaven.   (Estonian)

136

Taiyo [tigh-yoh] Sun, the sun. (Japanese)

Taji [tah-jee] Crown, symbol of a king. (Swahili)

Takane [tah-kah-nay] Mountain Peak. (Japanese)

Talor [tah-lor] Dew Light, dew sparkling in the dawn. (Hbr)
"Tal": "Dew" + "Or": "Light," morning light (dawn).

Talorc [tal-lork] Warrior Ready with Weapons. (Gaelic)
fr "Talorcan"; N of Pict King born in 595 AD; *see* Lorgan.

Tamon [tah-mohn] Good Listener, learns well. (Japanese)

Tane [tah-nay] Seed. (Japanese)

Tankan [tahn-kahn] Great, greatness. (Sioux)

Tapper [tap-pur] Brave, Courageous. (Swed, Nor)

Tarendra [tar-rehn-drah] Star Prince. (Skt)
"Tara": "Star" + "Indra"; N of a god (lord), a prince.
  Taranatha [tar-rah-nah-thah] Refuge in Liberation.
  "Tara": "Star" (rescuer) + "Natha": "Refuge" (protector).

Tarkan [tar-kahn] The Spiritual Path to God. (Turkish)
fr "Tarik" [tar-rihk] "Way," "Road," the way to God.

Tarkin [tar-kihn] Reasoning, skilled in logical thinking. (Skt)
fr "Tark": "Reasoning" (logic), conjecture and speculation.
  Tarkan [tar-kahn] Reasoning, logical, *fr* "Tarkana."
  Tarkus [tar-kuhss] Wisdom. (Estonian)
  Tarquin [tar-keen] Reasoning, logical. (Latin)

Tatewakan [tah-tay-wah-kahn] Sacred Wind, powerful. (Sioux)
"Tate": "Wind" + "Wakan": "Sacred."
  Tatewanyaggo [tah-tay-wahn-yah-goh] Visible Wind.
  "Tate": "Wind" + "Wanyango": "Visible."

Tawachin [tah-wah-cheen] His Mind, the thinker. (Sioux)
"Tawachin": "Mind," using his mind, he understands.

Teemant [tay-mahnt] Diamond. (Estonian)

Teg [teeg] Fair, good-looking lad, handsome. (Welsh)
  Tegen [teeg-gehn] Good-looking, *fr* "Teg." (OE)
  Tegan, **Teggan** [teeg-gehn] Good-looking. (OE)
  Teague, **Teag** [teeg] Good-looking. (ME)
  Teige, **Tigue** [teeg] Good-looking. (ME)

137

Tyge [teeg] Good-looking, *fr* "Teg." (ME)

Teagan [teeg-gehn] Good-looking. (ME)

Tego [tee-goh] Good-looking, handsome lad. (ME)

Tege, **Teeg** [teeg] Good-looking, *fr* "Teague." (Eam)

Tegwyn [teeg-gwihn] Good-looking and Fair. (Welsh)
"Teg": "Fair" (good-looks) + "Gwyn": "White" (fair).

Tecwyn [teek-kwihn] *fr* "Tegwyn." (OE)

Tehan Peta [tay-hahn pay-tah] Ancient Fire, still burning. (Sioux)
"Tehan": "Long Time" (ancient) + "Peta": "Fire."

Keyatehan [kay-yah-tay-hahn] Ancient Turtle.
"Keya": "Turtle" + "Tehan": "Ancient."

Tejan [tay-jahn] A Being of Light. (Skt)
fr "Tejas": "Light," fiery energy, to have magical powers.

Tejinder [tay-jihn-dur] Lord of Illumination.
"Tejas": "Light" + "Indra" (lord); N of the mightiest god.

Tej [tayj] Light, Nn *fr* "Tejinder."

Taj, **Tajan** [tahj, tahj-jahn] Light, *fr* "Tej." (Hindi)
The Taj Mahal palace means "Great Light" (great splendor).

Tekene [teh-keh-nee] Forest, *became* "Tokeneke." (Lenape)

Tekene Teme [teh-keh-nee tuh-may] Wolf of the Forest.

Teleon [tehl-lee-ahn] Perfection, *fr* "Teleios": "Perfect." (Grk)

Telemachus [tehl-leh-mah-kuhss] Perfect Warrior.
"Teleios": "Perfect" + "Machus": "Fighter" (warrior).
Telemachus was the prince of Ithaca in 1200 BC.

Tellurian [tehl-lur-ree-ihn] Earth Man. (Latin)
fr "Telluris" [tehl-lur-rihss] "Earth."

Temba, **Themba** [tehm-bah] Faith, Trust. (Zulu)

Temenus [teh-meh-nuhss] N for a sacred place. (Grk)

Temple [tehm-pehl] Place of Worship. (Frn)

Tenzin [tehn-zihn] Upholder of the Truth. (Tibetan)
"Tenpa" *fr* "Denpa": "Truth" + "Zin": "Holds," to hold up.

Tenzin Gyatso [tehn-zihn jaht-soh] Ocean Full of Truth.
"Tenzin": "Upholder of Truth" + "Gyatso": "Ocean."
RN of the Dalai Lama; *see* Gendun, Kundun, Ap1: Dalai.

138

Tenzin Yeshi [tehn-zihn yeh-shee] Holds Auspicious Truth. "Tenzin": "Truth Holder" + "Yeshe": "Auspicious."

Teom [tee-ohm] Twin, *became* **Thomas**.　　　　　(Hbr)

Tereus [tair-ray-uhss] Guardian, who looks at everything.　(Grk)
　fr "Tereo": "Look Over" (protect), a guardian.

Terran [tair-rehn] Earth, *fr* "Terra" [tair-rah] "Earth."　(Latin)
　　Terrance [tair-rehnss] Earth, of the earth.　　　(Frn)
　　Terron, Teran, Teren [tair-rehn] Earth, *fr* "Terrance.　(Eam)

Terton [tur-tuhn] Treasure Finder, treasure revealer.　(Tibetan)

Theodon [thee-oh-duhn] Ruler of the People.　　(Germanic)
　fr "Theuderic" [thoo-dair-rihk] "Ruler of the People."
　"Thiuda": "People" + "Ric": "Ruler"; *see* Reikan.
　　Theodric [thee-oh-drihk] Cmpd Nn *fr* "Theodoric."
　　Theuderic > **Theodoric** > Dederic > Derek > Dirk.
　　Derek [dair-rehk] Ruler of the People, *fr* "Theoderic."
　　Dirk [durk] Cmpd Nn *fr* "Derek."　　　　　(Ger)
　　Dirck [durk] Ruler of the People, *fr* "Dirk."　　(Danish)
　　Tedrick [tehd-drihk] Cmpd Nn *fr* "Theodoric."　(ME)

Theon [thee-ahn] God.　　　　　　　　　　　(Grk)
　fr "Theos": "God," *became* "Deos"; *see* Zatheon.
　　Theander [thee-ann-dur] Man like God.
　　"Theos": "God" + "Ander": "Man."

Theron [theer-rahn] Hunter, to be untamed and wild.　(Grk)

Tiandi [tee-ann-dee] Heaven on Earth.　　　(Mandarin)
　"Tian": "Heaven" + "Di" (earth); N for a divine emperor.

Tierney [teer-nee] A Lord.　　　　　　(OE *fr* Gaelic)
　fr "Tighearna" [tee-ur-nah] "Lord."　　　　　(Gaelic)
　　Tiernan [teer-nihn] A Lord, *fr* "Tighearnan": "Lord."
　　Ternan [tair-nihn] A Lord, *fr* "Tiernan."　　(ME)

Tigest [tih-gehst] Patience, one who is calm.　(Amharic)

Tigran [tee-grehn] Tiger, tiger man.　　　　(Russian)

Tiki [tee-kee] Hope, *fr* "Tikva" [teek-vah] "Hope."　(Hbr)

Timaeus [tihm-may-uhss] Honored Man.　　　(Grk)
　fr "Tima" [tee-mah] "Honor" + "-us" (man).

Timon [tee-mohn] Honored.

Timeon [tihm-mee-yuhn] Honored.

Timarchus [tihm-mar-kuhss] Honored Leader.
"Tima": "Honor" (honored) + "Archus": "Leader."

Timander [tihm-mann-dur] Honorable Man.
"Tima": "Honor" + "Ander": "Man" (brave).

Tivon [tihv-vohn] Nature, nature boy. (Hbr)
fr "Teva" [teh-vah] "Nature" (natural), to love nature.

Tevor [tehv-vor] Nature, nature boy. (New Hbr)

Tolun [toh-luhn] Full Moon. (Turkish)

Tomer [toh-mur] Palm Tree, to be tall and slender. (Hbr)
fr "Tamar": "Tall," "Slender," as the tall palm tree.

Tonde [tohn-day] God Listens to Us. (Shona)
fr **Tonderai** [tohn-dair-righ] Listens to Us, God does.

Tonitrus [toh-nee-truhss] Thunder, thunderbolt. (Latin)

Topden [tahp-dehn] The Power of the Truth. (Tibetan)
"Top": "Power" + "Denpa": "Truth."

Torden [tor-dehn] Thunder. (Danish, Nor, Swed)
fr "Tor": "Thunder"; N of the Scandanavian Thunder God.

Tordon [tor-duhn] Thunder.

Torvis [tor-vihss] Wise Thunder God.
"Tor": "Thunder" + "Vis": "Wise."

Torbjorn [tor-bee-yorn] Thunder Bear. (Swed)
"Tor": "Thunder" (thunderbolt) + "Bjorn": "Bear."

Torgund [tor-guhn] Thunder God Warrior.
"Tor": "Thunder" + "Gund": "Battle" (fighter), warrior.

Torgun [tor-guhn] Thunder God Warrior, *fr* "Torgund."

Torgen [tor-gehn] Thunder God Warrior, *fr* "Torgun."

Torgeir [tor-geer] Thunder Spear, a warrior.
"Tor": "Thunder" + "Geir": "Spear" (warrior).

Torger [tor-gur] Thunder God Spear.

Torgren [tor-grehn] Thunder God Spear, *fr* "Torger."

Torsten [tor-stehn] Stone of the Thunder God. (Danish)
"Tor": "Thunder" (Thunder God) + "Sten": "Stone."

Torbran [tor-brehn] Thunder Warrior, power of Thor.   (Nor)
"Tor": "Thunder" + "Brann": "Warrior"; *see* Brand.

   Torbram [tor-bruhm] Thunder Warrior, *fr* "Torbran."   (OE)
Tormi [tor-mee] Hurricane, man of great strength.   (Estonian)
Tovenaar [toh-vehn-nar] Magician, *fr* "Tover": "Magic." (Dutch)
   Toven [toh-vehn] Magician, Nn *fr* "Tovenaar."
Towakan [toh-wah-kahn] His Own Sacredness.   (Sioux)
"To" (his) + "Wakan": "Sacred," his sacred spirit.
Trevellyn [trehv-vehl-lihn] Town by the Lake.   (Welsh)
"Trev": "Town" (settlement) + "Llyn": "Lake."

   Trevlyn [trehv-lihn] Town by the Lake.

   Trevell [trehv-vehl] Town by the Lake, *fr* "Trevellyn."

   Trevyn [trehv-vihn] *fr* "Trevellyn"; *see* Ap1: Trevor.
Trillian [trihl-lee-yihn] Magic.   (OE *fr* Nor)

   fr "Trylling" [trihl-leeng] "Magic."   (Nor)

   Trilliam [trihl-lee-uhm] Magic.   (ME)
Troen [troo-wehn] The Truth.   (Nor)

   fr "Tro" [troo] "Truth" + "En": "The."

   Treowan [troo-wehn] Truthful.   (OE)

   fr "Treowe" [troo] "True," to be faithful.

   Trewen [troo-wehn] Truthful Man.   (ME)

   fr **Trew**, **Trewe** [troo] True, faithful.

   Treweman > **Trewman** > Trueman > **Truman**.

   Trune [troon] Truthful Man, cmpd Nn *fr* "Truman."   (ME)
Truver [troo-vair] Trustworthy, honest and true.   (Nor)

   fr "Truverdig" [troo-vair-dihk] "Trustworthy" (true).
Trygger [trihg-gur] Trustworthy.   (Swed, Nor)

   fr "Trygge" [trihg] "Secure" (sure), trustworthy.

   Trygg, **Tryg** [trihg] Trustworthy.

   Trigger, **Trigg** [trih-gur, trihg] *fr* "Trygger."   (OE)

   Tregaron [treh-gar-rehn] Trustworthy, *fr* "Trygger."   (ME)

   Tregan [treh-gehn] Trustworthy, *fr* "Tregaron."   (ME)
Tugan [too-gehn] Hard, muscular man, to be strong.   (Russian)

   fr "Tugo": "Tight," "Taut," hard muscles, great strength.

Tugi [too-gee] Support, to give strength.　　　　　(Estonian)

Tunkan [toonk-kahn] Sacred Stone, a medicine stone.　(Sioux)

　Tunkan Tuwa Mani [toonk-kahn too-wah mah-nee].

　Sacred Stone (medicine) Whom Walks, a medicine man.

　"Tunkan" + "Tuwa": "Whom" + "Mani": "Walks."

Tursam [tur-sahm] Lucky.　　　　　　　　　　　(Swed)

Tuvi, Tovi [too-vee, toh-vee] Goodness.　　　　　　(Hbr)

　Toviah [toh-vigh-yah] Goodness of God.

　"Tovi": "Goodness" + "Yah": "God."

　Toviah (Hbr) > Tobiah > **Tobias** (Grk) > **Toby** (OE).

　Tobian [toh-bigh-yehn] God's Goodness, *fr* "Tobiah."　(OE)

Tyven [tee-vehn] Calm and Tranquil.　　　　　　(Finnish)

Tzikin [see-keen] Eagle.　　　　　　　　　　(Mam Maya)

V

Vaering [vair-rihng] Strong as the Wind.　　　　　(Nor)

　fr "Vaer" [vair] "Wind," the power of the wind.

　Vaerin [vair-rihn] Strong as the Wind.

　Vaerian [vair-ree-ehn] Strong as the Wind, *fr* "Vaerin."

　Vaeran [vair-rehn] Strong as the Wind, *fr* "Vaerian."

Vajrin [vahj-rihn] Lightning, truth is the mightiest of all.　(Skt)

　fr "Vajr": "Hardest" (diamond), "Mightiest" (lightning).

　"Vaj": "Stone" (lightning) + "Rje": "King" (lord).

　Truth is an unstoppable force, like lightning; *see* Dorje.

Valente [val-lehn-tay] Strong, Valiant, brave man.　(Latin)

　fr "Valentis": "Strong," "Powerful," brave and valiant.

　Vallon [val-lahn] Valiant, brave man, *fr* "Valente."　(Frn)

Varshan [var-shahn] Rain, *fr* "Varsha": "Rain."　　　(Skt)

Vatren [vah-trehn] Fiery (ardent), very passionate.　(Sb-Cr)

Vedan [vay-dahn] Perception, a wise man.　　　　(Skt)

　fr "Veda" [vay-dah] "Perception," to see all and be wise.

　Vedi [vay-dee] Perceptive, wisdom.　　　　　　(Hindi)

Vedran [veh-drehn] Serenity.　　　　　　　　(Sb-Cr)

Veikko [vay-koh] Nice Guy. (Finnish)

Velimir, **Velemir** [vehl-lih-meer] Great Peace. (Sb-Cr, Russian)
"Velik" [vehl-leek] "Great" + "Mir": "Peace" (world).

Veranus [vair-rahn-nuhss] Truthful, truthful man. (Latin)
fr "Vero" [veer-roh] "Truth."
Vero > Veritas (Latin) > Verite (Frn) > Verdad (Span).
Veran [vair-rehn] Faithful, true friend. (Russian)

Verdan [vair-dahn] Green, green world. (Frn *fr* Latin)
fr "Viridis" [veer-ree-dihss] "Green," plants (life). (Latin)
Verdean [vair-deen] Green, green world.

Vesan [vay-sahn] Young Tree, vitality & strength. (Finnish)
fr "Vesa": "Sapling" (young tree), youthful strength.

Vianter [vee-ahn-tur] Traveller. (Russian *fr* Latin)
fr "Viator" [vee-ah-tor] "Way" (journey), a traveler. (Latin)

Vidin [vee-dihn] Vision, *fr* "Vid": "Vision." (Russian)
Vitan [vee-tahn] Man of Vision.
Vitomir [vee-toh-meer] Vision of Peace on Earth.
"Vit": "Vision" + "Mir": "Peace," a peaceful world.

Vidrik [vihd-drihk] Wide Ruler, great ruler. (Nor)
"Vid": "Wide" (great) + "Rik": "Ruler."

Viggo [vee-goh] Warrior, *fr* "Vig": "War." (Scand)

Vijay [vee-jay] Leading to Victory, conquest & triumph. (Skt)
fr "Vijaya" = "Vi" + "Jaya" [jigh-yah] "Victory."

Vikram [vihk-kruhm] To Step Beyond, to have courage. (Skt)
fr "Vikrama": "Step" (advance), valor and prowress.

Vinco [veen-koh] Conqueror (victor), to vanquish. (Latin)
Vinco > **Victor** > Vico (Latin) > **Vincent** (Ital).
Vico [vee-koh] Conqueror, *fr* "Vinco."
Vicente [vih-sehnt-tay] Conqueror, *fr* "Vincent." (Span)

Visandus [vih-sann-duhss] Bold Wisdom. (Nor, Scand)
"Vis": "Wise" + "Ande": "Spirit" (bold), to be spirited.

Vogan [voh-gehn] Warrior. (Russian)
fr "Voikin" [voy-kihn] "Warrior" (soldier).
Voyko [voy-koh] Warrior.

143

W

Waed [wayd] Wade, where to ford the river.   (OE)
   fr "Waed": "Water" (wade), fording rivers & shallow seas.
   Wayde, **Wade** [wayd] Wade, across the river.   (ME)
Waitzell [wayt-zehl] Wait Still, to have patience.   (Eam)
   fr "Waitstill": "Wait Still," being patient for God to answer.
   Waitstill > Waitstell > **Waitsell** > Waitzell.
Wajan Kuta [wah-jahn koo-tah] Shoots Light, like fire.   (Sioux)
   "Aojanjan": "Light" + "Kuta": "Shoots."
Wakan [wah-kahn] Sacred, power through sacredness.   (Sioux)
   "Wakan Tanka": "Great Sacredness"; N of the Great Spirit.
   Wakanojan [wah-kahn-oh-jahn] Sacred Light, a healer.
   "Wakan": "Sacred" + "Ojan" *fr* "Aojanjan": "Light."
   Wakan Dowan [wah-kahn doh-wahn] Sacred Singer.
   "Wakan": "Sacred" + "Dowan": "Singer."
   Wambdi Wakan [wahm-dee wah-kahn] Sacred Eagle.
   Idewakan [ee-day-wah-kahn] Sacred Blaze. "Ide": "Blaze."
   Tuwa Wakan Najin [too-wah wah-kahn nah-jeen].
   Whom Sacred Stands, upon the earth.
   "Tuwa": "Whom" + "Wakan" + "Najin": "Stands."
Weyland [way-lannd] Way Land, through the land.   (OE)
   "Weg" [way] "Way" (path) + "Land."
   Wayland [way-lannd] The Way, *fr* "Weyland."   (ME)
Wheeler [weel-lur] A Wheelwright, maker of wheels.   (OE)
   fr "Hweol" [weel] "Wheel," generating power.
Willem [wihl-lehm] Willful Warrior.   (Dutch *fr* Ger)
   fr "William" [wihl-yuhm] "Willful Warrior."   (Ger)
   "Wille": "Will" + "Helm": "Helmet" (warrior).
   Wim [wihm] Willful Warrior, cmpd Nn *fr* "Willem."
   Liam [lee-uhm] Willful Warrior, Nn *fr* "William."   (Gaelic)
Winstrom [wihn-strawm] Wind Stream.   (OE *fr* Ger)
   fr "Windstrom" = "Wind" + "Strom": "Stream."   (Ger)
Winzel [wihn-zehl] Friend's Hill, *fr* "Winselow."   (ME *fr* OE)

Winselow [wihn-sehl-loh] Friend's Hill. (OE)

"Wine" [wihn] "Friend" + "Hlaew" [loh] "Hill."

Win's-low > Winselow > **Winslow** (OE) > Winzel (ME).

Witton [wiht-tuhn] Wise. (Germanic)

fr "Witan": "To Know" (wise); *see* Ap1: Rune.

Witteric [wiht-tair-rihk] Wise Ruler, mighty wisdom.

"Witan": "Wise" + "Ric": "Ruler" (mighty).

Wittram [wiht-truhm] Wise Raven.

"Witan": "Wise" + "Ram": "Raven."

Witiza was King of the Visigoth Tribe in 700 AD.

Wolan [woh-lahn] Friendship, the traditional way. (Sioux)

Nn *fr* "Wolakota" [woh-lah-koh-tah] "Friendship."

"Wo" (to be) + "Lakota": "Friend"; *see* Dakoda.

Wulfram [wuhl-fruhm] Wolf Raven. (Germanic)

"Wulf": "Wolf" + "Ram": "Raven."

Wylfen [wuhl-fehn] Wolfish, *fr* "Wulf." (OE)

Y

Yable [yay-buhl] Able, capable man, *fr* **Able**. (Eam)

Yachay [yah-chay] Knowledge, wisdom. (Quechua)

Yadon [yay-duhn] He will Judge, God will judge me. (Hbr)

"Ye" (to) + "Dan": "Judge"; *see* Jadon.

Yaron [yar-ruhn] Singing Joyfully to God. (Hbr)

"Yah": "God" + "Ron": "Delight" (joy), joyful singing.

Jaron [jar-rahn] Singing Joyfully to God, *fr* "Yaron." (Grk)

Yasen [yah-sehn] Ash Tree. (Russian)

This tree is considered sacred in Scandinavian mythology.

Yashar [yash-shar] Upright & Honest. (Hbr)

Asher [ash-shur] Upright & Honest, *fr* "Yashar."

Yered [yair-rehd] Descending, like a river. (Hbr)

Jared [jar-rehd] River, *fr* "Yered," *became* "Jordan." (Grk)

Yeshayahu [yeh-shay-yah-hoo] God Saves. (Hbr)

"Yeshay" is *fr* "Le'hoshia": "To Save" + "Yehu": "God."

H(y)oshia-yah > Yeshayahu > Yesha(i)ah > **Isaiah** (Grk).

H(y)oshia-yah > Yoshiyahu > Yoshiah > **Josiah** (Grk).

Josias [joh-sigh-uhss] God Saves, *fr* "Josiah."   (Grk)

Joziah [joh-zigh-yah] God Saves, *fr* "Josiah."   (Eam)

Jessiah [jehss-sigh-ah] God Saves, *fr* "Josiah."   (Eam)

Yeshe, Yeshey [yeh-shay] Wisdom.   (Tibetan)

Yeshua [yeh-shoo-wah] Savior from God.   (Hbr)

 fr **Yehoshua** [yeh-hoh-shoo-wah] Savior from God.

 "Yehu" (yah): "God" + "Hoshea": "Save."

 Yehoshua > Ye(ho)shua > Yeshua (Hbr) > **Jesus** (Grk).

 Yoshua [yoh-shoo-wah] God's Savior, *fr* "Yehoshua."

 Yehoshua > Y(eh)oshua > Yoshua (Hbr) > **Joshua** (Grk).

 Joshuway [jah-shoo-way] Pron N for "Joshua."   (Eam)

Yodi [yoh-dee] Warrior.   (Skt)

 fr "Yoddhr" [yoh-dree] "Fighter" (warrior), *became* "Yoda."

 Ancient warriors are the teachers of the Jedi; *see* Jodha.

 Yodhrin [yoh-drihn] Warrior.

Yohanan [yoh-hahn-nahn] Graced by God's Mercy.   (Hbr)

 "Yehu" (yah): "God" + "Hanan": "Grace" (mercy).

Yonatan [yoh-nah-tahn] Gift from God; *see* Jonatan.   (Hbr)

 fr "Yehonatan": "God's Gift," Y(eh)onatan.

 "Yehu" (yah): "God" + "Natan": "Gift."

 Yanni, Yannis [yahn-nee, yahn-nihss] *fr* "Yonatan."   (Grk)

Yonten [yahn-tehn] Knowledge.   (Tibetan)

 Yonten Gyatso [yahn-tehn jee-yaht-soh] Knowledge Ocean.
N of the Fourth Dalai Lama, born in 1589.

Yoram [yor-ruhm] God is Exalted, elevated to glory.   (Hbr)

 Cmpd Nn *fr* "Yehoram": "God is Exalted," Y(eh)oram.

 "Yehu" (yah): "God" + "Ram": "Exalted."

 Joram [jor-ruhm] God is Exalted.   (Grk)

Yoshi [yoh-shee] Good Luck.   (Japanese)

Yosi [yoh-see] Storyteller of God, *fr* "Yosef."   (Hbr)

 Yosef [yoh-sayf] God's Storyteller, *became* **Joseph**.

 "Yah": "God" + "Sipur": "To Tell" (storyteller).

146

Z

Zadok [zad-dawk] Righteous, practicing justice. (Hbr)
    fr "Tsedek" [zeh-dehk] "Just" (righteous).
    Zaddock, Zadock [zad-dawk] Righteous, *fr* "Zadok."
Zafan [zah-fahn] Melody, the singer. (Amharic)
Zain [zayn] Beauty, to be handsome. (Moroccan Ara)
    Zein [zayn] Beauty, handsome, to be fine and alright. (Ara)
Zak, Zach [zak] Pure, pure enough for God. (Hbr)
    fr "Zax" [zak] "Pure," holy.
    Zakkai, Zaccai [zak-kay] Purity.
    Zaccheus [zak-kay-uhss] Purity, man of purity. (Grk)
    Zaqueo [zak-kay-yoh] Purity, *fr* "Zaccheus." (Span)
Zaki [zeh-kee] Preferable One, the chosen. (Ara)
Zalman [zal-mann] His Peace, *fr* "Solomon"; *see* Solomon. (Hbr)
Zamir [zah-meer] Singer, *fr* "Zamar": "Singer." (Hbr)
    Zemer [zehm-mur] Singing.
    Zimran [zihm-rahn] Singing, celebration through song.
    Zimri [zihm-ree] My Singing, My Song.
    "Zimra": "Singing" + "-i" (sheli): "My."
    Zemari [zeh-mar-ree] Singer, Chanter, teacher. (Amharic)
    Zimry, Zimre [zihm-ree] Song, *fr* "Zimri." (Eam)
Zandre [zann-dray] Defender of Men, *fr* "Alexander." (Frn)
    Xandre [zahn-dray] *fr* "Alexander"; *see* Alexin.
Zante [zahn-tay] Great Hunting God. (Grk)
    fr "Zacynthos" [zah-kihn-thohss] "Great Hunting God."
    "Za": "Great" + "Cyn": "Hunting" + "Theos": "God."
Zargun [zar-guhn] Golden Colored. (Persian)
    "Zar": "Golden" + "Gun": "Color."
    Sargon [sar-gahn] Golden Colored. (Sumerian)
    Sargon the Great was king of Mesopotamia in 2300 BC.
    Sumerian and Persian are ancient Indo-European languages.
Zatheon [zah-thee-uhn] Very Divine God. (Grk)
    "Za": "Very" + "Theos": "God" (divine); *see* Theon.

Zechariah [zeh-kar-righ-yah] God Remembers All.   (Hbr)
  "Zekar": "Remembers" + "Yah": "God."
  Zichri [zihk-kree] God Remembers, *fr* "Zechariah."
  Zacharias [zak-kar-ree-uhss] *fr* "Zechariah."   (Grk)
  Zachary [zak-kar-ree] God Remembers, *fr* "Zacharias." (Grk)
  Zachory [zak-kor-ree] God Remembers, *fr* "Zachary." (Ger)
  Zachry, Zackrey [zak-kree] *fr* "Zachary."   (Eam)
Zedekiah [zeh-deh-kigh-yah] God is Righteous.   (Hbr)
  fr "Tsadik" [zah-deek] "Righteous."
Zeke [zeek] Strengthened by God, *fr* "Ezekiel."   (Grk *fr* Hbr)
  Ezekiel [eh-zee-kee-ehl] Strengthened by God.   (Hbr)
  fr "Yechezkel" [yeh-hehz-kehl] "Strengthened by God."
  fr "Le'chizuk" (yechezk): "To Strengthen" + "El": "God."
  Zekial, Zikial [zeek-kee-uhl] Nn *fr* "Ezekial."   (Eam)
Zemko [zehm-koh] Little Earth.   (Russian)
  "Zemi": "Earth" + "-ko" (little).
Zenithan [zeh-nee-thehn] Zenith, a celestial man.   (Eam)
Zenji [zehn-jee] Little Zen Master.   (Japanese)
Zeno, Zenon [zee-noh, zee-nahn] Life, to be like Zeus.   (Grk)
  fr "Zeus" is *fr* "Zoe": "Life," Z(o)e-us.
  Zinovii [zee-noh-vee] Force of Life, Zeus's power. (Russian)
  "Zeno": "Zeus" (life) + "Bia": "Force" (power).
Zephyrn [zeh-furn] God of the West Wind.   (Eam *fr* Grk)
  fr "Zephyr": "West Wind"; N of a wind god.   (Grk)
  Zephin [zeh-fihn] God of the West Wind, *fr* "Zephryn."
  Zepheon [zeh-fee-yuhn] *fr* "Zephin."
Zeruko [zair-roo-koh] Sky, celestial.   (Basque)
Zewde [zoo-day] My Crown, the one who is king.   (Amharic)
Zhidian [zuh-dee-ehn] Earnest & Sincere.   (Mandarin)
Zhivan [jhih-vahn] Life.   (Russian)
  "Zhivago" [jhih-vah-goh] "Life," to love life.
  Zivon [jhih-vahn] Life.   (Sb-Cr)
  Zivotan [jhih-voh-tahn] Life.   (Sb-Cr, Slovak)
  Zivko, Zhivko [jheev-koh] Life, lively man.   (Bulgarian)

Ziah [zigh-yah] God's Burden, taking it from him.   (Eam *fr* Hbr)
   fr "Amaziah" [ah-mah-zigh-yah] "Burden of God."   (Hbr)
   "Amaz": "Burden" + "Yah": "God."

Ziggy [zihg-ghee] Victor, *fr* "Sigur"; *see* Sigur.   (Ger)
   Zeeger [zee-gur] Victor.   (Dutch)

Ziyad, **Ziad** [zee-yahd] Increase (growth), abundance.   (Ara)
   fr "Ziada" (zada): "Increase," surplus, abundance.
   Zidan [zee-dahn] Increase and Abundance.
   Zaiden, **Zaydan** [zay-dehn] Increase and Abundance.
   Zade [zayd] Increase and Abundance, Nn *fr* "Zaiden."
   Zidane [zih-dayn] Increase and Abundance, *fr* "Zidan." (Frn)

Zoeth [zoh-wehth] Life.   (Eam *fr* Grk)
   fr **Zoeteus** [zoh-wee-tee-uhss] Life, man of life.   (Grk)
   fr "Zoe" [zoh-wee] "Life," *became* "Zeus," Z(o)e-us.
   Educated Early Americans read the Greek classics.

Zohar [zoh-har] Shining, radiance.   (Hbr)
   Zoharon [zoh-har-rahn] Shining Singer, the teacher.
   "Zohar": "Shining" + "Oneg": "Delight" (joy), joyful sing.
   The chanter is teaching by singing sacred songs.
   Zoharon > Aharon > Aaron > **Aron**.
   Aaron [air-ruhn] Shining Singer (teacher), *fr* "Aharon."
   Zerach [zair-rahk] Shining Man. "Zer" is Nn *fr* "Zohar."
   Ziv [zeev] Shining, Nn *fr* "Zohar."
   Ziv Koren [zeev kor-rehn] Shining Light.

Zoran [zor-rehn] Dawn, *fr* "Zora."   (Sb-Cr)
   Zorin [zor-rihn] Dawn.

Zorion [zor-ree-ahn] Happiness.   (Basque)

Zowie [zoh-wee] Life.   (Frn *fr* Grk)
   fr "Zoe" [zoh-wee] "Life."   (Grk)
   Zoel [zoh-wehl] Life.
   Zowin [zoh-wihn] Life, *fr* "Zowie."   (ME)
   Zoey [zoh-wee] Life, *fr* "Zoe."   (Eam)

Zuran [zur-rehn] Powerful, *fr* "Zur": "Force" (power). (Persian)
   Zoran [zor-rehn] Powerful.

Appendices

Ap1 - Familiar Exotic Names

Aaliyah [ah-lee-yah] Elevated, the higher self. (Ara)
  Aliyah [ah-lee-yah] Ascending to a higher position. (Hbr)
Abigail [ab-bih-gayl] Energy from God. (Grk *fr* Hbr)
  fr **Avigal** [ah-vih-gahl] "Wave of Energy from God." (Hbr)
  "Avi": "Father" (God) + "Gal": "Wave" (energy).
  "Gal" [gahl] "Wave," wave of energy, like water; *see* Galet.
Adam [ah-dahm] Earth, *fr* "Adama": "Soil," "Earth." (Hbr)
  Man is made out of earth; Adama > Adam > Dam (blood).
Alan, Alain *is* Nn for "Alexander": "Defender of Men." (Frn)
Alana [ah-lah-nah] Great Awakening, to Arise. (Hwn)
  Alanna [ah-lahn-nah] Gift.
Allen [al-lehn] Stands Alone in Battle. (Scand *fr* Ger)
  fr "Allein": "Alone," the lone warrior, great strength. (Ger)
  A warrior strong enough to stand alone in battle.
  Allein > Allen (Ger) > Allin (Swed) > **Allinson** > Allison.
  Allison [al-lihss-suhn] Stands Alone in Battle, *fr* "Allinson."
Amazon [am-mah-zahn] Without Breast. (Grk)
  "A": "Against" (without) + "Mastos": "Breast."
  Women raised to be warriors from birth; their right breast
  was prevented from growing to free up their throwing arm.
  Andromache, Eurybe; *see* Antandra, Deianira, Evandra.
Aphrodite [af-froh-digh-tee] Bubbles, from sea foam. (Grk)
  The Goddess of Love; the origin of "Aphrodisiac."
Argentina [ar-jehn-tee-nah] Land of Silver; *see* Argenta. (Span)
Ariel is for boys; *see* Ari; **Ariella** is for girls. (Hbr)
Asher is *fr* **Yashar** [yash-shar] Upright, Honest. (Hbr)
Ashley [ash-lee] Meadow surrounded by Ash Trees. (OE)
  "Ash" (trees) + "Leah" [lee] "Meadow."
Austin [awe-stihn] Venerated. (OE *fr* Latin)
  Cmpd Nn *fr* **Augustine**: "Venerable." (Latin)
  Saint Augustine was sent by Rome to spread Christianity.
Avon [ay-vahn] River; N of a river. (OE *fr* Welsh)

fr "Afon" [ay-vahn] "River." (Welsh)

Aventon [ay-vehn-tuhn] River Town. "Avon" + "Town."

Bart [bart] Beard. (Ger)

Bethany [beh-thahn-nee] House of God. (OE *fr* Hbr)

   fr "Bethel" (OE) is *fr* "Betel": "House of God." (Hbr)

"Bet": "House" + "El": "God," a place of worship.

   Bethenia [beh-thehn-nee-yah] *fr* "Bethel." (Eam)

Bjork [bee-york] Birch Tree. (Swed)

Blaire [blair] Battlefield. (OE *fr* Gaelic)

   fr "Blar": "Flat," "Open Plain," used for battles. (Gaelic)

Blake [blayk] is *fr* "Blak": "Black." (ME *fr* OE)

   "Blak" (ME) is *fr* "Blaec" [blak] "Black." (OE)

Blythe is *fr* "Blithe" [blighth] "Joyful," "Cheerful." (OE)

Bradley [brad-lee] Wide Meadow. (OE)

   "Brad" is "Broad" + "Leah" [lee] "Meadow."

Britny is *fr* "Britian" *fr* "Brython," for native Celts. (OE *fr* Welsh)

Burt is *fr* "Bert" [burt] "Bright"; N for boys. (ME *fr* Ger)

   Birdina (ME) *fr* **Bertana** "Bright"; N for girls.

Cameron [kam-mur-rahn] Crooked Nose. (Welsh)

   "Cam": "Curved" (crooked) + "Sron": "Nose."

   Camron [kam-rahn] Crooked Nose.

Carmen [kar-mehn] Song, lyric poetry, a prophecy. (Latin)

Cassandra [kah-sawn-drah] Fragrantly Spiced Woman. (Grk)

   "Cassia": "Spices" + "Andra": "Man" (woman).

Cassidy [kass-sih-dee] Mound of Curly Hair. (Gaelic)

   "Cass": "Curls" + "Digh": "Mound."

Chandler [channd-lur] Chandelier, a candlemaker. (ME)

Charlize is a girls N *fr* "Charles" (ME) *fr* "Karl": "Man." (Ger)

Cher [shair] Dear one; a N *for* boys. (Frn)

   Chere [shair-ree] Dear one; a N *for* girls.

Chloe [kloh-wee] Blooming; the green, living world. (Grk)

Cindy [sihn-dee] Little Cinder. (Eam *fr* Frn)

   fr "Cinderella": "Little Cinder" (ashes). (Frn)

   Cindrell, **Cindra** [sihn-drehl, sihn-drah] Little Cinder.

Cindyanna [sihn-dee-yahn-nah] "Cindy" + "Anna."

Claire [clair] Clear, clarity. (Frn)

    Eclaire [ee-klair] Lightning, of great clarity.

Clayton [klay-tuhn] Clay estate, made of earth. (ME *fr* OE)

    "Claeg" [klay] "Clay" + "Tun": "Estate" (town). (OE)

Cole [kohl] Music, to love music. (OE *fr* Gaelic)

    fr "Coel" [kee-ohl] "Music." (Gaelic)

    Ole King Cole was a merry ole soul because of music!

Cynthea [sihn-thee-yah] Hunter Goddess, *fr* "Cynthos." (Grk)

    "Cyn" [kihn] "Hunter" + "Thea": "Goddess."

    Immortal twins, Artemis (Moon) & Apollo (Sun) were
    hunters whose arrows saved their worshippers. Their place
    of birth, Mount Cynthos [kihn-thohss], was sacred.

Dalai Lama [dah-ligh lah-mah] Superior Wisdom. (Mongolian)

    N of Third Dalai Lama was Sonam Gyatso, but in 1574
    a Mongol ruler said his wisdom was as vast as the ocean.
    "Dalai": "Ocean" + "Lama": "None Above" (Tibetan).
    Gendun Drup was the First Dalai Lama, reincarnating
    14 times in the past 600 years. Today he is Tenzin Gyatso;
    see Gendun, Jamphel, Kundun, Sonam, Tenzin, Yonten.

Dallas [dal-luhss] Noble Shield. (Eam *fr* Germanic)

    fr "Adallindis": "Noble Shield"; *see* Adela. (Germanic)

    "Adal": "Noble" + "Linde": "Shield."

    Adalinde > Adalindis > Adallindis > **Adallas** > Dallas.

Deepak [deep-pahk] Light, bringer of the light. (Hindi *fr* Skt)

    fr "Dip" [deep] "Light"; *see* Ap3: Randeep. (Skt)

Devon [deh-vuhn] N of a Celtic Tribe. (Latin *fr* Welsh)

    fr "Domnunii" [doh-vuhn] *became* the Devon Tribe. (Welsh)

    The Domnunii (Devon) were in the southwest of Britain.
    Among the 33 Celtic tribes there in 50 AD lived the
    Decantae and the Iceni. The Parisi tribe were refugees
    from the Romans, originally being from Paris, France.

Dimitri [dih-mee-tree] Loves the Earth Goddess. (Grk)

    fr "Demetrios": "Demeter," Goddess of the Earth.

Donovan [dahn-noh-vehn] Brown-brown Hair.   (Gaelic)
  fr "Donndubhan" [dahn-duh-vahn] "Brown-Black."
  "Donn": "Brown" + "Dubh" [duhv] "Black."
Duke [dook] Leader, *fr* "Dux": "Leader."   (Latin)
Dylan [dihl-luhn] Of the Sea; N for Son of the Sea God. (Welsh)
  "Dy" (of) + "Llanw" [lah-noo] "Tide" (sea) = "Of the Sea."
  Dillon [dihl-luhn] Of the Sea, *fr* "Dylan."   (OE)
Electra [ehl-lehk-trah] Brilliance; the orig N of Amber.   (Grk)
  Electricity was discovered by rubbing the "Electra" stone,
  so they changed the N of the electra stone to "Amber."
Elton [ehl-tuhn] Old Estate, old farm.   (OE)
  "Eald": "Old" + "Tun": "Estate" (farm), *became* "Town."
Erin [air-rihn] Western Island, to be from Ireland.   (Gaelic)
  fr "Iar": "West"; "Iar-land" (Ireland) is "Western Land."
Eve [eev] Life; N for Canaanite Goddess Asherah.   (OE *fr* Hbr)
  fr "Chawat": "Life"; Hbr N for the Goddess Asherah.   (Hbr)
  Co-creator goddess of the Canaanites, by the Tree of Life,
  who gave birth to many gods, became "Chawat" in Hebrew.
Fannie, **Fanny** is *fr* **Tiffany**; *see* Tephania.   (OE *fr* Grk)
Frodo is *fr* **Frodi** [froh-dee] Abundant Wisdom.   (Scand, Nor)
  "Frodi": "Lush" (abundance), much wisdom, very wise.
Gandalf [gann-dawlf] Elf Wizard, who has magic staff.   (Scand)
  "Gandar": "Magic Staff" (wizard) + "Alf": "Elf."
Gilbert [gihl-burt] Bright Angel.   (Ger)
  fr **Engelbert** = "Engel": "Angel" + "Bert": "Bright."
Godiva [gah-digh-vah] God's Gift.   (ME *fr* OE)
  fr "Godgifu" [gahd-geef] "God's Gift."   (OE)
  "God" + "Giefu" [geef] "Give" (gives), gift.
  Lady Godgifu (Lady Godiva) was loved by all the people.
  Born in 997 AD, she was influential & generous. During
  her legendary tax protest on horseback, out of respect
  everyone closed their windows, except for peeping Tom.
Grayham [gram] Gray Home, stone home.   (OE)
  "Graeg" [gray] "Gray" + "Ham": "Home," of gray stone.

Graham [gram] Grey Stone Home, *fr* "Grayham."

Graeme [gram] Pron N for "Graham." (ME)

Gwyndolyn [gwehn-doh-lihn] Shiny Armor. (Welsh)
"Gwen": "White" (shiny) + "Dolen": "Rings" (chain mail).
A white knight in shining armor.
"Gwyn" *for* boys; *see* Gwydion; "Gwen" *for* girls.

Gypsy is *fr* "Egyptian"; their RN is the "Rom." (Frn)

Halle [hahl-lee] Mansion, a home with many halls. (ME)

Hamilton [ham-mihl-tuhn] Home in the Mill Town. (OE)
"Ham": "Home" + "Mill" + "Ton": "Estate" (town).

Harley [har-lee] Meadow of Bunnies. (OE)
"Har": "Hare" (bunny) + "Leah": "Meadow."

Hayden [hay-dehn] Enclosed Valley, to be hedged in. (OE)
"Haeg" [hay] "Enclosure" (hedge) + "Dene": "Valley."

Haydn is *fr* "Hajdn" [hay-dehn] N of famous composer. (Sb-Cr)

Hendrix [hehn-drihks] Home Ruler. (OE *fr* Ger)
fr "Heimerich" [highm-mur-rihk] "Home Ruler." (Ger)
"Heim": "Home" + "Rik": "Ruler."
Heimerich > **Hendrich** > **Hendrick** > Hendrix.

Hercules [hur-kew-leez] Goddess Hera's Fame. (Latin *fr* Grk)
fr **Heracles** [hair-rah-kleez] Goddess Hera's Fame. (Grk)
"Hera": "Holy" + "Cleo": "Fame."

Hilary, Hillary *fr* **Hildegarde** "Hero Warrior." (Scand, Ger)
"Heldin": "Hero" + "Gard": "Protector" (spear warrior).

Hogan [hoh-gehn] Youth, vitality, strength. (Gaelic)
fr "Ogan" [oh-gehn] "Youth" (strength).

Hypatia [high-pay-shee-ah] Seat of the Soul. (Grk)
fr "Hypatos" [high-pah-tohss] "Under," under the heart.
The seat of the soul is under the heart, the hypatic place.
Hypatia was a genius who could have changed the world.
Hyppashia [high-pah-shee-ah] *fr* "Hypatia." (Eam)

Irene, Irenea [i-ree-nee, i-ree-nee-ah] Peace. (OE *fr* Grk)
fr **Eirene** [i-ree-nee] Peace; N of Goddess of Peace. (Grk)

Isaac (Isak) is *fr* "Yitzhak" [eets-zahk] "Laughter." (Grk *fr* Hbr)

155

Israel [ihz-rah-ehl] Wrestles with God, an angel of God. (Hbr)
"Isra": "Wrestle" + "El": "God."

Jade [jayd] Loin; N of curative stone for kidneys. (Frn *fr* Span)
fr "Ijada" [ee-hah-dah] "Loin," behind the kidneys. (Span)
Spanish conquerors saw jade for the first time in Mexico.

Jagger, Jagar [jag-gur] Hunter, *became* **Jaegar**. (OE *fr* Swed)
fr "Jagare" [yah-gar-rah] "Hunter," a great hunter. (Swed)

Jessica is *fr* **Jessamine** "Jasmin"; *see* Jessamine. (OE *fr* Persian)

Joel [joh-wehl] is *fr* **Yoel** [yoh-wehl] The Lord is God. (Hbr)
"Yah": "God" (lord) + "El": "God."

Jonah [joh-nah] Dove, *fr* "Yonah" [yoh-nah] "Dove." (Hbr)

Jude [jood] Thankful to God, *fr* "Yehuda." (OE *fr* Hbr)
"Ye" [yay] "To" + "Todah" [toh-dah] "Thank." (Hbr)
Yehudah > **Yudah** (Hbr) > Judah (Grk) > Jude.

Kahuna [kah-hoon-nah] Mystic Man. (Hwn)
"Ka": "The" + "Huna": "Expert," of greatest mysteries.

Kendra [kehn-drah] Ruling King, *fr* "Kendrick." (ME *fr* OE)
"Kendrick" (ME) is *fr* "Cynric": "Ruling King." (OE)
Cynric was a Saxon King in 534 AD; *see* Kenric.

Kiefer [kee-fur] Pine Tree. (Ger)

Kimberly is the "Welshman's Meadow." (ME *fr* Welsh)
"Cymry": "Welsh" + "Ley" [lee] "Meadow." (Welsh)
"Cymry" [koom-ree] is their original N for themselves.
"Cymry" *became* "Cambri," and the **Cambrian** Mountains.
Cymry > **Cymbry** > Cimberley > Kimberly.

Kojak [koh-jak] Brave. (Turkish)

Larry is *fr* **Laramie** [lar-rah-mee] The Mercy. (Eam *fr* Hbr)
fr "Laruhamah" [lah-roo-hah-mah] "The Mercy." (Hbr)
"La": "The" + "Ruhamah": "Mercy."
Laruhamah > Laruhamy > **Laramy** > Laramie > Larry.

Laurence is *fr* "Laurentius": "Wreath" (victor). (Frn *fr* Latin)
fr "Laureus": "Laurel" (wreath), symbol of victory. (Latin)
Lorenzo [lor-rehn-zoh] *fr* "Laurence"; *see* Renzo. (Ital)
Lonzo [lahn-zoh] Victor, the champion. (Span)

Lars [larz] Victor, *fr* "Laurence." (Nor)

Leah [lee-yah] My God, *fr* **Liya** [lee-yah] My God. (Grk *fr* Hbr)
"Li" is *fr* "Sheli": "My" + "Yah": "God." (Hbr)

Lennon is *fr* **Leannan** [lah-nahn] Sweetheart. (Gaelic)

Liv [lihv] Life. (Swed)

Lysandra [ligh-sann-drah] Liberator of Men. (Grk)
"Lys": "Loosen" (release) + "Andra": "Men."

Mahoney is *fr* **Mahon** [mah-hahn] Bear. (OE *fr* Gaelic)
"Mahon" is *fr* "Mathan" [mah-hahn] "Bear." (Gaelic)

Mamie is *fr* **Jemima**, a girl's Nn for "Jeremiah." (Eam *fr* Hbr)

Max [maks] Of the Highest Degree, the best quality. (Latin)

Miles, **Myles** [mighlz] An Army. (Latin)
fr "Mill": "Millions," millions of soldiers, an army.

Netanyahu [neh-tahn-yah-hoo] Gift from God. (Hbr)
"Netanyahu" is the reverse of "Yehonatan"; *see* Yonatan.

Nicholas [nee-koh-lahss] Champion of the People. (Grk)
"Nike": "Victor" (champion) + "Laos": "People" (nation).
Famous Saint Nick had a Greek name, and lived in Turkey.
Nielsson [neelz-suhn] Son of the Champion. (Swed)
Nielsson > Nilsson > **Nelson** (OE), **Neeson** (Irish).

Nirvani [nur-vahn-nee] Liberation, ultimate freedom. (Skt)
fr "Nirvana," liberation from the inside out, mind revelation.

Nissan [nee-sahn] Miracle, *fr* "Nes": "Miracle." (Hbr)

Opal is *fr* **Upala** [oo-pah-lah] Gem, precious stone. (Skt)

Oprah [oh-prah] Fawn. (Grk *fr* Hbr)
fr "Ofer" [oh-fur] "Fawn." (Hbr)

Orion [or-righ-uhn] Blooming (beauty), a handsome boy. (Grk)

Paris is *fr* "Parisii," a Celtic tribe; *see* Ap1: Devon. (Celtic)

Parker is a Cmpd Nn *fr* **Parkkeeper**. (ME)

Phaedra is *fr* **Phaenna** [fay-nah] Brilliance. (Grk)
Phaenna is the N of a moon goddess; *see* Phaedima.

Pleiades [plee-ay-deez] The Star Daughters of Pleione. (Grk)
Pleione [plee-oh-nee] Many Stars; N of a Star Goddess.
fr "Pleion": "More" (larger), to birth many stars.

157

Pleione gave birth to seven star goddesses with Atlas:
Alcyone, Asterope, Caleano, Electra, Maia, Merope, Taygete.

Polly is *fr* "Polyxena"; N known from the classics.   (Eam *fr* Grk)

   Polyxena [pahl-lee-zee-nah] Great Host.   (Grk)

   Daughter of King Priam, famous for the Trojan War.

   "Poly": "Many" (great) + "Xena" : "Hospitable" (kind).

   Pollyanna [pahl-lee-ann-nah] Many Thanks.

Presley is *fr* **Priestley** "Priest's Meadow."   (ME *fr* OE)

   "Priest" + "Leah" [lee] "Meadow."   (OE)

Ramona is *fr* **Rimona** "Sweet Pomegranate."   (Hbr)

Randall, **Randell** [rann-duhl] Wolf Shield.   (OE *fr* Germanic)

   fr "Randwulf": "Wolf-Shield."   (Germanic)

   "Rand": "Shield" + "Wulf": "Wolf."

Raphael [rahf-figh-ehl] God's Healing Power.   (Hbr)

   "Raf": "Medicine" + "El": "God" = God's Medicine.

Raymond [ray-muhnd] *fr* "Raimund."   (Frn *fr* Germanic)

   Raimund [ray-muhnd] Commanding Warrior.   (Germanic)

   fr "Raginmund" [rayn-muhnd] "Commanding Warrior."

   "Ragin" [rayn] "Opinion" (decree), a commander.

   "Mund": "Hand," symbol of trust, a protector, a warrior.

   Raginmund > Reginmund > Reinmund > **Redmond**.

Robert [rah-burt] Bright Red, a bloody warrior.   (OE *fr* Ger)

   "Rod" is *fr* "Rot": "Red" + "Bert": "Bright."   (Ger)

   A warrior survives battle covered with the blood of men.

   Robin [rah-bihn] Bright Red, *fr* "Robert."

   N given to the bird, Robin Redbreast, in 1400 AD.

Ronald is *fr* "Rognvald": "Counselor Wields" (power).   (Scand)

   "Rogn" (rad): "Opinion" (decree), battle counselor.

Rune [roon] Secret Wisdom; *see* Ronn.   (Scand)

   Here is an example of a Rune translated into Old English.

   "Wisdomes wrapu and witena frofur,"

   (A supporter of wisdom and comfort of wise men)

   "And eorla gehwam eadnys and toniht."

   (And a blessing and hope to every man)

Witena (wise man); Frofur (comfort); Eorla (every);
Gehwam (man); Eadnys (blessing); Toniht (hope).

Russell [ruh-sehl] Red-haired. (ME *fr* Frn)

fr "Rousse": "Red," *became* **Roussell** > Russell. (Frn)

Ross [rhass] Red-haired, *fr* "Roussell."

Shaq, Shaqira [shak, shah-keer-rah] Thankful, to God. (Ara)

Sherman is *fr* "Shire-man," for he watches over the shire. (OE)
"Sher": "Shire" + "Man" = Sherman, *became* **Sheriff.**

Sigourney [sihg-gur-nee] Way of the Victor. (ME *fr* Nor)

fr "Sigurveig" [sihg-gur-vigh] "Way of the Victor." (Nor)
"Sigur": "Victor" (champion) + "Veig": "Way."

Stacy is *fr* **Anastasia** [ann-nah-stay-see-ah] "Resurrection." (Grk)

Sylvia, Sylvani [sihl-vee-ah, sihl-vah-nee] Forest. (Latin)

fr "Silva" [sihl-vah] "Forest."

Timothy [tihm-moh-thee] *fr* "Timotheus." (OE *fr* Grk)

Timotheus [tihm-moh-thee-uhss] Honored God. (Grk)
"Tima": "Honor" + "Theos": "God"; *see* Timaeus.

Tori [tor-ree] Farm Bird, chicken. (Japanese)

Travis *fr* "Travers": "Traverse," to cross the river. (ME *fr* Frn)

Trevor [trehv-vor] Big Town. (Welsh)
"Tref": "Town" + "Fawr" [var] "Much" (bigger).
Trefawr > Trefar > Trefor > Trevor.

Trev *fr* "Tref" [trehf] "Settlement" (town), homestead.

Trey [tray] Nn *fr* "Trevor." (Modern Eng)

Twyla [twigh-lah] Little Twin. (OE)

Tyler *fr* "Tigele" [tighl] "Tile," a tile maker, a Tiler. (OE)

Tyrone [tigh-rohn] Military Recuit, a young soldier. (Latin)
fr "Tironis": "Recruit," into the military.

Wesley *fr* **Westley** = "West" + "Leah" [lee] "Meadow." (OE)

Windham [wihn-duhm] Home down the Winding Road. (OE)
"Vind": "Winding" (winding road) + "Ham": "Home."

Wynston [wihn-stuhn] Mansion of Joy. (OE)
"Wyn": "Joyful" + "Stan" [stann] "Stone" (mansion).

Zorro [zor-roh] Fox; N for boys; "Zorra" is *for* girls. (Span)

Ap2 – Extra-Exotic Girl Names

Achebe [ah-chay-bay] People Believe in You. (Igbo)

Aisling [ash-leen] Good Dream, dreams come true. (Gaelic)
  Ashling [ash-leeng] Good Dream, *fr* "Aisling." (OE)

Aiwen [i-wehn] Quiet Love. (Mandarin)
  "Ai" [i] "Love" + "Wen": "Quiet."

Almika [al-mee-kah] Sky. (Ixil Maya)

Anuhea [ah-noo-hay-yah] Cool Mountain Breeze. (Hwn)
  "Anu": "Cold" + "He": "Roaring," sound of wind.

Arabethia [ar-rah-beh-thee-yah] Altar in the Temple. (OE)
  fr "Arabethiah": "Altar in the House of God."
  "Ara": "Altar" + "Beth": "House" + "Yah": "God."

Asterope [ah-stair-roh-pay] Voice of the Stars. (Grk)
  "Astro": "Star" + "Ope": "Voice" (opera).
  Daughter of the Star Goddess Pleione; *see* Ap1: Pleiades.

Avali [ah-vahl-lee] Garden. (Ixil Maya)

Bilena [bih-lee-nah] Iris of the Eyes, pretty eyes. (Amharic)

Chakrasena [chah-krah-see-nah] Mystical Wheel Warrior. (Skt)
  "Chakra": "Wheel" (mystical wheel) + "Sena": "Warrior."

Coryphea [kor-ree-fee-yah] Goddess of the Mountains. (Grk)
  fr "Coryphe" [kor-ree-fee] "Summit" (mountaintops).

Deepamala [deep-pah-mah-lah] Pure Light. (Hindi *fr* Skt)
  "Dip" [deep] "Light" + "Amala": "Spotless" (pure). (Skt)

Deogracia [dee-oh-grah-see-ah] Thank God. (Span)
  "Dios": "God" + "Gracias": "Thanks."

Elveneigh [ehl-veh-nay] Elf Friend; *see* "Elfwina." (Eam *fr* OE)

Ezume [eh-zoo-may] Pure Water, a pond. (Japanese)

Farisha [far-ree-shah] Angel, *fr* "Farishta": "Angel." (Persian)

Fredirica [freh-deer-ree-kah] Peaceful Ruler. (OE *fr* Ger)
  fr **Frederich** = "Frid": "Peace" + "Rik": "Ruler." (Ger)

Gamuchirai [gah-moo-cheer-righ] To Receive with Joy. (Shona)

Julianther [joo-lee-ann-thur] Flower of July. (Eam)
  "July" (Latin) + "Anthea": "Flower" (Grk).

Kiku [kee-koo] Chrysanthemum, a beautiful flower. (Japanese)

Kumaripala [koo-mar-ree-pah-lah] Goddess Protector. (Skt)
"Kumari": "Living Goddess" + "Pala": "Protector."

Kusichina [koo-see-chee-nah] Happy Girl. (Quechua)
"Kusi": "Happy" + "China": "Girl" (feminine).

Menashen [mehn-nah-shehn] Beauty. (Cree)

Nain [nigh-een] Truth. (Mam Maya)
The Maya have no word for "Liar" in their vocabulary.

Nikamoon [nee-kah-moon] Song (chanting), prayers. (Cree)

Olenka [oh-lehnk-kah] Little Deer. "Olen": "Deer." (Russian)

Ooja [oo-jah] Star, *fr* "Oojahooch" [oo-jah-hooch] "Star." (Cree)

Paivanvalo [pigh-vahn-val-loh] Daylight. (Finnish)
"Paiva" [pigh-vah]: "Day" + "Valo": "Light."

Parvati [par-vaht-tee] Goddess of the Mountains. (Skt)

Priyada [pree-yah-dah] Love Gift; a mystical N for Earth. (Skt)
fr "Priyadatta" [pree-yah-dah-tah] "Love Gift."
"Priya": "Love" + "Datta": "Given"; the N of a Sage.

Rewa, **Reawa** [ray-wah] Hope. (Tibetan)

Sabra [say-brah] Cactus, *fr* "Tsabar" [zah-bar] "Cactus." (Hbr)
Tough on the outside, sweet on the inside.

Suyana [soo-yay-nah] Hope. (Aymara)

Tatewin [tah-tay-wihn] Wind Woman. (Sioux)
"Tate": "Wind" + "Win": "Woman."

    Tateyuha Mani [tah-tay-yoo-hah mah-nee] Wind Walker.
    "Tate": "Wind" + "Yuha": "Carries" + "Mani": "Walker."

Tesfaye [tehss-fah-yay] My Hope. (Amharic)

Tichafara [tee-chah-far-rah] We are Going to Be Happy. (Shona)

Tishka [teesh-kah] God uses this person. (Ixil Maya)
"Tishkatchahoonishsho" [teesh-kaht-chah-hoon-eesh-shoh].

Tizeta [tih-zee-tah] Memory. (Amharic)

Vitalia [vigh-tal-lee-ah] Vital, lives long, *fr* "Vita": "Life." (Latin)

Wubayehu [woo-bay-yeh-hoo] I Saw Beauty. (Amharic)

Xinmei [sheen-may] Happy Beauty. (Mandarin)
"Xin": "Happy" + "Mei": "Beauty"; *see* Meishan.

Ap3 – Extra-Exotic Boy Names

Atik [ah-teek] Brave. (Quechua)

Aviram [ah-veer-ruhm] Supreme Father. (Hbr)
  "Avi": "Father" + "Ram": "High" (supreme).

Buddharaja [boo-dar-rah-jah] Enlightened King. (Skt)
  "Buddha": "Awake" (enlightened) + "Raja": "King."

Chanku [chahnk-koo] Path. (Sioux)
  Chanku Ounye [chahnk-koo oon-yay] Path of Power.

Chotso [choh-tsoh] Dharma Lake, reservoir of truth. (Tibetan)
  "Cho": "Dharma" (truth) + "Tso": "Lake" (reservoir).
  Konchog [kahn-chawg] Triple Jewel, triad of wisdom;
  teacher (Buddha), teachings (dharma), & students (sangha).

Dinesh [deen-nehsh] Sun, a son of the Sun. (Skt)
  fr "Dina" [deen-nah] "Day" (Sun).

Ehud [eh-hood] Beloved, *fr* "Ahava": "Love." (Hbr)

Excelino [ehks-sehl-lee-noh] Excellence. (Span)

Farzan [far-zahn] Learned Scholar, the sciences, wise. (Persian)

Gamaliel [gah-mahl-lee-ehl] Rewarded by God. (Hbr)
  "Gemal": "Reward" + "El": "God."

Godleap [gahd-leep] God Leap, leap of faith. (Eam)

Greenhope [green-hohp] Green Hope, hopeful harvest. (Eam)
  Greenup [green-uhp] Nn *fr* "Greenhope."

Hakim [hah-keem] Wise Man, a doctor. (Ara)

Harvard [har-vard] Guardian Army, to stand guard. (OE)
  fr "Hereward" [hair-ward] "Guardian Army."
  "Here": "Army" + "Weard": "Ward" (protected).

Hezekiah [hehz-zeh-kigh-yah] Strength from God. (Hbr)
  "Xozek" [hoh-zehk] "Strength" + "Yah": "God."
  Hezokiah, Hezek *fr* "Hezekiah." (Eam)

Hopian [hohp-pee-ihn] Hope, *fr* "Hopa": "Hope." (OE)

Ichante [ee-chahn-tay] From the Heart. (Sioux)
  "I" (my) + "Cante" [chahn-tay] "Heart."

Juba [joo-bah] Respected, Honored. (Yoruba)

Jubane [joo-bah-nay] Swift. (Zulu)

Lhundrup [luhn-druhp] Natural Perfection. (Tibetan)
"Lhun": "Natural" + "Drup": "Accomplished, Perfected."

Marvic [mar-vihk] *fr* "Marvel": "Marvelous." (Modern Eng)

Masaru [mah-sar-roo] Surpassing, to excel. (Japanese)

Obinna [oh-bee-nah] Loved by his Father. (Igbo)
"Obi": "Heart" (beloved) + "Nna" [nah] "Father."

Ohana [oh-hah-nah] Family, a tribe. (Hwn)

Olushola [oh-loo-shoh-lah] God has Blessed Me. (Yoruba)
"Olu": "God" + "Shola": "Blessed."

Omani [oh-mah-nee] Traveler, *fr* "Mani": "Walker." (Sioux)

Randeep [rann-deep] Bringer of Light into Battle. (Hindi *fr* Skt)
"Ran": "Battle" + "Dip" [deep] "Light." (Skt)
The hero who brings light into the heart of battle.

Shantasena [shahn-tah-see-nah] Peaceful Warrior. (Skt)
"Shanta": "Peace" + "Sena": "Spear" (warrior).

Shingirai [sheeng-geer-righ] Be Strong; Nn is **Shingi**. (Shona)

Shoma [shoh-mah] Catching Truth, a champion. (Japanese)
People jumping up to the sky and catching truth.

Taisho [tigh-shoh] A Leader. (Japanese)

Tallock [tal-luhk] Tall Cut, a tall lad. (Eam)
fr "Tallcut" [tawl-kuht] "Cut Tall," made tall by God.

Tashunka, Taxunka [tah-shoonk-kah] Horse. (Sioux)
"Tanka": "Big" (great) + "Shunka": "Dog" = A Horse.
The Sioux though horses looked like big dogs.
   Tashunka Witco [tah-shoonk-kah weet-koh] Crazy Horse.
This world is made of shadows of the real world behind it,
and Crazy Horse entered it to survive all his battles.

Terton [tur-tuhn] Treasure Finder. (Tibetan)
Jewels are symbols of wisdom; many jewels make a treasure.

Wambdi [wahm-dee] Eagle. (Dakota Sioux)

Yochi [yoh-chee] Hope, *fr* "Yochiltay": "Hope." (Ixil Maya)

Zuya Hanska [zoo-yah hann-skah] Tall Warrior. (Sioux)
"Zuya": "Warrior" + "Hanska": "Tall."

163

Ap4 - Exotic Names in English

Acacia, Amber, Amberwren, Ambrosia, Angel, Apple, Asia, Aurora, Autumn, Azure, Brave, Brook, Buck, Buddy, Canyon, Carol, Cedar, Destiny, Dream, Earnest, Faith, Forrest, Fox, Gallant, Galore, Gardner, Gazelle, Ginger, Glen, Gloria, Golden, Grace, Grant, Haven, Hazel, Hero, Hope, Horizon, Hunter, India, Ivy, Jade, Jasmine, Jasper, Jay, Jazz, Jet, Jewell, Journey, Joy, Jubilee, Juniper, Lance, Laurel, Legend, Lightning, Lily, Link, Lotus, Lovie, Lyric, Major, Meadow, Melody, Mercy, Merrily, Miracle, Misty, Moon, Pearl, Persia, Pilot, Piper, Pony, Rain, Raven, Radiance, Reed, River, Rocker, Rose, Ruby, Rune, Saffron, Savannah, Serene, Shepherd, Shine, Sky, Sojourner, Starlight, Sterling, Stone, Summer, Sunny, Taylor, Teal, Temple, Tiara, Trinity, Venus, Victory, Walker, Willow, Windsong, Yarrow.

Ap5 – Early American Girl Names
Pilgrims 1600, Colonists 1700, Pioneers 1800

Airy, Aliveine, Alpha, Amaryllis, America, Angelic, Avis, Beautifila, Bliss, Celestia, Charity, Cinderella, Comfort, Commentary, Consent, Consolation, Constance, Content/Contenta, Copper, Daisy, Darling, Delight, Delphia (Oracle of Delphi), Desire (for God), Diademma, Dolly, Dovey/Dovie, Emerald, Euphamia, Eurica (Eureka), Experience, Fairy, Faithful, Fear (of God), Fortune, Freedom, Freegrace, Freelove/Frelove, Garland, Gowell (go well), Harmony, Highly, Honora, Hopestill, Humility (was on the Mayflower), Learned, Liberty, Light, Loveall, Loveasy (love easy), Loveday, Lovelace, Loveland, Loveth/Lovey, Marvella, Mercy, Merry, Minerva, Morning, Moxya, Obedience, Oceana/Ocenia, Opal, Parthenia (Parthenon), Patience, Peace, Precious, Promise, Providence, Prudence, Rangle, Reliance, Relief, Remedy, Remember (was on Mayflower), Remembrance, Renewal, Silence, Spicy, Stormy, Surprise, Sweet, Teaberry, Temperance/Tempe, Tenetta (Bible tenet), Thankful, Truelove, Utopia, Venus, Virtue, Wealthy/Wealthea, Wing, Wisdom, Wise.

Alpha Jane   **Alta Sweet**
America Bramble   **Happy Always**
Mercy Flowers   **Olive Wise**

Ap6 - Early American Boy Names

Pilgrims 1600, Colonists 1700, Pioneers 1800

Able, Aeon, Almond, Alpheus, Americus, Amiable, Archer, Armor, Armstead, Avis, Banner, Beach, Berry, Berryman, Birch, Bison, Bloomfield, Bold, Boon, Branch, Bridge, Brooks, Burden (taking God's), Center, Champion, Chance, Christhope, Clouds, Comfort, Conquest, Consider, Constant, Content, Converse, Creed/Creedance, Dependence, Dexterity, Drummer, Duty (to God), Eager, Eden, Edenton, Eminous, Emulous, Experience (was on the Mayflower), Fearnot, Fielden, Firmer, Fleet, Forrester, Fountain, Freeborn/Frebourne, Freedom, Freeland, Friend, Garnett, Gladden/Gladen, Goalman, Godleap, Godsgift, Green/Greene, Greenberry, Greengrove, Greenhope/Greenup, Greenleaf, Gusty, Halcyon, Hawkins, Heartwell, Hevier (heavier in values), Honest, Honor/Honner, Hopefor, Hopeful, Hopewell, Increase/Increas, Jubal (jubilee), Justice/Justus, Keys (to the kingdom), Kindler, Kindred, Kingman, Kingsberry, Knight, Level, Lightfoot, Lion, Listen, Liven, Loved, Lovel/Lovell, Loveright, Lucke, Makepeace, Memory, Merit, Messenger, Mindwell, Mountain, Oakes, Obedience, Oceanus (born on the Mayflower), Orange, Origin, Orisen, Pacific, Pardon, Planner, Playford, Pleasant, Pledge, Plymouth, Preserved, Price, Prime/Primus, Prince, Principle, Prospect, Prosper, Ransom, Reason/Reazen, Recompense, Record, Refine, Relefe, Remember, Remembrance, Resolve, Resolved (was on the Mayflower), Restore, Rider, Rising, Royal/Royall, Rubicon, Samarian, Saywell, Shade, Sharp, Sharpen, Sharper, Sheppard, Snow, Solitary, Sparks, Spear, Standfast, Sterling, Stokely, Storm, Strong, Submit (to God), Sunnier, Tallcut, Tempest, Temple, Thankful, Theoren, Train, Traverse, Treatise, Trotter, True, Trueman, Trueworthy, Truit/Truet (truth), Trust, Ulysses, Unicorn, Usual, Valorous/Valentine, Vinyard, Wait, Waitstill, Wakeful, Watching, Waters, Wayman/Waymon, Weaver, Welcome, Welthyen, Wheaton, Wheeler, Winder, Wing, Wisdom, Wiseman, Worthey, Wrestle, Wrestling, Zenith.

Able Greenleaf	**Archer Lightfoot**
Forest Foliage	**Grant Light**
Joseph Muchmore	**Noble Noah**

Ap7 - Language Locations & Notes

Amharic evolved out of Hebrew spoken by Jews that migrated down the coast of the Red Sea into Ethiopia, East Africa.

Basque people are actually the **Euskara** [yoo-skar-rah]. They have lived isolated in the mountains of Northern Spain, and speak the only remnant of Neolithic languages.

Cree people live in Canada, above the Great Lakes. My teacher was over six feet tall, like many in his tribe, because Native Americans in the Northeast (Mohican, Mohawk, Sioux) came over the North Atlantic 20-30,000 years ago, after a previous ice age. They are related to the ancestors of Scandinavians, and are much larger than West Coast Indians of Oriental stock.

Croatian is from Russian, and Serbian is a dialect.

Dutch is actually **Nederlands**, and comes from German.

Early American represents an era of creative naming for the Pilgrims (1600), Colonists (1700), & Pioneers (1800).

Estonian is related to Finnish, Estonia being a small Nordic country across from Finland that borders Northern Russia.

Finnish is Nordic. Long ago the Finnish Empire was so great it bordered the Persian Empire, spreading across Northern Russia to Japan; thus, they're related in many ways. They both believe that the elements of the Earth, every mountain, tree, and fish, are very much alive with Spirit.

Gaelic is **Irish-Gaelic**, here. The Celts once covered all of Southern Europe, until the invading Romans pushed the last Brythony Celt off the mainland and onto an island that would be named for them, and "Brythony" *became* "Britain."
Only minor differences in dialect give us:
Brythonic Gaelic – **Breton**, Cornish, **Welsh**.
Goidelic Gaelic – **Irish**, **Scottish**, Manx.
"Scotti" was the Roman N for Irish Celts, whom were never invaded because of their ferocity, their women fighting also.

Germanic was very influential in the Nordic world. Once their tribes spread throughout Europe, including the Ostrogoth (Eastern Goth), who went to Italy and took down the Roman Empire, and the Visigoth (Western Goth) who went to Spain. The Germanic language forms the foundation English, which began when Vikings took over the island called Britain and spoke Anglo-Saxon, otherwise known as Old English.

Greek has changed little. Most of the names are Ancient Greek.

Hausa tribe comes from the Niger River and Chadda River in Nigeria, a country in the middle of Western Africa.

Hebrew has not been spoken for 2,000 years, until Eliezer Benyehuda revived it. His son, Ehud, is credited with going into the streets as a child and teaching the other children how to speak it. At first, only the Arab children could understand him, because the Jews spoke Yiddish, which is from German.

Hindi is modern Sanskrit, it is the same with some additions.

Igbo (Ibo) are from the Niger River Delta, Nigeria, West Africa.

Ixil Maya [ee-sheel] live in the highlands of Guatemala.

Kamba tribe live at the base of Mt Kenya in Eastern Africa. Their name for the mountain, "Kilinya" *became* "Kenya."

Kikuyu tribe live at the base of Mt Kenya in Eastern Africa. Mt Kenya is called "Kere Nyaga": "Mountain of God."

Lenape are the oldest tribe in the U.S., arriving 20–30,000 years ago. They were called the Grandfathers by other tribes.
The Lenape are famous for trading Manhattan for beads.
They ended up being forced south, where they were renamed, "De La War" (Of the War), after the governor of the state.

Lithuanian is spoken in Lithuania, on the Baltic Sea. It's across from Sweden, wedged between Germany and Russia.

Mam Maya Indians live on the Yucatan Peninsula in Guatemala.

Mandarin Chinese is spoken in Northern China.

Middle English was spoken from 1066–1400 AD, when Britain was conquered by French-speaking Danes from Normandy, France. They took over Britain and changed its name to "Angland": "Angle-land" (England). Then, they transformed

Old English (German base) into Middle English (French influence), rendering the final product rather unphonetic.

Old English (Anglo-Saxon) was spoken from 450–1066 AD. The Germanic language forms the foundation of the English language, and began when Vikings took over the island of Britain. They were hired by Romans to push back Celts (Picts) trying to reclaim their land, but instead took over the island for themselves and all their Anglo and Saxon friends; thus, Old English is Anglo-Saxon. These Nordic Tribesmen began to replace runes with the local Gaelic script; *see* Ap1: Rune.

Persian is the ancient N for Iranian, an Indo-European language.

Russian is written in Cyrillic letters, like Greek.

Sanskrit is the ancient Indo-European language that spread as far as India, making it cousin to English. "Star": "Tara."

Shona people live in Zimbabwe, South Africa.

Sioux tribe lives in the Dakota states, and their RN is **Dakoda**. They divided into 3 groups, adding the Lakota & Nakota.

Swahili is a unifying language from North Africa.

Welsh is the Gaelic (Brythony) of the surviving Celts of Britain.

Wolof people live in the country of Senegal, West Africa.

Yoruba is spoken in Southwest Nigeria, West Africa.

Yucateco Maya indians are the dominant tribe (out of 20), thus, the Yucatan Peninsula is named after them.

Zulu is a Bantu language from South Africa.

Indo-European Languages

Italic – Latin, Italian, French, Spanish, Portuguese, Romanian.

Celtic – Gaulish, Galatian, Welsh, Gaelic, Cornish, Breton.

Iranian – Persian (Farsi), Kurdish, Pashto.

Sanskrit – Hindi, Bengali, Punjabi, Nepali, Kashmiri.

Slavic – Bulgarian, Croatian, Russian, Czech, Slovak, Polish.

Germanic – Yiddish, German, English, Dutch, Danish, Swedish, Norwegian, Icelandic.

Isolates – Greek, Albanian, Armenian.